CIRENCESTER: ANGLO-SAXON CHURCH AND MEDIEVAL ABBEY

CIRENCESTER EXCAVATIONS IV

CIRENCESTER
ANGLO-SAXON CHURCH
AND
MEDIEVAL ABBEY

by David J. Wilkinson and Alan D. McWhirr

Excavations directed by J. S. Wacher (1964), A. D. McWhirr (1965)
and P. D. C. Brown (1965-6)

WITH CONTRIBUTIONS FROM

R. Brownsword, R. M. Bryant, T. C. Darvill, G. Egan, A. K. B. Evans,
C. M. Heighway, C. A. Ireland, R. D. H. Gem, N. Griffiths, M. Harman, D. R. Hook,
J. Keely, N. Mayhew, E. E. H. Pitt, J. F. Rhodes, L. Viner, A. G. Vince

Cotswold Archaeological Trust Ltd
Cirencester
1998

ISBN 0 9523196 2 4

The publication of this volume has been supported by English Heritage.

Cover illustration: the Spital Gate of Cirencester Abbey. *Copyright: Cirencester Town Council*

Produced by Past Historic, King's Stanley, Gloucestershire
Printed in Great Britain by J.W. Arrowsmith Ltd., Bristol

CONTENTS

LIST OF FIGURES

ACKNOWLEDGEMENTS

Many people assisted on the 1964-5 excavations, some on site, others behind the scene. Supervisors included, Anna Bachelier, Peter Bellwood, Peter Broxton, Christine Butcher, Philippa Cullen, Maggie Heewitt, Helen McWhirr, Christine Mahany, Marion Overs, H. Smith, Anna Wacher. Photography on site was carried out by Gilly Jones (1964) and Roger Rumens (1965). After the close of the summer season in 1965 photographs during the rest of the year and in 1966 were taken by David Brown.

Considerable help was given throughout the excavations by officers of Cirencester Urban District Council, in particular its surveyor and engineer Mr Jack Elliott and clerk Mr Stan Esland, and the custodian of the Corinium Museum, Mr Jack Real. Members of the Cirencester Archaeological and Historical Society helped with the digging and also acted as guides to the many visitors who came to see the excavations. The guides were organised by Miss D. M. Radway. A great deal of organisational work was undertaken locally by Miss J. Barker. The presence of Mr W. I. Croome during the excavations in 1964 and 1965 was a constant source of encouragement to all who directed the work. He regularly brought books from his library in the back of his car and left them for people to read. The directors also benefited from the visits of Dr Joan Evans, Mr R. Gilyard-Beer, Mr R. Neville Hadcock, Dr C. A. Raleigh Radford, Mr Arnold Taylor, Dr H. M. Taylor and others whom we may have forgotten. The chairman of the Excavation Committee, Sir Ian Richmond, was most supportive and his regular visits and advice were eagerly awaited. Sadly a number of those named above are no longer with us to see this volume in print.

Financial support for the excavations came from a variety of sources. The bulk came from the Ministry of Public Buildings and Works. Other grants were made by Cirencester Urban District Council, the Society of Antiquaries, the British Academy, the Haverfield Trust and Craven Fund of the University of Oxford, the Bristol and Gloucestershire Archaeological Society, the Cirencester Archaeological and Historical Society and Gloucestershire County Council. This volume has been published by Cotswold Archaeological Trust as successor to the Excavation Committee, with the support of English Heritage.

Post-excavation work was undertaken by various people who were at one time employed by the Cirencester Excavation Committee. They included Janet Keely, Caroline Ireland, Valery Rigby, and Linda Viner. Conservation work was undertaken by Gill Juleff and Martin Read, HMBC conservators, based at City of Bristol Museum and Art Gallery. The difficult task of making sense of the excavation records fell to David Wilkinson who was employed by the Excavation Committee to write reports on the excavations and on groups of finds. His work forms the backbone of this report. Final editing was carried out by Alan McWhirr, Linda Viner, Carolyn Heighway and Richard Bryant. We are also grateful to those who have contributed sections in this report and whose names will be found at the relevant point in the pages which follow and where the value of their contribution is apparent.

Nick Griffiths has been responsible for the drawing of small finds and for professional advice relating to the other illustrations. The architectural stonework was drawn by David Wilkinson. The topographical drawings were done by Richard Bryant. The floor tiles were drawn by David Wilkinson and retraced by Nick Griffiths. The drawings were finalised by Peter Moore of Cotswold Archaeological Trust. The index was compiled by Susanne Atkin.

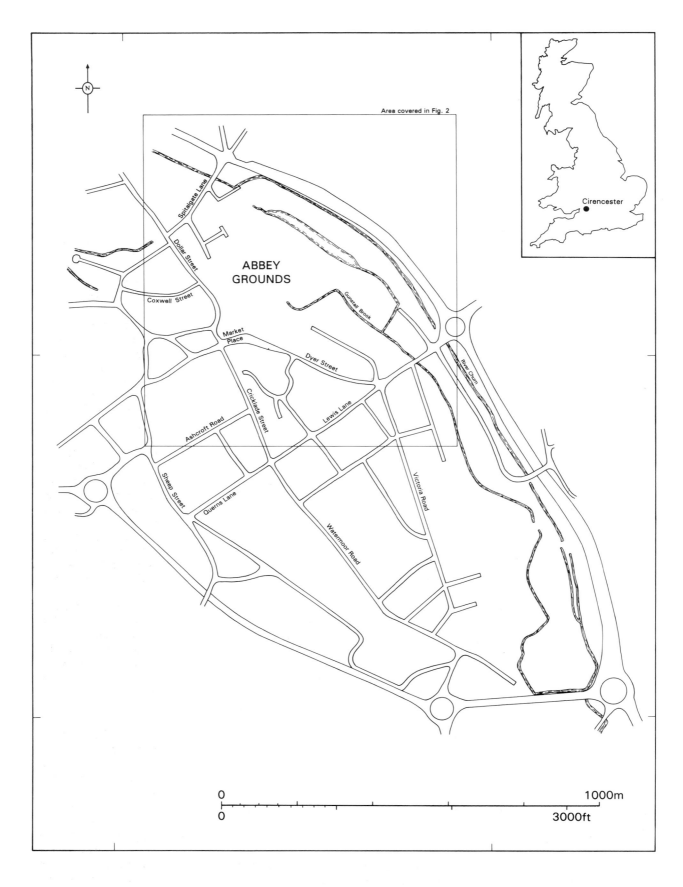

1. The location of Cirencester, and of the Abbey Grounds

INTRODUCTION

A. D. McWhirr

Background

Excavations on the site of the Augustinian abbey of St Mary, Cirencester (fig. 1) were directed by David Brown (1965-6), Dr Alan McWhirr (1965), and Professor John Wacher (1964), for the Cirencester Excavation Committee, on behalf of the then Ministry of Public Building and Works. Development proposals threatened a large part of the open space surrounding Abbey House, which stood in 41 acres (16.4 hectares) of landscaped parkland, stretching from the centre of the town to the River Churn on the east. In the event planning permission was withdrawn, with only minimal housing allowed on the site of Abbey House, demolished in 1964, and around the periphery of the park, the greater part of which remains as a public open space, the Abbey Grounds, in the care of Cirencester Town Council.

The presence of a large Augustinian abbey is well attested from documentary sources, but demolition following the dissolution of the monasteries in 1539 was so effective as to remove all trace of the site of the abbey church and attendant buildings. The only extant structure of the abbey complex is the Abbey Gateway in the northern corner of the Abbey Grounds, which formerly provided access to the Whiteway. The line of the precinct wall can be traced, with stretches of wall surviving in Gosditch Street and to the east of the present churchyard in the Abbey Grounds. Until the turn of the century one of the abbey barns still stood near the Abbey Gateway (fig. 2).

Local opinion had always placed the church below Abbey House, with the high altar under the apsidal front porch. Beecham, working on this hypothesis and taking the measurements provided by William Worcestre (1480), published a plan of the church, cloisters, and chapter house (1887, opp. p. 66). In 1964 Professor Wacher took this as his initial point of reference and a large area beyond the semicircular carriage-drive in front of Abbey House, presumed to cover the east end of the church, was stripped of topsoil and excavated (areas 64 BG, BH and BJ, figs. 3 and 4). Previous archaeological work on the site had been confined to three small-scale investigations carried out by W. St Clair Baddeley and Richard Reece (Reece 1962).

St Clair Baddeley undertook limited excavations in an area that appears to have located the rear of the northern range of the cloisters (Wacher 1965, 105). No record of this work, in about 1930, remains save a few photographs in the Corinium Museum, which show substantial foundations (Reece 1962, 198). In April 1959 Dr Reece dug six small trial trenches to the south and north of the balustraded forecourt. Those to the south of the forecourt revealed a hard courtyard-like surface of mortar and gravel at a depth of 3ft 6in (1.07m), while that to the north produced the lower courses of a fine ashlar wall, 2ft (0.61m) wide, running east-west, with flooring on either side of it (Reece 1962, 198-203). Stratification and finds suggested the 16th century destruction of an ornate (?ecclesiastical) building. Further work in the spring of 1964 by Dr Reece was inconclusive, but finds included two stone heads (Wacher 1965, pl.xxxix; Evans 1993, 131, Fig. 5, where the caption, owing to editorial error, wrongly describes one of the heads as that of a king, instead of a pope).

During the summer of 1964, as work proceeded under the direction of Professor Wacher, it became apparent that the range of buildings revealed was not part of the church, but part of the conventual buildings. Ultimately the church was found to lie well to the south-east of the main excavations (Wacher 1965, 106; trench 64 BK I, fig. 4). The 1964 excavations revealed the north transept of the church, the chapter house, the undercroft of the calefactory and dormitory, the east ambulatory of the cloisters, and the east end of the buildings of the north range (Wacher 1965, 105-10).

Work in 1965, begun by Professor Wacher and completed by David Brown and Dr McWhirr, concentrated on the area of the abbey church itself, with trenches laid out to investigate the nave, choir, presbytery, east end and south transept (trenches 65 BK, BL, BM and BN, fig. 4). Progress was impeded by the presence of mature trees and a yew hedge which effectively cut the nave in half. Towards the end of the summer season the substantial remains of a pre-Conquest church, comprising nave, aisles and apsidal eastern end with a crypt beneath, were revealed below the nave of the abbey church (Brown and McWhirr 1966, 245-54). Excavations continued in April 1966, directed by David Brown, to reveal

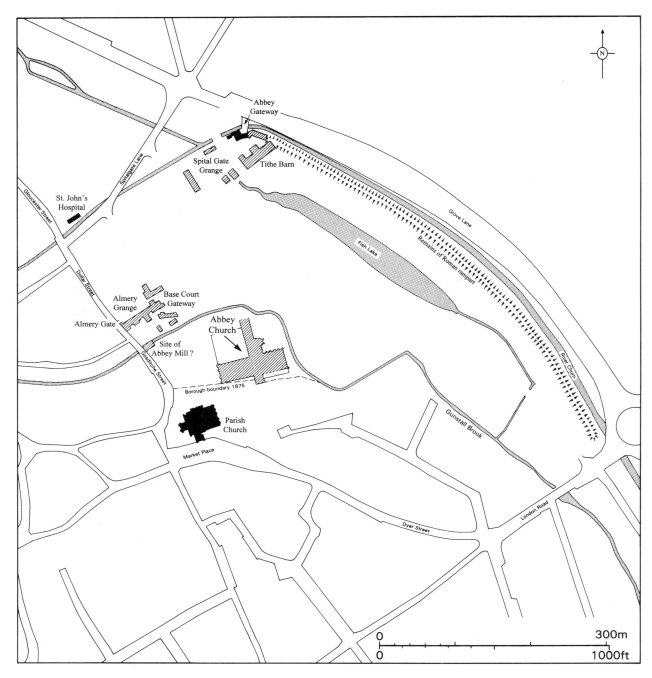

2. Cirencester: the abbey precinct and north part of the town

more of this early church (sites BP, BT and BV; Brown and McWhirr 1967, 195-7).

In 1975 a research seminar was held in Cirencester at which various papers were given including one by David Brown on the Anglo-Saxon church and another by Dr Evans on the historical background to both the abbey and Anglo-Saxon church. These papers were duly published (McWhirr 1976).

In 1979 grants from the then Inspectorate of Ancient Monuments of the Department of the Environment were made available to support detailed post-excavation analysis. David Wilkinson was appointed to undertake the task of collating,

analysing, and cataloguing all records and finds, and to write final reports. His work forms the basis for this report, and the contributions from specialists also rely on the considerable time and effort which he expended in post-excavation analysis. His contract of employment terminated in 1982. It was hoped that David Brown would contribute a revised chapter describing the pre-abbey features excavated 1965-6, but unfortunately in 1989 David Brown had to withdraw from the project. In 1986 a seminar of invited specialists was held, including Dr John Blair, David Brown, Dr Babette Evans, Prof Eric Fernie, Dr Richard Gem, Dr Alan McWhirr, Dr David

3. General view of the 1964 excavations, the east cloister range including the chapter house, looking south; the balustrade of Abbey House is on the right

Parsons, and David Wilkinson. With the help of notes taken by Dr Evans, the pre-Conquest features have been reassessed.

The authors and editors apologise to all contributors to this volume for the delay in publishing their work. Many specialist reports were written over ten years ago and whilst some have been rewritten, others remain unchanged, as they still contain significant and useful material.

This report is, therefore, a compilation by many hands. David Wilkinson's draft texts have formed the basis of several chapters and his overall phasing and layout have been maintained. Editing has been carried out over the years by several people including Alan McWhirr, John Wacher and Linda Viner. Final editing, and some rewriting following investigation of the original records, was carried out in 1997 by Carolyn Heighway and Richard Bryant.

In parallel with the analysis of the archaeological record, Dr A. K. B. Evans carried out exhaustive research into the documentary sources. A summary is presented here; her work has been published in full elsewhere (Evans 1989, 1991, 1993).

Some categories of finds have not been studied. Only a small proportion of the considerable quantity of worked stone has been reported on (below p 156); there is scope for a major study. There is a collection of window glass in poor condition which remains unstudied.

Many of the problems of interpretation raised in this report have the potential to be resolved by more extensive excavation. There is a possibility for instance, that there are 5th to 8th-century features which remain unexcavated. There are many questions

about the Anglo-Saxon church which further excavation could solve; the nature of the junction between the nave and the chancel apse, the plan of the southern half of the church, details of the Roman architectural fragments re-used in the foundations. For the 11th-century plan it might be possible to elucidate further the rebuilding of the west end of the Anglo-Saxon nave and the date and nature of the pre-abbey domestic buildings. There is considerable potential to study the burials of earlier centuries related to the first Anglo-Saxon church. The plan of the medieval abbey church is far from complete and there are a number of complexities which remain unresolved; the buried evidence must also include abbey buildings. As the area of the Abbey Grounds is a Scheduled Ancient Monument it is protected for the forseeable future; this report should serve to emphasise the national importance of this site.

Excavation strategy

When the Abbey site was excavated in 1964 and 1965 the area was marked out into a series of trenches, each one measuring c. 23 x 10ft (7 x 3m) although during the course of excavation many were amalgamated. A group of trenches was allocated a site code and a site supervisor and the basic record for each site was the site notebook. In addition sections were drawn by each supervisor and an overall plan produced by the director of excavations.

A bulldozer was used in the early stages of the 1964 and 1965 excavations to remove some topsoil, but subsequent work was carried out by hand. Trenches were excavated to varying depths; sometimes only post-dissolution levels were removed; in others all levels were removed to expose natural brown clay or gravel.

The following site codes were used (see fig. 4):-

Trenches excavated in 1964:-
    BG I - VII
    BH I - XI
    BJ I - XV
    BK I - IV
In the text these will appear as prefixed 64; for example, 64 BK I.

Trenches excavated in 1965:-
    BK I - XI
    BL I - X
    BM I-VII
    BN I-VIII
In the text these will appear as prefixed 65, for example, 65 BK I.

Trenches excavated in 1966:-
    BP I-VIII
    BT I-III
    BV I-III

Because of potential confusion between upper case Roman numerals and upper case letters, lower case Roman numerals have been used for trench numbers in the illustrations.

In this report the term 'early medieval' refers to the period immediately following the Norman Conquest.

The Archive
All records of the excavations are catalogued and include notebooks, plans, photographs and artefacts. These have been deposited in, and are available for study at, the Corinium Museum, Cirencester.

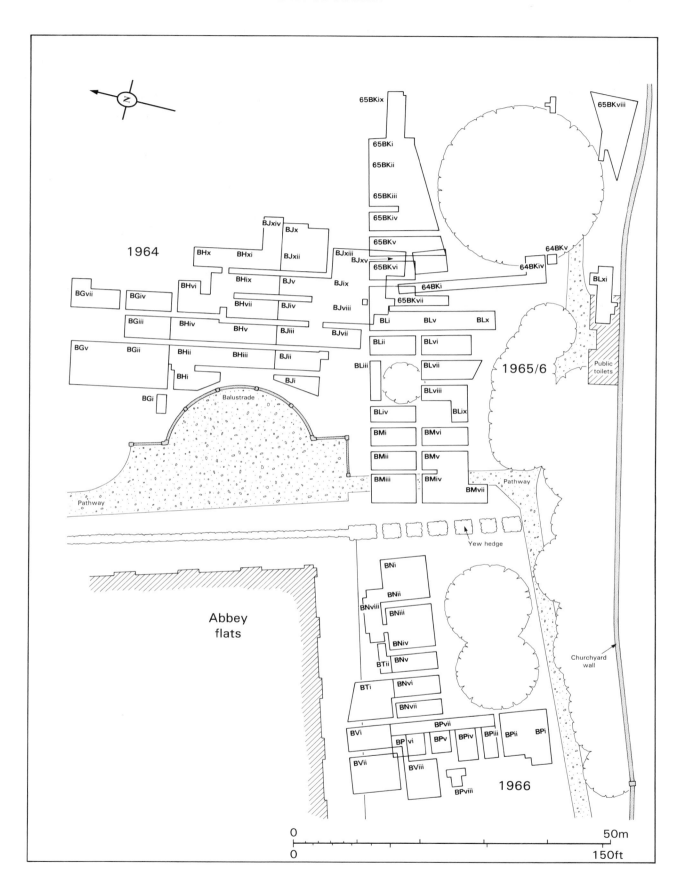

4. Trench outlines with excavation codes

HISTORICAL AND TOPOGRAPHICAL BACKGROUND

THE TOPOGRAPHICAL DEVELOPMENT OF THE SITE

R. M. Bryant and C. M. Heighway

Roman (fig. 5a)

The town of Cirencester lies on river-laid gravel at the point where the river Churn, flowing from the north-east through a winding valley cut into the oolitic limestone of the Cotswolds, meets the flood-plain of the river Thames. A slightly higher north-west to south-east ridge of ground may have formed a spine along which Ermin Street was aligned (Holbrook and Wilkinson, forthcoming). Ermin Street entered the town roughly on the line of Dollar Street (street A: Holbrook and Salvatore, forthcoming) and passed under the west end of the present parish church to cross another street in the present market place (Zeepvat 1979, 72). A Roman street of less substantial nature crossed the abbey site presumably parallel to Ermin Street; on either side of this street were domestic buildings used from the 2nd to the 3rd centuries (McWhirr 1986, 222-233; below p. 19).

Early post-Roman (fig. 5b)

Two of the site sections (section 121, fig. 19, and section 123, fig. 31) show a shallow 3ft (1m) deep linear feature, probably a ditch, which cuts Roman layers and some Roman destruction layers but was covered by layers connected with the construction of the Anglo-Saxon church. This ditch also had stake-holes on the southern berm (section 120, fig. 19) and was on roughly the same alignment as the Anglo-Saxon church. Its purpose is unknown. It could be a very late Roman feature but in that case its alignment seems curious. This ditch could not be located in other sections as intervening sections were not drawn.

Anglo-Saxon (fig. 6a)

The minster church founded in the 9th or 10th century (below p. 14) was probably a royal foundation (Evans 1989, 116). The minster acquired precinct land in the north-east quadrant of the Roman town in a peripheral position to the Roman centre (a similar situation prevailed at Gloucester when the minster there was founded in 679).

There may have been, in the 9th century, some vestige of the principal Roman roads. Certainly the north section of Ermin Street continued in the middle ages, though shifting by some metres to the east. The new minster could have originally occupied approximately the blocks of Roman town land of Insula XXV and XXVI (McWhirr 1986, fig 2), though not, it would seem, as far south as the cross-roads; this cross-roads was later to develop into the market place. It might be speculated that at the time of the foundation of the minster, the cross-roads area was already significant to the secular power, and only peripheral land was allocated to the minster (again, the analogy is with Gloucester, where the minster precinct was drawn well short of the central market area).

Fig. 6a shows the borough boundary as recorded in 1875 (OS 1875). Though first mapped only at this late date, the borough boundary is likely to perpetuate that of the boundary of the township in 1571 (Slater 1976, 103); the medieval abbey precinct was then not only outside the township but was also extra hundredal (ibid, 104). The borough boundary (in its general course though not in detail) could go back still further to the original minster foundation and could mark the division between minster and secular land. The area later to be occupied by the parish church was also south of and outside the minster boundary.

The buildings of phase 1b: late 11th to early 12th century (fig. 6b)

The Anglo-Saxon church, it is suggested below, survived into the 12th century but with a modified and shortened west end of the late 11th to early 12th century. Some burials, many in stone-lined graves, belong to this period. There is also evidence north-east of the church for domestic occupation of some kind (p. 41); other domestic buildings lay west of the church, although the date of these is more problematic (p. 41). Some of this activity could relate to temporary accommodation of the Augustinian canons from 1130 onwards. However, some activity in the 11th century is suggested by the large collection of pottery of that date (p. 103); this presumably related to buildings associated with the old minster.

The building of the 12th century abbey (fig. 7a)

Cirencester Abbey was founded in the early 12th century by Henry I as a house of Augustinian canons, who inherited both the endowments and the parochial

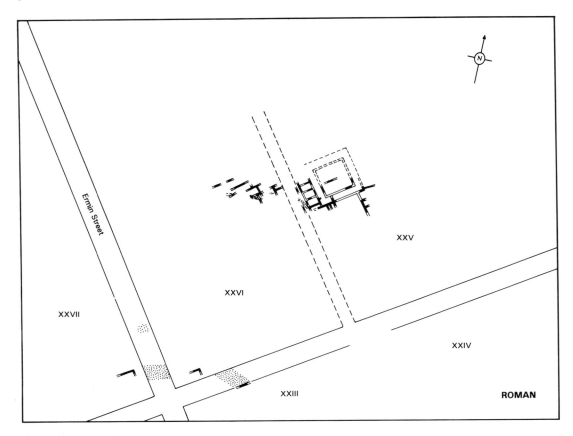

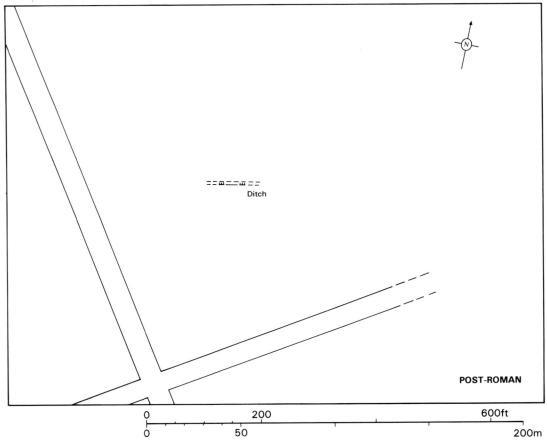

5. Topographical development: Roman and Post-Roman

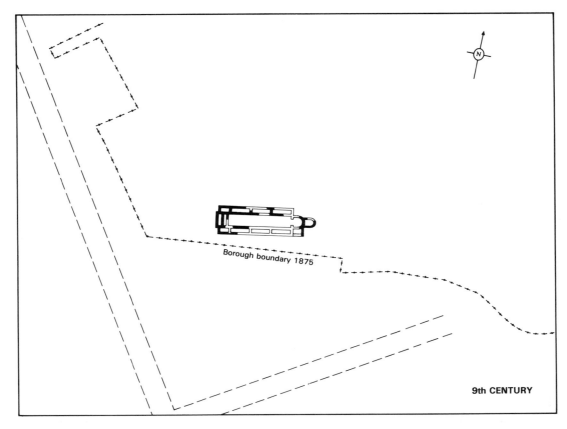

9th CENTURY

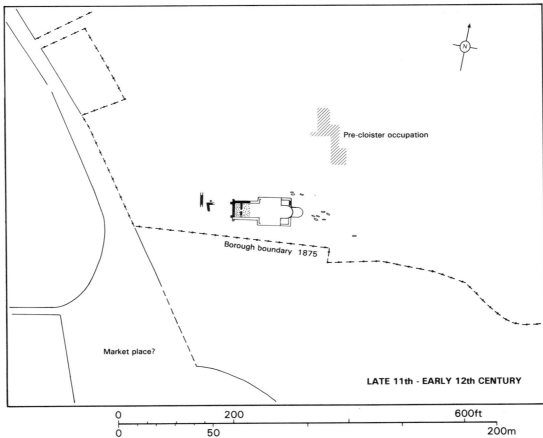

Pre-cloister occupation

Borough boundary 1875

Market place?

LATE 11th - EARLY 12th CENTURY

6. Topographical development: 9th to early 12th century

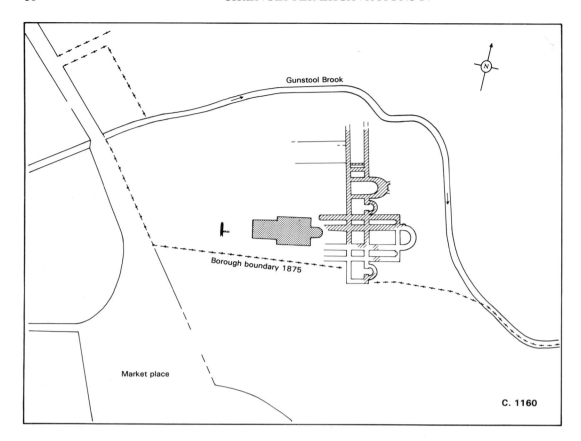

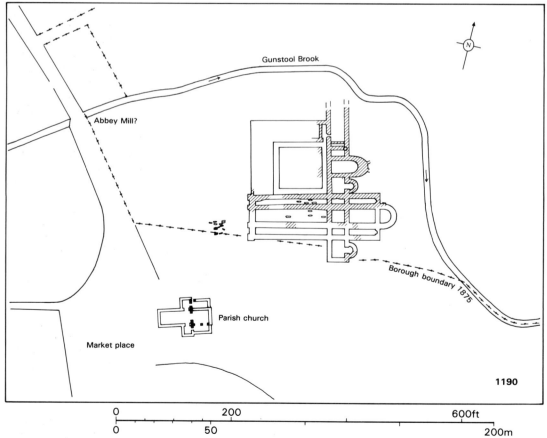

7. Topographical development: 12th century

obligations of the former minster (Evans 1991, 99). Building work may have begun in 1117, but more probably in 1130 (ibid., 100). The new abbey was probably begun when the old church, albeit shortened, was still standing (below p. 41). When the east end of the new church was completed, the abbey's own services could be held there, but the old church might have been left standing to serve the needs of the parish until it had to come down to make way for the nave of the abbey (Evans 1991, 101).

It may have been at this time that the Gunstool Brook was diverted across the town to flush the reredorter of the new abbey (Holbrook and Wilkinson, forthcoming; Slater 1976, fig 6.7).

The late 12th century (fig. 7b)
The abbey church was dedicated in 1176 (Evans 1991, 101); the tomb of a respected founder or benefactor (H118; below p. 165) was placed at the centre of the nave. Only fragments of walls survived, and the plan is, therefore, based upon foundations or robber trenches. This explains some of the irregularities in plan, and the presence of continuous 'sleeper' walls at the crossing, across the transepts, and on the line of the nave and presbytery arcades.

The earliest work in the parish church dates to the mid 12th century (McLees 1988, 38; Fuller 1893a, 35-6; Brown and McWhirr 1966, 250). The earliest known reference to a separate parish church is between 1182 and 1195 (Evans 1991, 101). The vill of Cirencester was first granted to Cirencester abbey in 1155 and the grant was made permanent in 1189. The abbey would then as the church's proprietor have had responsibility for the chancel. The chancel was provided with a south aisle c. 1180, with an arcade of two round columns, one re-used Roman (Fuller 1893a, 35-6), and the chancel north aisle had an external door of 12th-century date which could have been for access from the abbey (Evans 1991, 101-2).

The abbey in the 13th to 16th centuries (fig. 8a)
The church walls have been reconstructed to the thickness of the surviving wall of the north presbytery aisle extension; the 14th-century Lady chapel is reconstructed according to the paced measurements of William Worcestre (Harvey 1969, xvii, 284; Evans 1993, 139, n.9); if it took in the south transept, the east end of the Lady chapel extends to the east end of the chancel (Evans 1993, 133). The parish church is shown after its final addition: the south porch of the end of the 15th century (Evans 1993, 133). In the 13th century the wide market streets south and west of the parish church had been colonised by a number of shops (Slater 1976, 101).

A building shown over the stream on the map of 1795 could represent the medieval abbey mill (Fuller 1893a). The abbey had had a plot of land for a mill since the time of Henry I (Evans 1993, 116).

A cluster of 13th-century burials west of the abbey includes children. The interment of an evidently lay population suggests that the boundary between the burial ground of the canons and that of the parish church did not always run on the line of the borough boundary as later recorded, or on the parish churchyard boundary of the 19th century. It may have been that since the abbey also held the parish church, the zoning of parish and canons' burial grounds could fluctuate.

A burial pit found south of the 'borough boundary' may have been in the parish churchyard (see 'Burials', below). There were late medieval burials over the pit.

A building north of the cloister, which survived the Dissolution to appear in Kip's views, alongside the stream, could have been either the infirmary or the abbot's lodging (Fuller 1893a). The abbot's lodging is described as being between the cloister and the Spital Gate Grange and to have been recently extended when the abbey was dissolved (Evans 1993, 134).

The area c. 1700 (fig. 8b)
After the Dissolution the abbey church and claustral buildings were demolished, retaining at first the abbot's house and other buildings of practical use (Evans 1993, 134). Soon after the 1570s, when Camden described the site as uninhabited and having only the ruins of the abbey (Camden 1586, 195), a mansion (later called 'The Abbey') was built on the site, and this house with its formal garden is shown in two views by John Kip (figs. 65, 66). This house was in turn rebuilt as 'Abbey House' c. 1780 after a fire (Reece and Catling 1975, 19). Kip's view of The Abbey is too faulty in perspective for the position of this house to be identified with certainty. However the 18th-century gateway survives today, and another survivor from the garden appears in the map of 1795, which shows a row of dots west of the house (fig. 9a). These, from their position in relation to the gateway, can be identified as the row of trees on the north side of the western garden of The Abbey. It is thus possible to reconstruct the garden, placing The Abbey on the same plan as Abbey House. This reconstruction also fits with the various garden walls found in the excavations. It is clear that the 18th-century Abbey House was indeed built directly on the foundations of the Elizabethan mansion.

Kip's view of The Abbey shows a property between The Abbey and the parish churchyard. The north boundary of this property appears to have been on the line of the borough boundary. The area of this property had, in the 15th to 16th century, contained burials (fig. 8a), presumably of the parish churchyard. Perhaps this tract of land had been leased by the abbey as a burial ground, and later transferred as a dwelling plot by the secular owners.

The area c. 1795 (fig. 9a)
The 1795 map (Anon 1795) shows the market is still fully colonised by buildings. The Abbey House of 1780 has a new wing to the west which Fuller (1893b) labels as 'modern servants wing'.

The area in 1966 (fig. 9b)
The market place south of the parish church was cleared of its buildings in 1830 (Slater 1976, 101). Abbey House has been demolished and Abbey Flats built. The area of the excavations is shown.

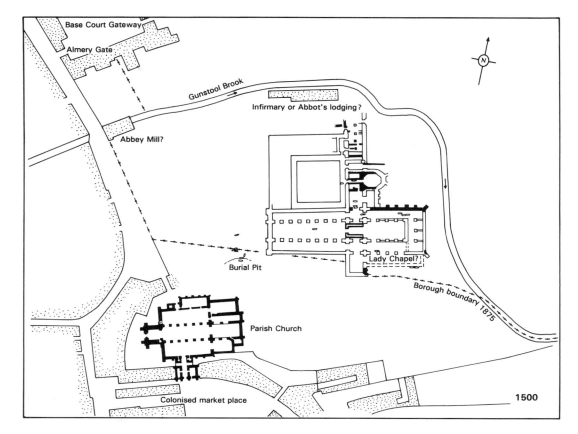

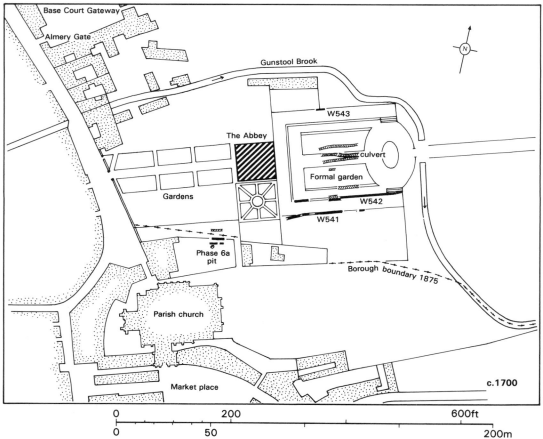

8. Topographical development: 13th-18th centuries

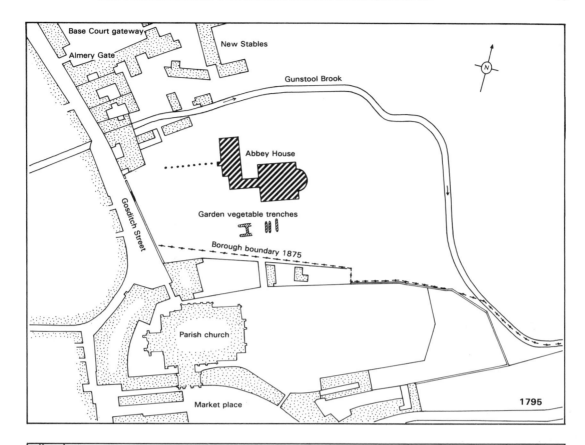

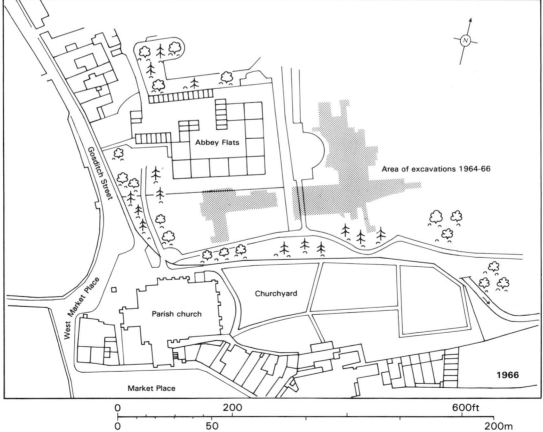

9. Topographical development 1795 and 1966: excavated area in relation to modern features

HISTORICAL EVIDENCE FOR THE ANGLO-SAXON CHURCH AND MEDIEVAL ABBEY

A.K.B. Evans

The Pre-Conquest Church

Cirencester church receives its earliest recorded mention in Domesday Book, compiled in 1086. It has an entry under its own name, as a tenant-in-chief of the Crown:

Land of the Church of Cirencester (*DB* **1**, 166c)
In Cirencester hundred.
The Church of Cirencester holds two hides from the king in alms, and it held them from King Edward free from all customary dues. There are 6 acres of meadow. It was and is worth 40s.

Domesday Book has two further references to the church, one under the heading of Roger of Lacy's lands, and the other in the account of the king's property in Gloucestershire:

Land of Roger of Lacy (*DB* **1**, 167d)
In Bisley hundred.
Roger holds Painswick...On this land St. Mary of Cirencester has one villein and part of a wood. King William gave this to it. It is worth 10s.
Land of the King (*DB* **1**, 162d)
In Cirencester hundred.
... From the new market 20s, of which St. Mary has the third penny.

From these entries it is apparent that on the eve of the Conquest the church had a two-hide endowment, which was comparatively modest if for a group of priests.[1] To this William I added a small property in Painswick and a third of the tolls of Cirencester market. The church's status as a tenant-in-chief under William suggests that it was an old minster with royal connexions. Cirencester was certainly a royal vill in the 10th and 11th centuries, when it is mentioned in charters and in the Anglo-Saxon Chronicle as a place where on occasion the king resided and met his Witan[2] It is likely that it was royal property long before.

Domesday Book is the only surviving historical record of the existence of Cirencester's pre-Conquest church. There is no reliable evidence for the date or circumstances of its foundation. No local tradition concerning it had survived into the sixteenth century, since when Leland visited Cirencester in *c.* 1540 his inquiries on this matter elicited no response. He remarked that 'of what Saxon's foundation no man can telle' (*Itin.* **1**, 128). However, the Rev John Collinson, writing in the late 18th century, stated that it was 'founded by Alwyn, a Saxon, in the time of King Egbert'. Collinson cited as the source of this information a chronicle of Cirencester Abbey in his own possession.[3] This manuscript chronicle has never been traced. If, as will be suggested below, its own date was no earlier than the fifteenth century, it would not necessarily be a reliable source for the pre-Conquest period.

Egbert was king of Wessex from 802 until 839. At this time Cirencester was in the neighbouring kingdom of Mercia. For one year, 829-30, Egbert annexed and ruled Mercia, but both before and after that year Mercia's king was Wiglaf (827-9, 830-40), who refers to the period from 830 as 'my second reign' (*CS* 400). It cannot be suggested that Cirencester was retained by Wessex after Wiglaf's restoration, for the Anglo-Saxon Chronicle records that it was to Cirencester that Guthrum and his army went in 879 when they left Wessex after the Treaty of Wedmore. Cirencester was in the border area between Mercia and Wessex. If Wiglaf recovered his kingdom from Wessex by military force, it seems unlikely that a major church (as its excavated foundations have shown Cirencester's to be) would be founded in this vulnerable location: there was already a royal minster at Winchcombe, 16 miles further from the border, where the Mercian royal archives were kept (Finberg 1961, 11 n.2, 229; Finberg 1957, 59). Moreover, if the church was a Mercian foundation, it would be attributed to the reign of the king of Mercia, not of Wessex. But if, as Dr S. D. Keynes has suggested[4], Wiglaf's restoration was by agreement with Wessex, and perhaps accompanied by an alliance, it is possible that a church might have been founded in Cirencester under West Saxon patronage.

There remains the problem of the founder, who, Collinson's source implies, was not royal. No known Alwyn (Alhhun, Alhwine or Æthelwine) of this period had any connexion with Cirencester. Consequently, although the date given in Collinson's manuscript chronicle may be appropriate (and the archaeological evidence could well support it), the name of the founder could be mythical, perhaps based on an Alwyn mentioned in Domesday Book (Evans 1989, 108-9). It remains uncorroborated and unexplained.

The cartulary of Cirencester Abbey has no statement or document which might throw light on the foundation of the church which preceded the abbey on its site. But the cartulary does contain a marginal comment which could have given rise to the date mentioned in Collinson's source. In the margin next to the dating clause of the copy of the abbey's foundation charter (Reg. A, f.14v), a memorandum was added in a 15th-century hand: 'Note that the monastery of Cirencester has been established for about 300 years'. The date given in the abbey's foundation charter was 1133: a date 300 years before that would be in the 830s when Egbert was reigning in Wessex. It could be that the compiler of the chronicle Collinson used took this marginal comment to refer to a church which was established 300 years before the abbey's foundation. But, as the editor of the Cirencester Cartulary pointed out (*CC* **1**, p. 23), the marginal memorandum was written in the

15th century and did not refer to the pre-Conquest church at all: it referred to the abbey. The 15th-century annotator of the cartulary was drawing attention to the fact that the abbey had been founded 300 years before his own time. If this was the origin of the supposed date of the pre-Conquest church, it would be no more than a lucky chance that Egbert's reign comes within the period suggested for it by the archaeological evidence.

The Danish invasions of the 9th, 10th and early 11th centuries involved Mercian churches in impoverishment, through obligatory contributions to tributes and Danegelds, and in physical destruction, if in the path of a Danish army. Cirencester experienced a year of Danish occupation in 879-80; and probable raiding in 893, when the invaders were based in the Severn valley, and in 1015 when they rampaged through Gloucestershire: consequently, it could have suffered on both counts. This might be an explanation both of the church's limited resources in 1066, and of a truncated rebuilding (to the Phase 1b of the archaeological picture) whether this occurred in the 11th or the 12th century. Failure to recover both size and endowment was in tune with a general movement towards more numerous but smaller churches, for the most part served by only one priest.

It is not known whether the two hides belonging to Cirencester's church at the time of the Norman Conquest supported one priest or more. By the 1130s, when it was replaced by Cirencester Abbey, it had a community of priests (secular canons), who were compensated for losing their church and their livelihood. William I had augmented its resources, though not lavishly. It is likely that it had been further endowed by Regenbald[5], a well-rewarded king's clerk under both Edward the Confessor and William I, who had family connexions with the Cirencester area. A much later tradition, which first appears in the 13th century, credits him with being the dean of the church's community of priests (Evans 1989, 116-18); if so, he was probably an absentee, but there seems little doubt that he was a benefactor.

The Abbey

The Worcester chronicle records under the year 1117 that according to the command of Henry I a new work was begun at Cirencester.[6] This refers to building works, which may (but may not) be connected with the abbey the king later established there.

The date of the foundation of the abbey is noted in the contemporary chronicle of John of Worcester, and there are two versions. In the original version, the appointment and blessing of the first abbot, Serlo, appears under the year 1131 (Lambeth Palace MS 42, f.153). In the final version, John altered it to 1130 (*John of Worcester*, 31). Since his revised dates were sometimes less accurate than those in the original version, and since the consecration of Robert, bishop of Hereford, was similarly but erroneously altered from 1131 to 1130, it has been usual to attribute Serlo's appointment to 1131. But

the abbot of Cirencester is mentioned in the Pipe Roll of 1129-30 (*PR 31 Henry I*, 80, 126): he must, therefore, have been appointed no later than 1130.

The abbey's foundation charter is dated 1133 (*CC* **1**, 28). Although internal discrepancies show that the original text has been tampered with, the date is not unlikely; many monastic foundation charters were drawn up some years later than the actual foundation gift. Henry I in this charter granted to his new abbey all the property which had been held by Regenbald. It seems probable that Regenbald was the original donor of this benefaction to Cirencester church. Some of his former properties had fallen into other hands: in the charter the interests of these holders were protected for their life-times, as were the incomes of the existing priests of Cirencester church, which by Henry I's foundation now became an Augustinian abbey of regular canons. The abbey would have taken over the endowment and pastoral responsibilities of the church it replaced.

By a writ dated between 1130 and 1133 (*CC* **1**, 55), Henry I granted exemption from tolls on materials to be bought by the abbot and canons of the new abbey for the building of their church. However, it appears that little progress had been made by Henry I's death in 1135; and the work must have suffered a setback under Stephen, when Cirencester was in the front line of the civil war. In 1142, when Stephen temporarily took the town from the Empress Matilda's adherents, Cirencester Castle, which adjoined the abbey, was burned down (*Gesta Stephani*, **2**, 70).

It was left to Henry II to press forward what his grandfather had begun. In 1155, soon after his accession, he made a generous grant of the revenues of his royal vill of Cirencester to help finance the building of the abbey church (*CC* **1**, 66). The work was sufficiently advanced for the dedication ceremony to be held on 17 October 1176 (*Howden*, **2**, 101; *Gesta Henrici II*, **1**, 127), when the four bishops who were present granted an indulgence (*CC* **1**, 164), no doubt intended to encourage pilgrims whose donations would enable the church to be completed[7]. As a further subvention to the funds, Henry II even gave up his right to the abbey's revenues during the vacancy which occurred when Abbot Andrew died shortly after the dedication of his church (*CC* **1**, 70).

Although building work was still proceeding, the king's generosity did not extend to a similar sacrifice at a later vacancy, in 1186. On this occasion he took from the abbey the £433 17s 11d balance of income over necessary expenditure, as well as the contents of the late abbot's treasure-chest. Among the expenses of this year was an item of £7 7s 0d for roofing the church and repairing the workshops (*PR 33 Henry II*, 26-7).

Henry II's grant of the revenues of the royal manor of Cirencester, to fund the completion of the church, expired with him in 1189. To retain this useful income, the abbey had to approach the new king, Richard I. An agreement was reached by which the abbey paid £100 down and £30 a year in perpetuity for Cirencester manor plus the vill of Minety and the lordship of the Seven Hundreds (*CC* **1**, 32). Eventually, in 1214, these former royal demesne lands were recognised as exempt from tallage (*PR 16 John*, 56; *CC* **1**, 17, 39).

During the long period while the abbey church was in building, and before the cloister with its domestic ranges could have been begun, the Augustinian canons must have had living quarters somewhere on the site, temporary in the sense that they would eventually be replaced by the cloister buildings, but substantial enough to last for more than half a century. The pre-Conquest church would have continued in use while the chancel and transepts of the abbey church, well to the east of it, were being constructed. This could be the context (as is suggested below, pp. 39-42) for the structural alterations to the early church (Phase 1b) involving not only a new west front for its shortened nave but also readier access to its reliquary crypt. Relics, like Indulgences, attracted pilgrims and funds.

In the 1220s the abbey was preparing to build a conduit to bring water to the washing place (*lavatorium*) in the cloister (*CC* **1**, 235-8) which presumably by then was nearing completion; and in 1248-9 the abbey treasurer's accounts mention £9 8s 8d spent on the dormitory, perhaps for repairs. The abbot's lodging and the guesthall, which normally occupy the west range of a monastic cloister, receive incidental mention in the accounts of the abbot's chaplain in 1248-9; and the cellarer's accounts for that year record expenditure on modifications to an upper room adjoining the Great Hall (the refectory), which at Cirencester, where the cloister was on the north side of the church, would be in the cloister's north range (Obedientiaries' Accts., ff. 7,7v). Water for the refectory was brought by conduit from the spring called Letherwell at a date between the 1220s and the 1280s (*CC* **3**, 288-9).

A prison, built with royal permission granted in 1222 (*Rot. Claus.* **1**, 490), was ready to hold royal prisoners from Gloucester Castle in 1223 (*Rot. Claus.* **1**, 543b, 556). Possibly, like that at Bridlington Priory, it lay next to the abbey gate (Caley 1821, 271).

According to William Worcestre, two bells were consecrated at Cirencester in 1238 (Harvey 1969, 285). Perhaps they were for the tower of the abbey church, but they could have been for the parish church.[8]

Leland states that the heart of Sanchia of Provence, wife of Henry III's brother Richard of Cornwall, was buried in Cirencester Abbey church (*Itin.* **1**, 129). She died in 1261, and left £100 to the abbey in her will (*CC* **3**, 283).

Small items of expenditure on the abbey buildings are recorded in the third quarter of the 13th century; and in 1276-7 £4 10s 2d was spent on roofing part of the abbey church (Obedientaries Accts., f. 35v), perhaps after some structural alteration. A rebuilding project is likely to have prompted the papal grant in 1292 of an indulgence of a year and 40 days to those who visited Cirencester Abbey each year during the octaves of the feasts of the Nativity, the Annunciation, the Purification, and the Assumption of the Blessed Virgin, and on the anniversary of the church's dedication (*CC* **1**, 171). Donations arising from the indulgence would have provided funds for new building. Possibly this was for the construction of the new square-ended chancel with its eastern chapels, where the three new altars consecrated in the abbey church in 1309 might have been placed (*Reg. Reynolds*, 10).

Whatever income was generated by the papal indulgence was apparently vastly overspent, for when William Hereward became abbot in 1335 the abbey was deep in debt and parts of the church were in danger of collapse. Within ten years Abbot Hereward's efforts had restored the abbey to solvency and its church to stability. In gratitude, his community established a chantry to him in the Lady Chapel which he seems to have constructed (*Reg. Bransford*, 144-6). The Black Death of 1348-9 must have interrupted building operations, but more extensive reconstruction of the church was apparently planned, for in June 1351 Pope Clement VI granted another indulgence, valid for ten years, specifically to those who contributed to the fund for the rebuilding of the abbey church (*Cal. Pap. Lett. 1342-62*, 456).

Not only Abbot Hereward but three more abbots died between 1352 and 1363, no doubt owing to recurrences of plague. This meant not only changes of leadership but also four expensive vacancies in just over eleven years. Again the abbey was plunged in debt, with its buildings threatening collapse (*CC* **1**, 140). Finances apparently recovered by the 1370s, but the abbey's administration and morale incurred severe criticism from the bishop in 1378 (*Reg. Wakefield*, 155-8). Nevertheless, Pope Urban VI consented in January 1379 to a petition to make Cirencester a mitred abbey[9]; he was informed by the abbot that its annual income was one thousand marks (*CC* **3**, 120).

This revenue was dramatically reduced in Henry IV's reign when the townsmen of Cirencester, enjoying the king's support after quelling the incipient rebellion of January 1400, withheld their services from the abbey, causing losses which amounted to an estimated £6000 before, under Henry V, judgment was given in the abbey's favour in 1413 (*CC* **1**, 12; Fuller 1885, 330-8; Fuller 1894, 45-9, 58-74).

Henry IV's reign was a prosperous time for the townsfolk, who between 1402 and 1413 added the great west tower to Cirencester parish church. When the abbey's prosperity returned in the reign of Henry V, it is likely that building activity on the abbey church was resumed. William Worcestre visited Cirencester in 1480 and made the following notes (Harvey 1969, 284-5: blank spaces occur in two places, for measurements which he had intended to fill in):-

> The great church of Canons Regular of the order of St. Augustine is 140 paces or [ ] yards long; its nave with two aisles is 41 paces or 24 yards wide, apart from the east chapel whose length is [ ]. The very old chapel of St. Mary on the south side of the choir of the abbey church, with an aisle anciently annexed to it, is 44 yards long, and the width of the said old chapel is 22 paces including the old aisle.

The length of the cloister is 52 paces.
The length of the Chapterhouse is 14 yards and its width is 10 yards. And it has six windows glazed with three lights; and in the whole Chapterhouse are 10 lights filled with quarries, each light having three *orle* [?roundels].

When Worcestre gave dimensions in yards they were measurements, not estimates (Harvey 1969, xvii). Since his measurement of the nave's width is given in both yards and paces, it is apparent that his pace at this time was 1ft 9in. Consequently his description is of a church 245ft long and 72ft wide, with an elongated Lady Chapel, 132ft long and 38ft 6in wide, on the south side of the choir. The length of the cloister was 91ft, which is likely to represent the length of the nave west of the transept, less the width of the east and west cloister walks. The Chapter House was 42ft by 30ft, with six three-light windows and ten windows in all. Worcestre refers to a chapel at the east end of the nave; this may be the chapel built by Henry Morton which is mentioned in a will of 1403 (Reg. Arundel **1**. f.205; Wadley 1886, 78): Henry Morton occurs as canon at Cirencester in 1349-50 and as prior in 1353-4 (*Cal. Pap. Lett. 1342-62*, 328, 420; *CC* **2**, 574; *Cal. Pat. 1354-8*, 116). Since Worcestre said that this nave chapel was additional to the stated width of the nave, it must have projected; and it was presumably on the south side, for the cloister lay on the north side. Perhaps the chapel occupied the angle between south transept and nave, as did the Lady Chapel at Rochester Abbey half a century later.

Cirencester's last two abbots, John Hagbourne (1504-22) and John Blake (1522-39), were concerned with building work in the parish church's chancel, for which as rector the abbey was responsible. Probably they were also rebuilding the nave of the abbey church, for Leland in *c.* 1540 described the abbey church west of the transept as 'but new work to speke of'. The eastern part, on the other hand, appeared to him to be 'of a very old building' (*Itin.* **1**, 129).

When the abbey was dissolved in December 1539 there were 17 canons (*LP* **14**, no. 705). Numbers had been declining since 1307 when there were 40 (*Worc. Reg. s.v. 1301-1435*, 101). In 1498 there were 24 (Reg. Morton **1**, f.171; *VCH Gloucs* **2**, 83 gives the date erroneously as 1428); in 1534 there were 21 (*Dep. Keeper's Rep.* **7** (1846), App. ii, 283). But the abbey's income remained high. It was assessed in 1522 at £1333 6s 8d (*LP* **3**, no. 1047; Goring 1971, 701); and in the *Valor Ecclesiasticus* of 1535, when some abatements were allowed, at £1053 16s 8d (Lindley 1957, 113-4). After the Dissolution, the revenues were valued at £1131 1s 5d a year (*Mon. Angl.* **6**, 178-9). It was the richest of nearly 200 Augustinian houses in the kingdom.

The Dissolution Survey of 1539 gives lists of the buildings deemed to be superfluous and therefore to be demolished, and of those which were permitted to remain undestroyed. Reprieve from demolition was allowed only to purely domestic constructions, all of them standing detached from the church and the cloister, which were to be completely removed (P.R.O. E 315/494, f.61; Fuller 1893a, 45-6).

Assigned to Remayn undefaced

The late Abbottis lodging with the New lodging adioyning and the houses of Office to the seid lodging Annexed as they be sette betwene Spittell gate Grange and the lodging called the Squiers lodging. The Baking Bruying and Malting houses The late Abbotts Stabull The Barne in the Spittell gate Grange with ii entrees in the same. The Garner in the Base Courte The Gate that Closith the Quadraunte of the Base Courte. The Wollehouse with the Stable by the Mille And the Almery Grange for husbandry.

Demed to be superfluous

The Church with the Chapelles Adioynyng
The Cloister[10] with the Chaptrehouse Dormytory Frayter Library. the Hostery The Fermary with alle the Lodgings to theym adioynyng. The Cellerers Chambre. the Squiers Chambre The Sextery. The Convent Kitchyn with the houses adioyning. The Storehouse in the Courte. The Slatehouse. The Stywards Chambre. The Gesten Chambre. and Stabulles And the Heyhouse.

The site of the abbey and its lands in Minety were leased in 1540 to Roger Basing, the lease to include all the buildings except those which the king had commanded to be pulled down and carried away (P.R.O. E 315/212, ff. 138-40; *LP* **16**, 720). Lead from the roofs of the doomed buildings was reserved to the king: it was stripped off by July 1541 (Youings 1971, doc. 31a). The stone, timber and other materials were sold to Sir Anthony Hungerford and Robert Strange for removal (P.R.O. E 321/17/48). In January 1565 the reversion of the site of the abbey was purchased from Elizabeth I by her physician, Richard Master (*Cal. Pat. 1563-6*, 201), who presumably built there the late Elizabethan mansion shown on John Kip's drawing made in *c.* 1700 (in Atkyns 1712, **2**, pl. 18, and here fig. 66). When Camden visited Cirencester in the 1570s the abbey ruins were still visible (Camden 1586, 195), but no trace of the abbey church, the cloister, or the conventual buildings is visible in Kip's drawing: and Browne Willis, writing before 1718, stated that memory of the abbey church had entirely perished, together with the church itself; the materials having been so wholly removed that the local inhabitants could not give any satisfactory account even of where it had stood (Willis 1718, 58).

Richard Master's house was pulled down in 1776 when a new house was built, re-using the Elizabethan house's foundations (Bigland 1791, 344). It was thought that these successive houses stood on part of the site of the demolished abbey church, and attempted reconstructions of the abbey's lay-out by 19th-century antiquarians placed the church in this position (Beecham 1887, facing p. 66; Fuller 1893a, pl. II). But the excavated foundations of the abbey church lie clear of the site of Abbey House, which was built west of the cloister.

Notes

1. Two hides could have supported a group of priests, as at Tettenhall in Staffordshire (*DB* **1**, 247d); but other communities of priests had much larger endowments, for instance Wolverhampton, with 20¼ hides in 1086 (*VCH Staffs* **3**, 315-16, 321-2).

2. In 935 (Gibbs 1939, 5 no. J10); in 956 (Finberg 1961, no. 280); in 985 (Finberg 1961, nos. 141-2 with *ASC s.a.* 985); and in 1020 (*ASC s.a.*).

3. 'Chronicon Abbat. Cirencest. MS penes Edit.' (Collinson 1791, **2**, 191).

4. Dr S. D. Keynes suggests that the alliance between Wessex and Mercia, which was so important in the wars with the Danes, had its roots in the second quarter of the 9th century, in an understanding between Egbert and Wiglaf, and between their successors Aethelwulf of Wessex and Berhtwulf of Mercia whose coins were similar and struck by the same moneyers (Keynes and Lapidge 1983, 12, citing J. J. North, *English Hammered Coinage* **1** (2nd edn, London 1980), 70-71, 89-90; see also Keynes, 'King Alfred and the Mercians' in M. Blackburn and D. Dumville (eds), *Kings, Currency and Alliances* (Woodbridge, 1995).

5. Regenbald seems to have been given the church of Cirencester the 21¼ hides for which it was exempted from tax in 1128-9 (Evans 1989, 118). Probably he bequeathed all his property to the church, but more than half of it had fallen into other hands (Evans 1991, 100). For a consideration of Regenbald's possible career, see Keynes 1988.

6. The Worcester Chronicle has only this bare statement and gives no further information: *Secundum regis Henrici praeceptum apud Cirenceastre novum opus est inceptum* (Florence of Worcester, **2**, 70).

7. The dedication of a church did not wait until its completion. It could occur as soon as the walls were standing (Cheney 1973, 363).

8. The parish church, which stands just outside the abbey precinct, has its earliest known mention in 1182 x 95: J. E. Sayers, *Papal Judges Delegate 1198-1254* (Oxford 1971), 50. However, surviving Romanesque arches suggest a mid-12th century date. It appears among the churches belonging to the abbey in 1222 (*CC* **1**, 161). Although the abbey was responsible for the chancel, the nave was the responsibility of the parishioners, who twice rebuilt it, in *c.*1235-50 and in 1515-30.

9. The privileges granted by Urban VI to Cirencester Abbey raised its status. Its abbot was given the right to use the seven pontifical insignia normally belonging to bishops (mitre, ring, sandals, pastoral staff, gloves, tunicle and dalmatic), and to bestow solemn benediction after mass, vespers and matins if no bishop or apostolic legate was present.

10. The survey apparently proceeds round the cloister anti-clockwise. Thus the chapter-house and dormitory are in the east range, and the refectory (since Cirencester's cloister was on the north side of the church) is in the north range. The library could be in the upper storey of the refectory range, as at Walsingham (Evans 1993, 122). However, many monastic libraries, purpose-built in the 14th and 15th centuries, were located above the book-rooms and slypes (passage-ways) with book-cupboards which they replaced (T. Tatton-Brown, 'The Medieval Library at Canterbury Cathedral', in *Canterbury Cathedral Chronicle* no 82, 1988). At Cirencester, this would be over part of the east range.

THE EXCAVATIONS

SUMMARY OF PHASES

Roman
1. Post-Roman/pre-abbey construction
   1a Anglo-Saxon church
   1b Post-conquest features, late 11th to early 12th century
2. Construction of abbey, early 12th century-early 13th century
3. Use of abbey, early 13th-early 16th century
   3a robbing & pits outside west front, courtyard and ditch
   3b repairs to undercroft
   3c eastern extension including tombs; cobbled area outside west front
   3d pit, BP I 19
   3e latest abbey contexts, remodelling of chapter house

4. Demolition and robbing of abbey, early 16th-17th
   4a robbing pre-rubble
   4b primary rubble deposits
   4c pits and robbing through rubble
5. Garden activity, 17th and 18th century
   5a garden features
   5b redeposited rubble
   5c rubbish pits pre-1710
6. Early to mid 18th-century pits
   6a pit BP I 4
   6b stone structure and drain, BP I
   6c late rubble spreads, BJ XIV 2, late 18th-19th century
   6d late stony layer, BP I 8

ROMAN BUILDINGS BENEATH THE ANGLO-SAXON CHURCH AND MEDIEVAL ABBEY

J. Keely and L. Viner

During excavation Roman artefacts were frequently encountered in medieval levels and when time permitted the Roman deposits were examined. In 1964 only one trench was taken down to, and through, Roman levels (64 BK I), but in 1965 and 1966 time allowed for a more detailed examination of the Roman stratigraphy lying beneath the Saxon and medieval churches, particularly in areas 65 BK, BL, BM, BN, BP, BT, and BV.

Inevitably the Roman levels were much disturbed and many relationships destroyed by substantial Anglo-Saxon and medieval wall foundations. A detailed discussion of the excavated Roman structures, finds and pottery has been published elsewhere (McWhirr 1986, 222-33).

The area chosen for the Anglo-Saxon church and medieval abbey straddled two *insulae* of the former Roman town of *Corinium Dobunnorum,* XXV and

XXVI, lying in the north-eastern sector of the walled town (McWhirr 1986, fig. 2).

Building XXV. 1 (figs. 5 and 10)

The structural remains belonging to the Roman period found beneath the eastern part of the abbey church in *insula* XXV represented a courtyard building. At least four rooms of the west wing were uncovered with indications of further rooms to the east and south (fig. 10, areas 65 BK, BL and BM). The rooms and associated verandah were ranged around a courtyard, the inner wall of which was decorated with wall plaster painted to resemble marble. The courtyard wall itself was formed of massive stylobate blocks which originally carried pillars set at regular intervals.

The west side of the building lay parallel to the assumed line of street XXV/XXVI. The remains of two drains were found, one of which (in BM IV/V) may have linked with the drain found to the west on sites BN and BV. The robber-trench of this stone-lined drain cut through the gravel surfaces of the street. The second, a brick-lined drain in BM III, may have been a drain alongside the street. Evidence (undated) of structural alterations was found in several places and there are indications to suggest an earlier building on the site.

Dating evidence for the construction of the courtyard building was sparse. Several walls cut through earlier floor and make-up levels containing pottery dated no later than the 1st century. The layer cut by the stylobate blocks contained pottery of probable 3rd-century date. This evidence could be taken to indicate that the verandah wall was a later addition to the building. Alternatively, in the absence of closer dating evidence, it could be taken as the *terminus post quem* for the construction of the whole building.

The dark earth covering all Roman levels in trenches 64 BK I, BL I, BL II and BL V and the fill of several robber trenches contained pottery generally dating to after AD 350/370. Coins recovered from these deposits included issues of Gratian, Valentinian I and II and Arcadius. This suggests that these sealing levels began accumulating during the second half of the 4th century and into the 5th, by which time the building had probably been abandoned. Alternatively, these levels could represent redeposited material for levelling-up prior to Anglo-Saxon building work.

Building XXVI. 1 (figs. 5 and 11)
The destruction of Roman contexts in *insula* XXVI by Anglo-Saxon and medieval structures was even greater west of the street XXV/XXVI than it had been to the east in *insula* XXV. Phasing of wall construction was difficult and the walls shown on the plan (fig. 11) cannot all have been in use at the same time. The differences in alignment of the walls in this area also made it difficult to be certain of their relationship one with another.

Those walls in trenches BN I and II, with associated hypocaust system, clearly belonged to a structure fronting onto street XXV/XXVI. Two rows of *pilae* survived set in a grey clay layer. Charcoal, ash and black soil filled the hypocaust channels while tile and tesserae found in the overlying layers suggest that the floor above had been tessellated. It is probable that the walls in trenches BN IV, V, VIII and BT II also belonged to this structure although walls in one area were not aligned exactly with walls in the other. Furthermore, there was evidence to suggest later structural alterations. Disparate lengths of drains were associated with the structure and it may be that they ran under the building as in building XXV. 1. The partially robbed-out drain in BN IV can probably be linked with that in BM IV/V. Its fill contained pottery belonging to the second half of the 4th century and coins of post AD 388 date, together with a single sherd of possible Anglo-Saxon or Saxo-Norman date (BN IV 36, fabric 255).

The short sections of walls seen in trenches BV I and BV II may have belonged to a separate structure west of the one containing the hypocaust, since they were on a different alignment. However, this does not preclude the possibility that all the walls found in this *insula* may have belonged to the same building.

Dating evidence for the construction of the walls is again sparse but it suggests that building began during or soon after the late 1st century, judging by the lack of obvious 2nd-century pottery types in any of the construction levels, although a later date cannot be ruled out. Floor sequences found in the south of trench BN IV dated to after *c.* AD 120, while material sealing the hypocaust suggests that it was in use in the 2nd-3rd centuries. In the west of the area an *opus signinum* floor, unrelated to any structural features, was laid down after AD 250/270.

Residual Roman finds
The Roman pottery and small finds recovered from post-Roman levels are fully recorded in archive, available for consultation on application to the Corinium Museum, Cirencester.

The study of the Roman pottery could draw few conclusions from such an amorphous group of residual pottery and any discernible characteristics are unlikely to have much significance. However, a number of comments may still be made. Taking the groups (defined by trench assemblage) overall there was a slightly higher proportion of 1st and 2nd-century grey wares than those coarse ware types characteristic of the 3rd and 4th centuries, yet there were more fine wares belonging to the later period than the earlier one. There was just a handful of vessels characteristic of the military period while products typical of the later 4th century were also few in number, particularly local copies of B.B.1 forms which are usually relatively common in stratified 4th-century contexts in Cirencester.

One might also have expected larger numbers of mortaria which were not frequent in any of the groups and which were mostly from the Oxfordshire potteries. The disparity in the quantities of samian recovered from each site is also difficult to explain since it is not known what factors may have possibly influenced its retrieval - factors such as partial recovery during excavation and discarding during the initial stages of sorting.

One consistent characteristic of all the groups of residual pottery is the predominance of B.B.1 vessels, which serves to emphasise the tremendous importance of this industry in all but the earliest and latest groups of Roman pottery in Cirencester and elsewhere.

With regard to residual Roman small finds, 117 Roman coins were noted in post-Roman deposits, compared with 21 from Roman levels published by Richard Reece (in McWhirr 1986, 230). In date they ranged from issues of Claudius I (AD 41-54) to House of Theodosius (AD 383-451), and, as would be expected, a site plot shows a concentration in areas corresponding to deepest disturbance of Roman levels in areas BK, BL, BN and BT.

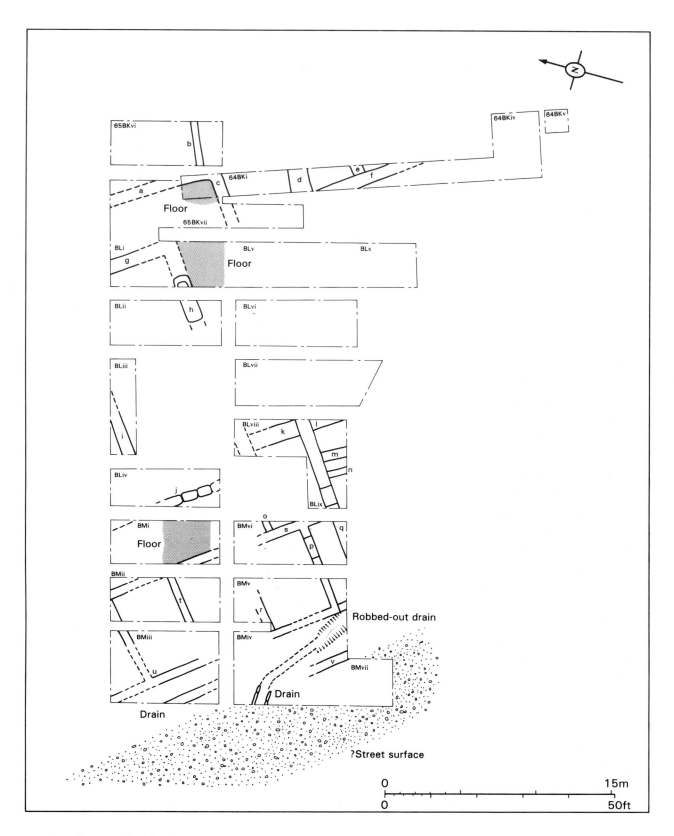

10. Plan of Roman Building XXV.1

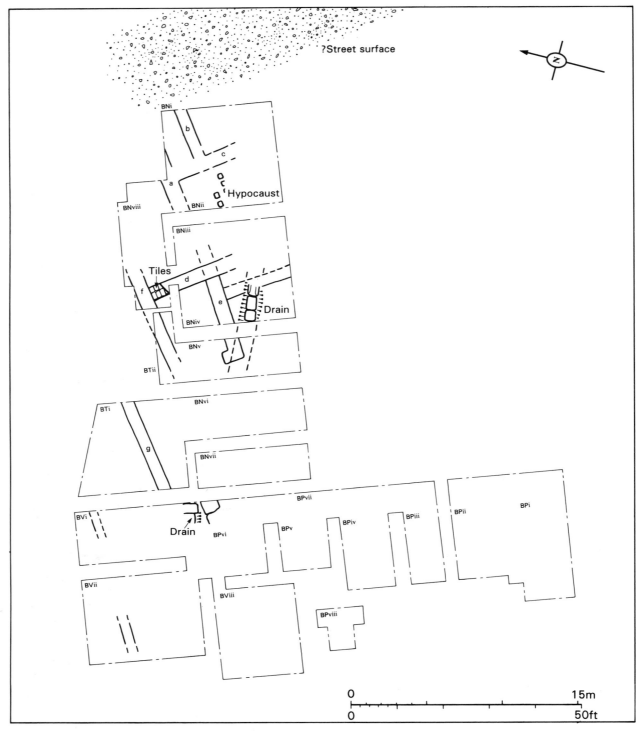

?Street surface

Z

BNi

b

c

a

Hypocaust

BNviii

BNii

BNiii

Tiles

d

f

e

Drain

BNiv

BNv

BTii

BTi   BNvi

g

BNvii

BPvii

BVi

Drain

BPvi   BPv   BPiv   BPiii   BPii   BPi

BVii

BViii

BPviii

0   15m

0   50ft

11. Plan of Roman Building XXVI.1

Fourth-century issues accounted for 87% of the total identified by Richard Reece.

Of the Roman brooches studied by Don Mackreth, the three residual finds were a Colchester Derivative, a Trumpet/Unclassified and a Zoomorphic flat plate brooch in the shape of a fish. Other recognisably Roman finds in residual contexts included spoons, nail cleaners, a pair of tweezers, a spatula, rings, bracelets (all made of copper alloy), and glass beads.

The builders of the Anglo-Saxon church used quantities of Roman masonry in the foundations of their church, blocks of a size and quality of finish that would suggest their origin in a prestigious public building. A fragment of a Roman tombstone was found in 1966, as filling in a foundation trench for the Anglo-Saxon church (Hassall 1973, 211, fn. 2).

THE ANGLO-SAXON CHURCH
THE ARCHAEOLOGICAL EVIDENCE

P. D. C. Brown

with A. K. B. Evans

The plan of the building excavated in 1965 and 1966 (figs. 14, 15) shows a church with an aisled nave and an apsidal eastern end. The full details are obscured for two reasons. The building was excavated as fully as possible, within the permitted area; this included the west end and the north side of the nave, and the east end. However, the south side of the church has barely been touched, and a vital space about 30ft (9m) wide between the east end and the nave, between sites BM and BN remains entirely unexcavated because of the presence of a yew hedge which could not be removed.. The second reason for incompleteness derives from the fact that the building had been extensively robbed, particularly at the west end. At no point was there any piece of walling standing even to floor level, and in most places even the foundations had been robbed to a considerable depth; nowhere within the church was any patch of the original flooring found intact, except in the crypt. The plan revealed is thus one of the foundations and the foundation trenches.

The foundations are massive, a double line of large stone blocks with an infilling of smaller stones, tiles and lumps of broken-up concrete - all recognisable as material plundered from Roman ruins; the smaller pieces could have come from one of the Roman buildings encountered on the site, but the large blocks may have been brought from some monumental building or one of the gates. The foundation trenches were cut down through earlier Roman layers until they reached the natural gravel subsoil. This pattern was followed even where the foundations crossed hard rammed gravel surfaces - all were cut away to subsoil level. There was a single exception to this pattern. A large stone-built Roman drain crossed the site, passing beneath the Roman buildings (figs. 12, 20). This was built of the same sort of large stones as the Anglo-Saxon foundations; it was left in position by the Anglo-Saxon builders and incorporated into their foundations. The plan gives an indication of the considerable scale, the large size of the stones used, the breadth of the foundations and the length of the building. To these should be added the sense of depth; the foundations were dug down about 6ft (1.8m) from the ancient ground surface: 10ft (3.05m) from the present ground level.

The Anglo-Saxon church lies west of and under the medieval abbey church (see fig. 6a, 7a); its east end lies roughly under the centre of the nave of the abbey church, and its west end lies outside the west end of the abbey church. In a few places the abbey walls overlie the Anglo-Saxon walls, but there is no confusion between them. The abbey walls are of a distinctly different construction, built of smaller stones and extensively mortared, and the foundations do not go down so deep. This last point means that, in the majority of instances, even where an abbey wall has entirely obscured an earlier Anglo-Saxon wall there still remains, below the abbey wall, the bottom of the foundation trench of the Anglo-Saxon wall.

The foundations of the main body of the Anglo-Saxon church indicate a nave with aisles divided into compartments, all in one style of construction, and so far as can be seen, all of one build (figs. 6a, 14, 21, 22, 23, 24). The layout shows best on the north side. At the west end there is a small compartment; then, moving eastward, two larger ones of about the same size, followed by a fourth whose eastern limits are unknown, but which could well be as large as the two preceding it. At the west end of the nave there is the foundation of a substantial structure - a tower perhaps or a two-bay narthex - which takes the form of three parallel walls. The foundation trench at the extreme west of the building curves westwards on the centre line of the building and it seems probable that the central tower structure or narthex stood forward of the side aisles. At present the southern half of the church is best seen as a reflection of the northern half; the little that is known of it easily fits into this pattern (fig. 15).

The foundations of the eastern end of the church show an apsidal end projecting eastwards from a substantial raft of massive foundations (fig. 12). This raft formed the basis for a crypt just a small part of which survived intact on the south side (figs. 20, 21). The northern limit to the east end is indicated by the clear edge to the foundation raft, while on the south side (only) there is an additional stretch of foundation of similar construction (W103) branching off southwards, indicating a wall in this position.

The unexcavated gap occupied by the yew hedge creates a problem for there appears to be a slight degree of non-alignment between the two parts of the church. This is best seen by following the line of the wall (W106, W117) on the north side of the nave. A straight 3ft (0.9m) wall can be placed quite comfortably on this line of foundations; but when extended towards the east, it is seen to arrive at a point slightly to the north of the edge of the foundation raft. This could be explained adequately by saying that the east end was slightly narrower than the nave, and that somewhere in the unexcavated area, presumably at the position of the chancel arch, there is an angle in the line of the wall; and if this is so

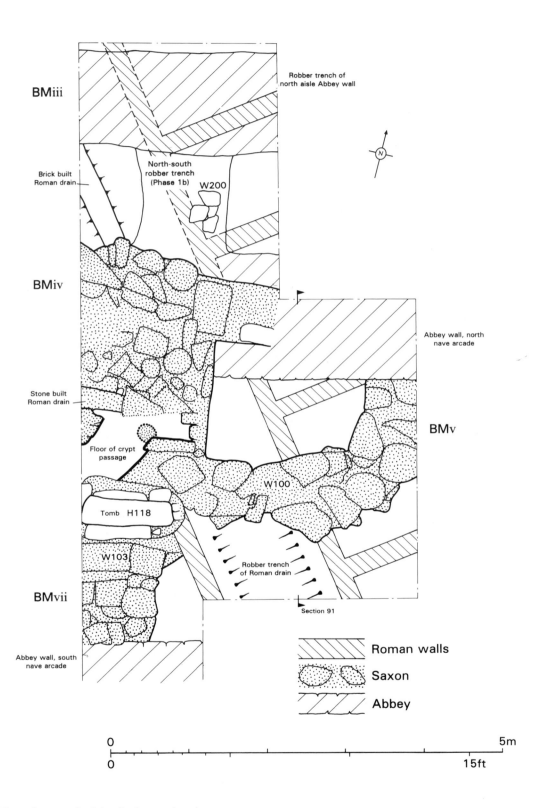

BMiii

Robber trench of
north aisle Abbey wall

Brick built
Roman drain

North-south
robber trench
(Phase 1b)

W200

BMiv

Abbey wall, north
nave arcade

Stone built
Roman drain

BMv

Floor of crypt
passage

W100

Tomb H118

W103

BMvii

Robber trench
of Roman drain

Section 91

Abbey wall, south
nave arcade

	Roman walls
	Saxon
	Abbey

0   5m

0   15ft

12. Plan of east end of Anglo-Saxon church

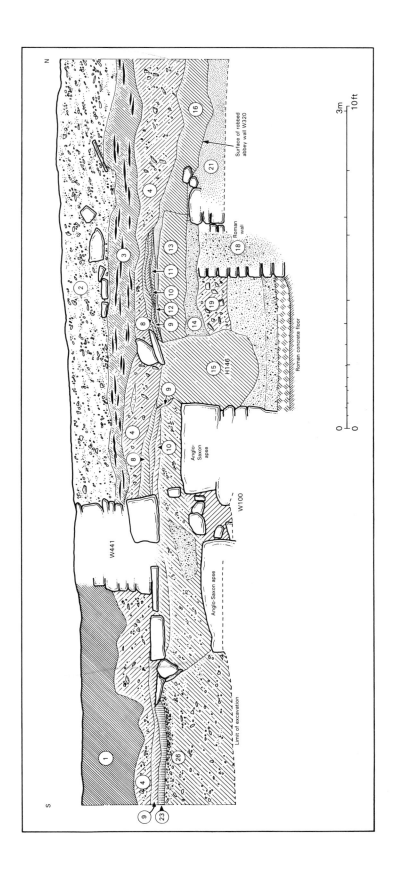

13. Trench 65 BM v, Section 91 through Anglo-Saxon apse and Roman features (see fig. 12)

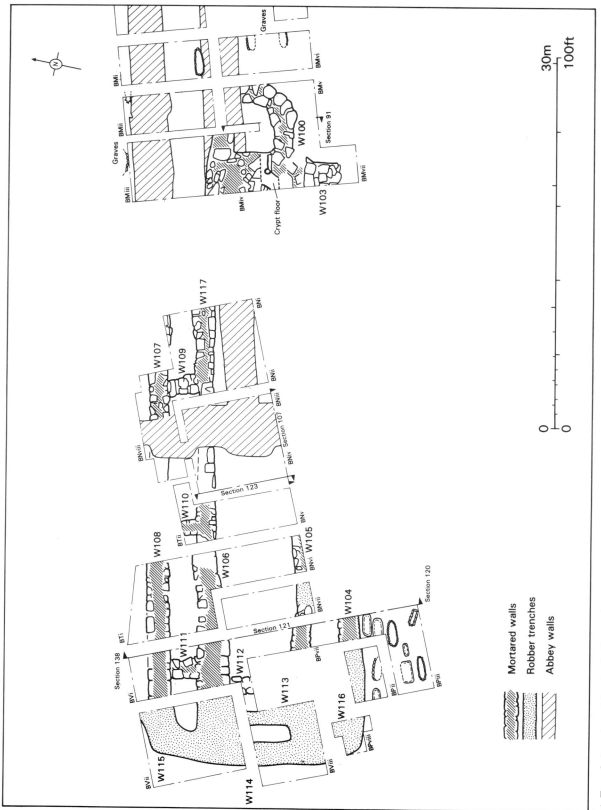

14. Foundation plan of the Anglo-Saxon church. The graves shown are probably 11th-12th century: see burial report

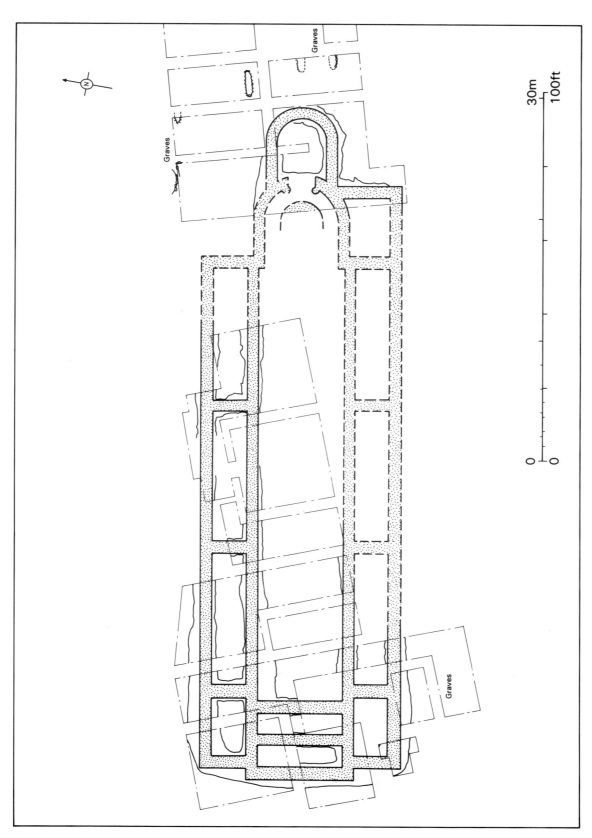

15. Suggested ground plan of the Anglo-Saxon church

16. Roman and Anglo-Saxon
walls in BN i and ii

17. Roman walls and grave H156 under nave north arcade
in BL viii

18. View of Anglo-Saxon south aisle wall and
Anglo-Saxon south nave wall, with burials of 11th-12th
century beyond

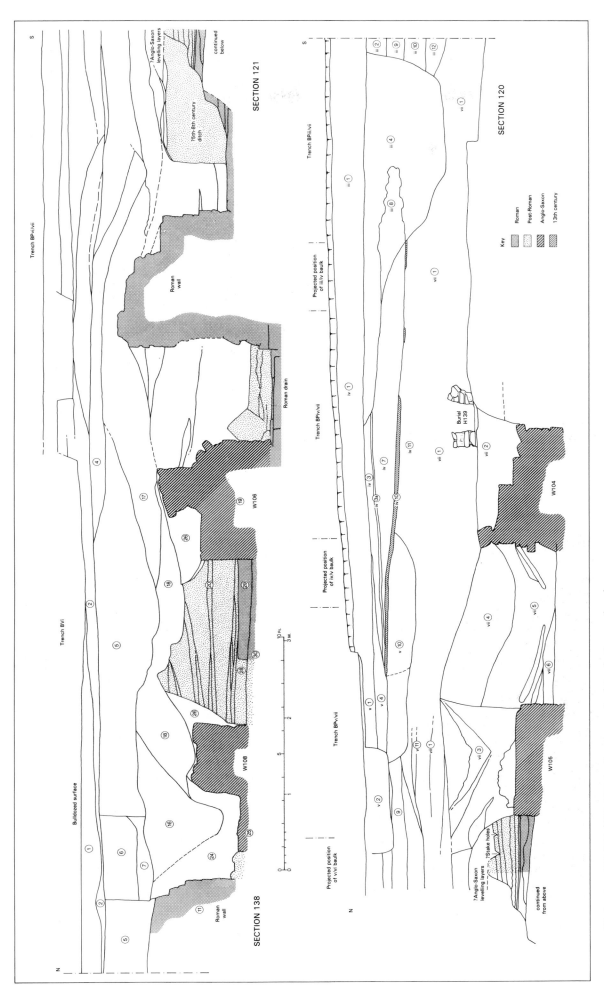

19. Section 120/121/138, BP vi, vii; west end of Anglo-Saxon church

it seems natural to think that this angle would narrow the east end down to the width of the apse. But, in effect, there are three different widths to be reconciled. There is the width of the nave; there is the width of the eastern apse; and there is the width of the foundation raft which seems to fall between the other two. A single angle in the line of the wall, at the chancel arch, might resolve the difference between the lines of the nave wall and the apse wall, but such an arrangement would leave very little room for the crypt and would also suggest that the foundation raft had been made wastefully wide at this point. This problem could only finally be solved by the excavation of the area between the two parts of the church, but Richard Gem suggests an hypothesis which resolves this problem (p. 32 below). The curve of the crypt passage is indicated by the surviving patch of crypt floor and part of its inner wall (figs. 15 and 25). The outside wall of this crypt passage could have been followed by the line of a chancel apse standing above it. A reconstruction based on this curve produces a main apse slightly narrower than the nave: the crypt passage beneath would lie within and against the curved wall of this apse. This would mean that the apse (W100) at the extreme east end of the church did not belong to the chancel but to a chapel to the east of it, representing an outer crypt, with its floor at a level a few feet above that of the crypt passage, and approached by steps leading up from the chamber in the centre of the curve of the passage which is described below.

The crypt passage consisted of a short length of floor bounded on the south-east by the wall, which, on Dr Gem's interpretation, carried at a higher level the outer wall of the chancel apse, and on the north-west by its own retaining wall. This passage leads to a chamber opening off it to the east. On the south side of this chamber is a large stone slab set upright and cut at an angle on the corner (fig. 20). The corner was covered by an engaged column, the setting for which, a circle of pink mortar, remained on the floor of the passage. Reconstructing these remains symmetrically about the axis of the church gives a rectangular stone chamber about 7ft (2.1m) wide and 4ft (1.2m) deep, opening off the curved crypt passage which varies between about 3 and 4ft (0.9-1.2m) wide. On the south side the passage was cut away by the later construction of a tomb (H118). On the north side all traces of the crypt have been removed by the building and later robbing of one of the abbey walls. Unfortunately this robbing removed the central part of the crypt and it is not possible to say whether or not there was an opening off the passage to the west below the area of the chancel. Such an opening would be normal in a crypt of this type for that was the position for the most sacred relics.

Comparison of the levels of various features in different parts of the church gives some indication of the levels of the floors. The minimum level of the floor in the nave is given by the highest surviving piece of Roman walling there, and this is incidentally higher than any of the Anglo-Saxon foundations.

20. Anglo-Saxon apse (top) and crypt floor (centre) above Roman drain (bottom left); one side of medieval tomb H118, bottom right (trenches BM iv, BM v)

21. Anglo-Saxon apse cutting Roman wall (right); part of medieval tomb H118, centre bottom

The tops of the Roman levels within the eastern apse (W100) and the top of Anglo-Saxon foundations at the east end are slightly lower than the highest Roman levels, and the floor of the crypt passage is about 2ft (0.6m) lower still. The floor level in the chancel must have been at least 8 or 9ft (2.4-2.7m) above the crypt floor, which brings it up to the level of, or slightly above, the present ground surface, and several feet above the level of the medieval abbey floor. There must have been a considerable flight of steps up from the level of the nave to the floor of the chancel and there must have been steps down to the passage and the crypt.

So far all interpretation has been based on the assumption that the plan was symmetrical. The only detail to suggest otherwise is the short stretch of foundation, W103, extending southwards at the east end. This is on the same massive scale as all the Anglo-Saxon foundations and looks, in its partially explored state, like the east end of the line of compartments along the south side of the nave. If this is so, this line of compartments extended further east than those on the north, for there is no sign of any comparable wall on that side, and the Roman levels survived higher than the level of the Anglo-Saxon foundations where such a wall might have been expected, to the north of the crypt foundation raft.

If the church was built everywhere with walls 3ft (0.9m) wide, the overall dimensions become approximately 179ft (54.6m) long by 52ft (15.8m) wide overall. The narrow eastern apse measures 13ft (4m), the nave 21ft (6.4m) and the aisle compartments are 8ft 6in to 9ft (2.55 to 2.7m) in width, all internally. The lengths of the compartments on the north side are 15ft (4.6m), 35ft (10.7m), 34ft (10.4m), with the fourth one at least 20ft (6.1m). The western structure measures 22ft (6.7m) by 28ft (8.5m) overall.

The dating evidence for the church is very sparse. Stratigraphically it is post-Roman, but there is not one single post-Roman object in a pre-church context; and there are virtually no deposits of this date either. The structures and associated levels attributed to the Anglo-Saxon period produced no contemporary pottery and only four residual sherds, recovered from the general area of Anglo-Saxon activity, may belong to early to mid-Saxon ware (p.103). The evidence of burials can only show that there were burials pre-dating the 12th-century abbey church (below, p. 164).

As far as the construction of the Anglo-Saxon church is concerned, we are thus left with a completely open date between the time when such a church is first conceivable in England, perhaps late in the 8th century, and the middle of the 11th century when its existence is attested by Domesday Book, though there is a good case to be made on architectural grounds for an early 9th-century construction date (below, p. 37).

The date of the destruction and robbing of the Anglo-Saxon church is also not given by the archaeological evidence. It is obvious that, being

22. The bonding of the north porticus wall 109 with nave wall 117

23. View north in trench BN ii showing Anglo-Saxon walls 117 and 107 joined by W109; Roman wall to right; abbey nave foundations W320 in foreground

under the nave of the abbey church, the Anglo-Saxon church must have been demolished at the latest when the abbey nave was built. The building of the nave is, however, also of uncertain date. Though building of some kind may have begun before 1130 when the first abbot was appointed, Henry I, in a writ dated between 1130 and 1133, granted exemption from tolls on building materials which the abbot was about to buy for the abbey church (*CC* **I**.55). Since the east end of a church was always built first, the nave would have come later. When the abbey church was dedicated in 1176, although it need not have been completed (roofing was still going on in 1186), all its outer walls would have been standing (Evans 1991, 101, 103-5). By then, the Anglo-Saxon church which preceded it must have been demolished. If, as seems probable, the nave was a long time in building, the demolition could have occurred in the middle years of the 12th century.

There is no dating evidence for the robbing of the east end of the Anglo-Saxon church; the robber trenches at its west end however contain the locally-made limestone-tempered ware of late 11th-century date onwards (p. 103). The construction levels of phase 2, the 12th-century abbey church , contain in addition 3% of Minety ware which is supposed to be produced from the 12th century onwards. It is just possible that the absence of Minety wares in the western robber trenches of the Anglo-Saxon church indicates a late 11th-century date both for the robbing of these, and also for the date of the possible rebuild of the west end of the Anglo-Saxon church (see phase 1b, below).

24. View south in trench BV i showing north porticus wall 111 joining W106 and W108

THE ANGLO-SAXON CHURCH AT CIRENCESTER: A RECONSTRUCTION AND EVALUATION

R. D. H. Gem

The reconstruction of the Anglo-Saxon church proposed here (fig. 26) was first formulated in 1986 on the basis of the evidence published in 1976 (Brown 1976). It was then discussed at a seminar held at Cirencester, where a number of issues were raised by the participants which it was hoped would lead on to a further detailed analysis of the excavation records. No significant new information has become available, and the suggested reconstruction thus remains based on the interim report and the further information adduced by the excavator at the 1986 seminar.

Reconstruction

A reconstruction of the superstructure of the church is set about with a number of difficulties. In the first place, the excavation encountered only the lower parts of the foundations and none of the walls that stood upon them - with the exception of a small area in the deepest part of the crypt. The excavator's suggestion that the main walls were in fact about 3ft (0.9m) wide seems perfectly reasonable: but the relationship of solid wall and of openings through it must remain conjectural. The second principal difficulty derives from the fact that the excavation could not investigate at all the area covering the more easterly part of the nave and the westerly part of the sanctuary, the area occupied by the yew hedge. Here again we can only hypothesise - but in the hope that further archaeological work may be carried out in the future to investigate meticulously this crucial area.

The nave of the church seems to have been 21ft (6.4m) wide internally and was flanked by aisles about 9ft (2.7m) wide; giving a total internal width of 45ft (13.7m). From the inner west wall the nave as excavated stretched eastward at least 100ft (30.5m)

25. Anglo-Saxon crypt floor looking west showing floor of crypt and curving inner crypt wall, cut by construction for tomb H118 on left

but the original termination lay still further east. The key to the original length is probably given by the aisles which are divided by transverse walls into compartments approximately 34ft 6in (10.5m) long: if the eastern, partly excavated, compartment was of the same length, then the total length of the nave was about 115ft (35m). The nave had no structural cross-wall separating off a distinct choir bay at its east end; but this does not preclude a non-structural screen. Between the nave and the aisles are likely to have been open arcades, while the position of some of the piers to carry these arcades are determined by the transverse walls in the aisles. It is here suggested that the nave was divided into nine bays at 12ft 6in (3.8m) intervals, such that each compartment of the aisle corresponded to three bays in the nave arcade. The dimensions of the piers and arches themselves can only be speculative: they are shown here as 4ft 6in (1.4m) and 8ft (2.4m) respectively. The piers corresponding to the position of the transverse walls across the aisles must have been rectangular; but the intermediate piers could have been either rectangular or columnar. It is suggested that the transverse walls across the aisles were themselves pierced by arches.

At its west end the internal length of the nave was prolonged a further 17ft to 18ft (5.2 to 5.5m) by a fore-building, which was itself divided into two compartments by a transverse wall running north and south. The aisles were also prolonged by compartments of similar length but these lateral compartments do not seem to have reached as far west as did the central block. The result is likely to have been a façade with the central unit in advance and the side units stepped back. Quite how this

quadripartite fore-building functioned, or what it was like in elevation, can be little more than matters of speculation in the absence of better surviving parallels elsewhere. The oblong plan and cross-wall of the central unit do not suggest a simple west-tower structure: but that there were one or more upper storeys seems highly plausible. On the ground floor it may be thought likely that an entrance arrangement was accommodated, and a sequence of three portals on the axis is thus shown in the reconstruction: these portals could have been flanked by minor openings (to permit a freer circulation) or by solid walls. If access were required to upper levels then stairs could have been provided either in the lateral units or to either side in the central unit. Any upper levels could have accommodated chapels and a gallery towards the nave.

At the east end of the nave the junction with the sanctuary has not been excavated (as already indicated), so the interpretation of the plan must proceed from the 'substantial raft of massive foundations' representing the easternmost extremity of the building. This raft incorporates surviving elements of a ring-crypt, such as would be expected to be associated with the main apse of a church. Following up this expectation, it can indeed be seen on the excavator's plan and in photographs (figs. 12 and 14) that the foundations incorporate on the south side, to the west of the minor eastern apse, a second curved setting of fairly massive stones which must represent another apse: the main apse of the church. This curved setting might at first sight suggest an apse of the same width as the nave; but this cannot be reconciled with the north side of the

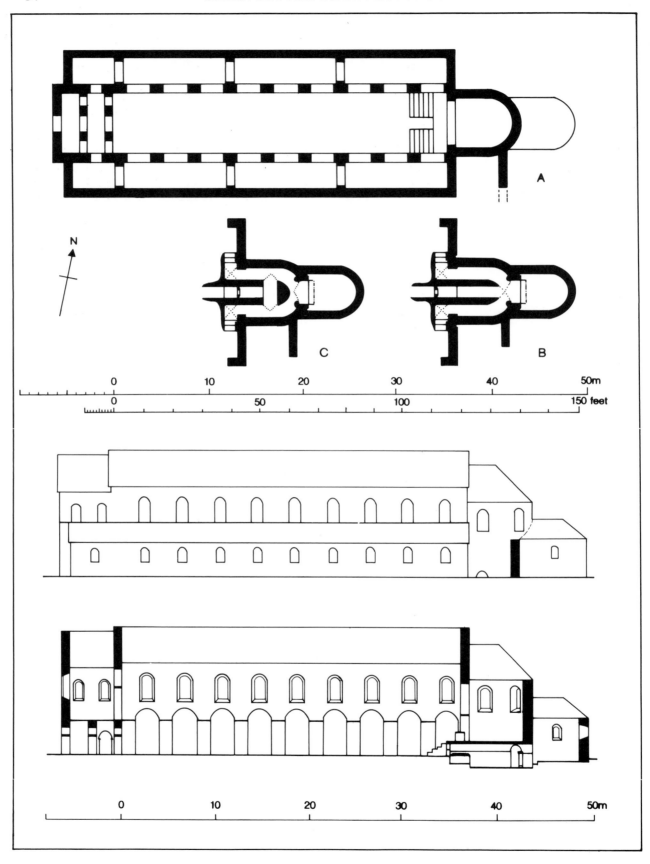

26. Top: reconstructed ground plan of the Anglo-Saxon church with alternative east ends (R Gem)

Bottom: Hypothetical reconstruction of the elevation of the Anglo-Saxon church (R Gem)

foundation where the 'clear edge to the foundation raft' shows that the apse must have been narrower than the nave. If the maximum diameter of apse compatible with the foundation is plotted and an apse wall 3ft (0.9m) wide is projected, then the inner face of the apse wall coincides very closely with the outer wall of the ring-crypt. This relationship is precisely what one would expect and may be taken as confirming the position of the main apse, with an internal diameter of 17ft (5.2m) and extending l9ft (5.8m) beyond the nave gable wall. To the east of this main apse lay a second apse with an internal diameter of 13ft (4m) and projecting eastward a further 18ft (5.5m): this is perhaps best seen as part of the crypt complex rather than of the main upper-level church.

In reconstructing precisely how the crypt worked, the limited extent of the excavations is a problem that cannot be wholly overcome and various options are presented and evaluated here (fig. 26 B and C). The surviving masonry and section of floor of the ring-crypt defined an annular passage about 4ft (1.2m) wide circumscribed on its outer edge by the main apse wall, and on its inner edge by a separate curved wall. This passage may be presumed to have led westward on either side from the chord of the apse and to have emerged somewhere in the main space of the church to provide access to the crypt: the most economical supposition is that it proceeded west until it had passed under the gable wall of the nave and the two sections then returned north and south respectively to emerge in the north and south aisles. What is unknown without further excavation is whether the crypt also contained a relic-chamber or *confessio* in the central area circumscribed by the annular passage and its westward extension - such chambers being a standard feature of crypts of this type where they occur on the Continent. The *confessio* if it existed might be expected to be found in the area underlying the western part of the apse and perhaps extending just west of the boundary between the apse and the nave (two alternatives are shown in B and C): in this position the relics would be visible through a window (a *fenestella*) from the nave as well as being accessible from within the crypt. The access from within the crypt might have been provided by means of a standard arrangement of a passageway running eastward from the *confessio* to join the annular passage (as in B). In the specific case of the

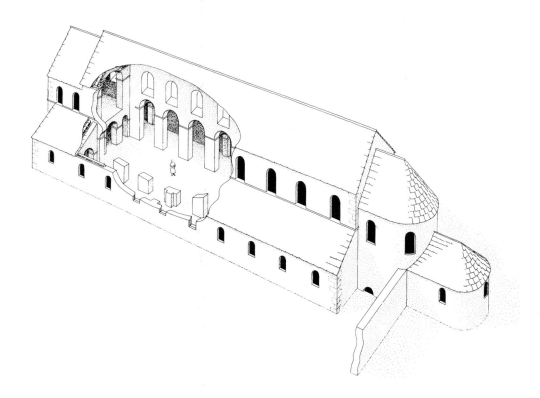

27. Reconstruction of the Anglo-Saxon church, by Simon James. Copyright: British Museum

Cirencester building, however, the main apse is quite narrow and when the width of the outer annular passage is subtracted this leaves only 9ft (2.8m) for a central passage and its side walls: but a central passage of 4ft (1.2m) width could be accommodated with side walls 2ft 6in (0.8m) thick. An alternative would be to have had not a passage running east and west, but one returning north and south between the two arms of the annular passage, with the *confessio* opening directly off this (as shown in C). The various passages of the crypt, whatever their precise arrangement, were probably barrel-vaulted.

As suggested already, the crypt seems to have comprised not only the ring-crypt itself but also an outer element to the east; yet the inter-relationship between the two is not altogether clear. At its easternmost point the annular passage was pierced by a stone-slab-revetted opening with decorative colonnettes framing it (figs. 12, 20). This opening was taken by the excavator as a chamber, but it is here suggested that it was in fact a passageway leading to an outer, apsidal crypt chamber, lying eastward of the main apse of the church. The floor level in this eastern crypt lay at least 2ft (0.6m) above that in the annular passage and so steps up to it might be expected; none were observed by the excavator in the area of the supposed entrance, where the Anglo-Saxon floor level survived, though at the 1986 seminar he did not consider the evidence ruled out the former existence of such steps. The main ring-crypt and the eastern outer-crypt seem to have had their floor levels only slightly below ground level - that is, they were only semi-subterranean features and could have been lit externally by windows at ground level. If the ring-crypt thus had its floor about 3ft (0.9m) below ground level, the top surface of the crowns of its passage vaults may have risen some 6ft (1.8m) above ground level. It is clear thus that a significant flight of steps must have risen from the nave of the church up to the sanctuary in the apse above the crypt. It is here suggested that these steps were arranged in two flights with a passage left between them to provide access to the *fenestella* into the *confessio*. The principal altar of the church could have been set at the top of these steps directly over the relics in the *confessio* below. To the east of this altar the space in the main apse (and possibly an upper storey to the outer-crypt) would have provided space for the liturgical use of the clergy, and possibly for further altars. One excavated feature that has not so far been accounted for here is the wall running southward from the main apse at its point of junction with the outer crypt. At first it appeared tempting to see this as the east wall of a chamber continuing the line of the south aisle eastward to flank the apse, and perhaps serving as a sacristy. However, the excavator was clear that there was no comparable original wall on the north side of the church (though there was a later wall in this position). The wall therefore belongs to an asymmetrically placed annexe and is perhaps best seen as part of a subsidiary structure, rather than of the church itself.

As far as any decorative details of the building are

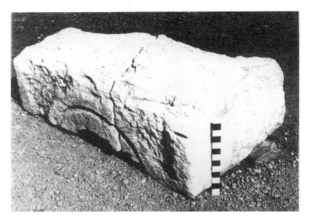

28. Carved stone built into wall 201

concerned the excavations provided almost no evidence. In the crypt the excavator thought (1986 seminar) that the impression in the mortar floor might be for a moulded base carrying a column. The impression appears from the plan to be lft 6 in (0.5m) in diameter and if this represents the size of the base then the column itself must have been somewhat less: this perhaps may be classified as a slender column rather than a large baluster. However, since neither base nor shaft survive it is unknown whether these were of Anglo-Saxon or Roman manufacture. Doubt also hangs over the only piece of surviving decorative worked stone that could conceivably come from the Anglo-Saxon church: a moulded window head rebuilt into the 11th-century W201 (fig. 28). This belongs to a type in which the circular head for a window is cut in a rectangular slab with a decorated border. The type is known from Anglo-Saxon buildings; but the prototypes for it lie in Roman architecture.

One further observation on the archaeological evidence may here seem in order. The ring-crypt with its *confessio* was presumably constructed to house important relics and these, if they had not already been removed at an earlier date, were presumably transferred into the new 12th-century abbey church. But what of the outer-crypt? - was it for further relics or for the burials of important personages who wished to be in close proximity to the main relics? In this connexion it may be wondered whether the tomb (H118), which contained the remains of two or three individuals and was cut down on the axis of the 12th-century church into the foundations of the main Anglo-Saxon apse at its point of junction with the outer-crypt, was not provided for relocating such burials from the old outer-crypt in a place of honour in the new church and as close as possible to their original position.

Evaluation

With so little evidence, either from the archaeological stratigraphy of the site or from the stylistic details of the building, an evaluation of the dating and significance of the building is not easy. Yet the fact that the Cirencester church is one of the largest

Anglo-Saxon buildings known to us makes it of considerable importance in the study of the architecture of the period .

The buildings with which *prima facie* Cirencester seems to show some affinity are a group of churches attributed to the 8th and 9th centuries and including Brixworth (Northants), Wareham (Dorset) and Wing (Bucks). These buildings show the characteristic of naves flanked by aisles or quasi-aisles, but having no transeptal feature: they stand in contrast with the early 10th-century church of the Winchester New Minster, which was an aisled building but which had developed transepts of some form. The origins of this group may go back to such late 7th-century Northumbrian churches as Hexham, Wearmouth and Jarrow, where the long narrow naves seem to have been flanked by rows of porticus; but the scale of these early buildings was much more modest. Brixworth shows a transformation of scale towards something much more ambitious, but the articulation of the design is rather cumbersome in the relative proportions of the piers and arcades and in the heavy screen wall separating the nave and choir. The ring crypt at Brixworth (if it is a primary feature, which is not certain) is also rather tentative insofar as it runs round the exterior of the apse rather than being incorporated beneath it. The date of Brixworth is uncertain and little reliance can be placed on the range of radiocarbon dates that have so far been obtained during the study of the fabric. At Wareham a plan similar to Brixworth was adopted, but it was interpreted with a great deal more architectural sophistication in the elevation: the nave was separated from the aisles by regular arcades carried on slender rectangular piers, with responds towards the aisles carrying transverse arches; the arch between the nave and choir was now of a single span.

Unfortunately we know little about the eastern termination of Wareham, but the idiom of the western portions could well belong to the same world of ideas as Cirencester. It may be noted also that the width of the nave and aisles at Cirencester and Wareham are similar, whereas Brixworth is much broader. In its exaggerated length, however, Cirencester greatly exceeds Wareham (but exaggerated length in relation to width - albeit on a smaller overall scale - was characteristic of one late 8th-century church at Edenham, Lincolnshire). Wareham unfortunately is not a dated building, though inscribed stones of 7th to late 8th or 9th-century date were reused in the fabric and suggest some *terminus post quem*. In contrast to the parallels between this group of churches and Cirencester, there are no good parallels known from the 10th or 11th centuries, when aisled churches seem to have been in less favour. Exceptional in being a major 10th-century aisled church is the Winchester New Minster; but the plan type has already been contrasted with that of Cirencester, while the overall proportions of the building seem to bear little comparison either.

In turning to some of the details of the building, it should be noted first that the ring-crypt, considered as a phenomenon of Europe north of the Alps, is essentially a Carolingian characteristic with a date span between the late 8th and the early 11th centuries, and with many examples falling in the 9th century. In England apart from Cirencester there is the undated example of the Brixworth ring-crypt, and a documentary description of such a crypt at Canterbury Cathedral, which on historical indications could belong to the early 9th or to the mid or late 10th century. The outer-crypt to the east of the apse is a feature that again became characteristic of Carolingian architecture in the 9th century (though like the ring-crypt itself going back to an earlier origin in St Peter's in the Vatican), and sometimes served as a Lady chapel and as a place for burials. In England in the late 10th century an extended eastern chapel and rectangular outer crypt was added to Winchester Cathedral; while at Wells a rectangular Lady chapel was built and subsequently linked westward to the main apse (which probably had its own crypt). Neither of these examples is a precise parallel to Cirencester, but rather they suggest a development of the tradition.

At the west end of the nave the plan of the fore-building may be contrasted with that of Brixworth which has five chambers of equal projection in a line north and south - a formula that may be traced back to the 7th century and earlier in England and on the Continent. The stepped façade and the broad central unit with its internal subdivision speak rather of a more developed and experimental milieu, such as that which on the continent was to lead to the creation of the westwork formula in the later 9th century (though Cirencester is certainly not itself a 'westwork'). However, it should be noted that on a much smaller scale the west porticus of Deerhurst church (Gloucs) had a transverse wall north and south already before its 9th-century rebuilding in its present form.

The clear dissimilarities between Cirencester and known buildings in England dating from the early 10th century onwards suggests that we should be looking for a date before 900 for its construction. On the other hand its relationship to a group of buildings that are generally assigned to the 8th and early 9th centuries, especially to the most sophisticated member of that group which should be one of the later examples (Wareham), suggests a date not much before *c.* 800 AD. A date in the 9th century would also provide an appropriate context for the influence from Carolingian architecture manifested by the crypts (and possibly, but much less certainly, by the fore-building). If one were to press further the apparent continuity with 8th-century architecture and the discontinuity with that of the 10th century, it might appear more likely that the building is in fact a creation of the early to mid 9th century rather than of the later part of the same century. This evaluation of the date is arrived at independently of specific considerations of the early history of Cirencester: but in the absence of early written documentation the architecture is itself perhaps a key document.

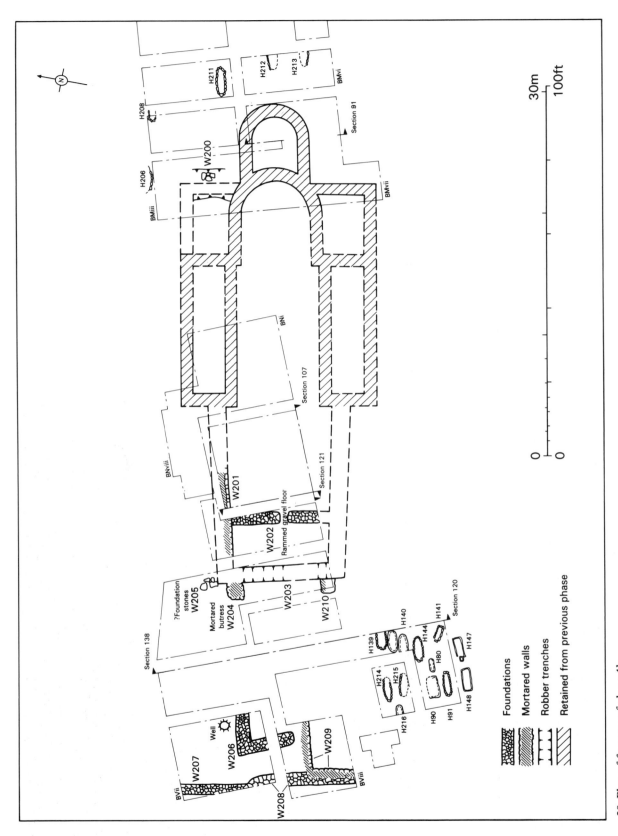

29. Plan of features of phase 1b

Postscript

A wider analysis of the Anglo-Saxon architecture of the period (Gem 1993) has emphasised that the group of churches to which Cirencester belongs is to be compared more generally in plan and scale with Carolingian architecture on the Continent. A particularly close parallel in this respect may be drawn between Cirencester and the abbey of Werden an der Ruhr as rebuilt from *c.* 840 to 875. More recently, excavation of the Anglo-Saxon cathedral of Canterbury (Blockley et al. 1997) has revealed another major building that may be interpreted as belonging within this group of churches. The date of the Canterbury building is uncertain, but may plausibly be attributed to Archbishop Wulfred (805-832). This would strengthen the evidence for a 'Carolingian eposide' in the Anglo-Saxon architecture of the period, with Cirencester being a major representative of the trend.

THE STRUCTURES OF PHASE 1b

R. M. Bryant

Immediately to the west of the abbey church (trenches BN IV, V, VI and VIII, and BT I, II) lies a series of structural features that seem to belong to a single building (fig. 29).

On the north side, built into the half-filled robber trench of the Anglo-Saxon nave wall, is a well-built wall, 201, of evenly coursed stones on rubble foundations with a neat offset and three courses of masonry above it (fig. 30). In trench BN VI a north-south wall, 203, is represented only by a robber trench, and robbing has obscured the corner where the two walls meet. To the west of W203, at its junction with W201, lies a substantial, roughly square, mortared foundation 204 which is interpreted as a buttress. At the south end of trench BN VI a deeper cut was dug to establish the position of the south wall of the Anglo-Saxon nave, and in the north face of this cut lies a foundation W210. This foundation is similar to W204 and is probably the corresponding southern buttress. A shallower stone foundation W205, running north from the north-west corner of the building, may be a further buttress. Within this building there is a

30. Wall 201, view north

secondary line of foundations, W202, running north-south and broken only for a doorway. The building extends southwards into the unexcavated area, while, on the east side, it is cut by the surviving foundations of the abbey's west front. The entire area within the structure is covered with a hard, rammed gravel 'floor' (BN IV 17 and 27 and BN V 16, fig. 31). This floor overlaps the offset on W201 and is continuous through the doorway, where there are signs of burning (Brown 1976, 41-2 and site records).

All these features are sealed by a 'courtyard' surface (BN IV 14 and 15, and BN V 13) which was laid over a large area outside the west end of the abbey church. This layer sealed the construction trench and foundation offset for the west wall of the abbey

church and abutted the only surviving stone (stone B, figs. 33, 41 and 42) in the west face of the church. The courtyard surface also sealed burials further to the west (below p. 164), and is said to have sealed a small group of structures, including a well, at the extreme west end of the site (below and Brown 1976, 42-3).

On the north side of the foundation raft of the Anglo-Saxon apse there was a short length of robber trench, W200, running northwards towards the north aisle wall of the abbey nave (figs. 12, 29). The bottom of this trench was not as deep as the Anglo-Saxon foundations. The trench cut the Roman levels, and there were still three large stones in position in the bottom (Brown 1976, 42).

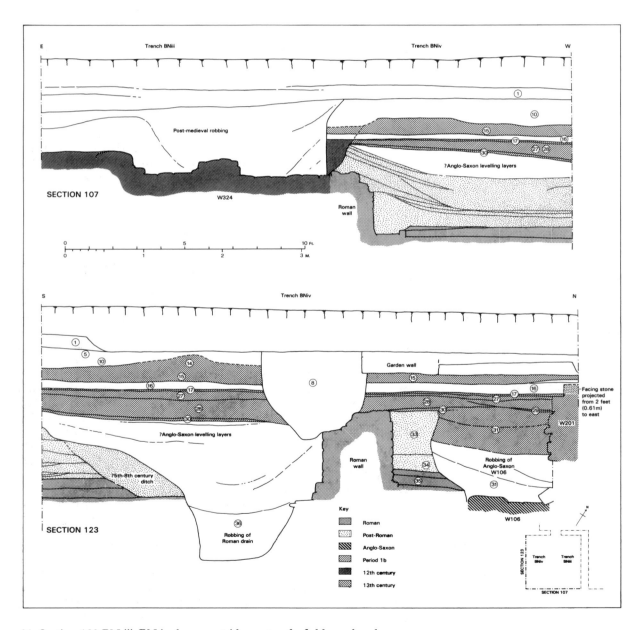

31. Section 123 BN iii, BN iv layers outside west end of abbey church

This complex of walls was originally interpreted as a church of the mid to late 11th century (Brown 1976, 41). Subsequent analysis led to the proposal that all these phase 1b features were of the 12th or early 13th century, and that the building was a 'Galilee Chapel' outside and contemporary with (or added to) the original west end of the abbey church (Wilkinson 1983a). This interpretation was based on two main points: (1) the suggestion that the west end of the abbey church betrays two phases of construction (Brown and McWhirr 1966, 249), and that it was the later of these phases that cut W201 and the floor of the building. The surviving facing stone of the church (stone B, fig. 33) would thus also belong to this later period. Therefore, the courtyard surface that abutted stone B and sealed the building would also belong to this later period; (2) pottery from layers that were considered to be part of the courtyard surface, in trenches in areas BP and BV, suggested a date in the 13th century or later (below, p. 100).

The hypothesis that these walls might represent a 12th or early 13th-century 'Galilee Chapel' is not inconsistent with the evidence. However, there are some difficulties with this interpretation.

1. The suggestion that the west wall of the abbey church was rebuilt and that the evidence survives in the excavated foundations is a hypothesis which cannot be substantiated with any certainty (see below).

2. No dating evidence whatsoever was recovered from the courtyard layers immediately next to the abbey west end (BN IV 15, fig. 31, and BN V). The dating evidence for the courtyard surface relies on evidence from layers 50ft (c. 15m) or more to the west of the abbey church's west wall (trenches BP VII and BV I, II, III). While the correlations may be correct, none was tested by the removal of baulks and some of the sections of the western trenches show more than one surface (fig. 19).

3. Beneath the courtyard surface lies another layer (fig. 31, BN IV 16) which is up to 6 inches (150mm) thick. This layer also seals the construction trench for the west wall of the abbey church, and at least part of the destroyed wall W201. There is no dating evidence from this layer, but it must represent an earlier surface outside the abbey church.

4. The west section of trench BN IV (fig. 31, Section 123) shows that W201 was built into the robber trench of W106 of the Anglo-Saxon church before the robber trench was completely backfilled. This must indicate a relatively short period between robbing and new building. Indeed it might be suggested that they were two parts of a single campaign. Layer 30 in trench BN IV (fig. 31), which covers most of the trench west of the abbey church footings, filled the top of the W106 robber trench and ran up to the faced foundations of W201.

5. The pottery evidence for the robbing of the western half of the Anglo-Saxon church is consistent with a late 11th-century date, or even an early 12th-century one (see above p. 32).

6. Most importantly, these walls make little sense architecturally in relation to the abbey church. The orientation of Wall 201 lies midway between that of the Anglo-Saxon church and that of the 12th-century abbey. As the excavator originally remarked, the position of this building in relation to the nave of the Anglo-Saxon church, and the similarity of axis suggested by the position of the doorway in W202, point to the influence of the Anglo-Saxon church rather than the abbey church (Brown 1976, 42).

It is therefore suggested that this building should be interpreted as the construction of a new west end onto the surviving east end of the Anglo-Saxon church, and that it belongs to the late 11th or early 12th century (possibly even representing the 'new work' of 1117).

Wall 200 also seems to require the eastern end of the Anglo-Saxon church to be still standing. Wall 200 could be seen as part of a reorganised access to the crypt after the church had been taken over by the Augustinian canons, allowing a flow of pilgrims through from north to south without the need for intrusion into the canons' choir in the church.

Whatever form the late 11th-century church took, it is likely that the canons left it standing while they started to build their new (phase 2) church to the east of the old minster, a solution that would have allowed worship to continue in the old church until the eastern part of the new work was completed. This first part of phase 2 would have included the eastern arm with the transept and crossing, together with the first and second bays of the nave (Brown and McWhirr 1966, 250).

Structures at the west end of the site

About 35ft (10m) to the west of the 11th-century building (BV II and III), lies a small group of walls and a well (fig. 29). These are said to be covered by the same courtyard surface that sealed the destruction of the 11th-century building. At least two phases are indicated by the fact that W206 is cut by W209, and W207 is cut by W208. Pottery from the foundations of W208 suggests a date in the late 12th century for the later of these two phases. The presence of the well and significantly greater amounts of pottery than from the area of the church suggest that these buildings were domestic. The earlier of the two phases may have been late 11th century, as suggested by the excavator, but there can be no certainty about this, in view of the difficulty about dating the courtyard surfaces described above.

Structures in the area of the later cloisters

Significant remains, also apparently of a domestic nature, were found over a large part of the area covered by the east range of the 12th-century cloister (trenches BG I, II, III, V and BH IV, V, VII). These remains consisted of a hearth (BH IV, fig. 32), walls, beam slots, post holes, and floors. The pottery from this and other areas, though in phase 2 contexts, includes a quantity of the locally-made F202 (below, p. 99) which implies the presence of late 11th-century occupation.

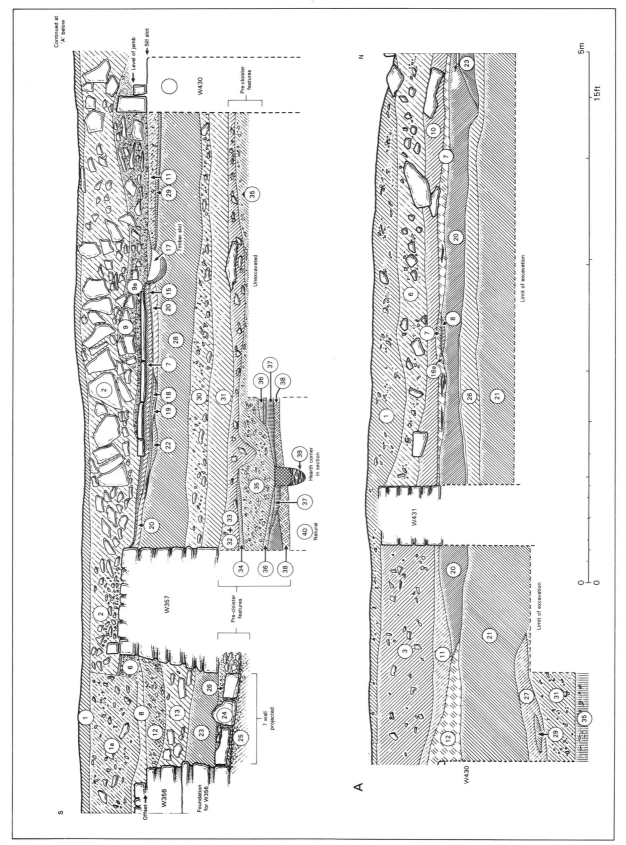

32. Section 26 and 15 through undercroft and slype, showing later floors and flagstones (trench BH iv), later partition walls, and pre-abbey levels; for section positions see fig. 57

THE AUGUSTINIAN ABBEY OF ST MARY

D. J. Wilkinson

THE TWELFTH-CENTURY BUILDING

In this account of the 12th-century abbey the church and the cloisters are considered separately: this division corresponds to the areas excavated in 1965-66 and 1964 respectively.

The church

The church of the 12th century was a cruciform building, with an apse at the east end and in each transept. The **presbytery** was aisled, and probably divided into three bays (if 14th-century buttressing on the north side represents the earlier arrangement). The east end of the presbytery was apsidal. Part of a curved wall 300 (figs. 33 and 47) was bonded into the east end of the north presbytery aisle. Very little of the apse was excavated, but enough to establish that it was probably slightly stilted, with the remains of a strip buttress on the outside.

The nave of the presbytery was 25ft 6in (7.7m) wide and 47ft 6in (14.3m) long at foundation level. The earliest floors in the presbytery consisted of a mortar base for a flagstone floor.

The south presbytery aisle was 12ft (3.6m) wide. The trench-built foundation of W303 dividing the south aisle from the presbytery was heavily robbed and only four courses remained. A short section of W302, the external wall of the south presbytery aisle, was investigated. A tomb H59 had been built into the foundations and was entered from the aisle down steps. The tomb is not part of the original layout as is shown by the orange mortar used for the main wall, in contrast to the brown clay used to bond the lining of the grave shaft. Apparently when the south wall was first built in the 12th century it was solid, load-bearing and external. W302 was of rough rubble construction with undressed facing stones bonded with orange mortar.

34. View across north presbytery aisle looking south, showing burial H201; a buttress on the apse of the presbytery is just behind the scale (trench 65 BK iii)

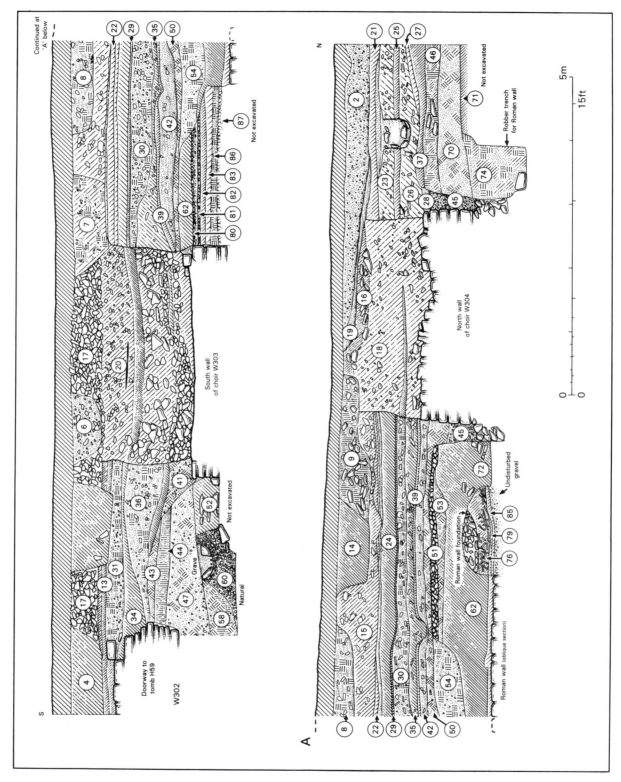

35 Section 49 across presbytery and aisles (trench 64 BK 1); for section positions see fig. 33

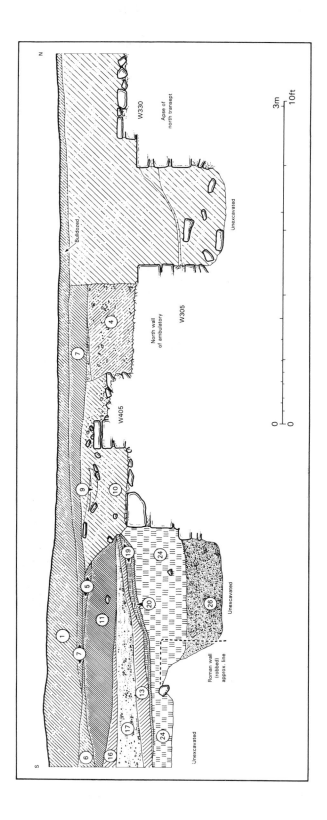

36. Section 60 north-south through the north presbytery aisle (trench 65 BK vi); for section positions see fig. 33

37. North transept apse cut by later wall 400 of chapel (trench BJ xiii) looking north-west

The north presbytery aisle was approximately 10ft (3m) by 47ft (14.1m) at foundation level. The east wall 306 was roughly made using undressed stone for the facing, of which seven courses survived externally with the lowest providing an irregular offset. It is possible that W306 contained an apsidiole within its thickness, indicated by the mismatch of courses on its internal face. Later alterations have obscured details (Brown and McWhirr 1966, plate XLa).

The north wall 305 of this aisle was also poorly constructed with irregular courses of roughly dressed stone (fig. 36). At the west end, five thin foundation courses were overlain by a course of large stones, forming an external offset, above which two courses of the superstructure survived. At the east end thin courses alternated with thick and were frequently broken. The wall was generally at least 8ft (2.4m) wide, with a very solid, mortared rubble core of sufficient quality to be prized by later builders, whose robbing penetrated below floor level. The earliest floors in the north presbytery aisle were of mortar. Much of W304 dividing the presbytery from its north aisle had been robbed, but five courses of the foundation survived in trench 64 BK I, where it was 11ft (3.3m) wide.

The internal dimensions of the **north transept** were 28ft (8.5m) by 21ft (6.4m) the width being the same as for the crossing (figs. 37, 43 and 45). The walls, like most of the walls of this period, were built

38. North transept showing junction between west wall of transept W333 and sleeper wall of ambulatory wall 314 looking south. The slab south of W314 must be an unexcavated tomb (trench BL ii)

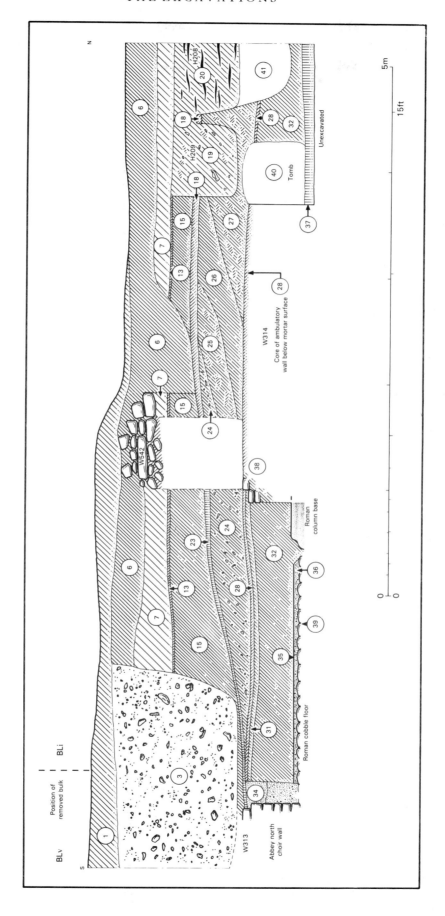

39. Section 70 through crossing (trench 65 BL i); see fig. 52 for continuation of this section; for section position see fig. 33

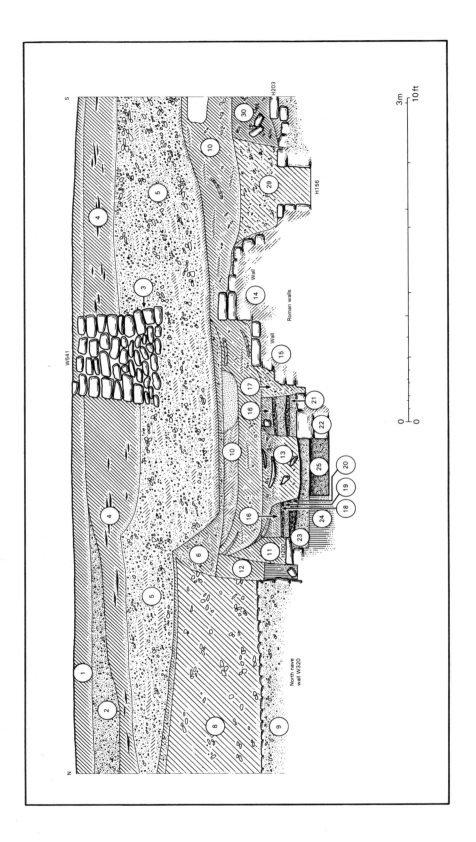

40. Section 72 through abbey nave (trench 65 BL viii, BL ix); for section position see fig. 33

with mortared rubble cores and undressed facing stones. An early floor of flagstones had been mostly taken up and replaced by a white mortar floor. The few surviving flagstones were approximately 18in square (457mm) and 3in (76mm) thick, with straight and flat edges displaying little sign of wear.

Much of the sleeper wall 314 dividing the crossing from the transept was overlaid by a mortar floor. However, at the junction of the transept wall 333 and the crossing sleeper wall 314, there was part of a pier-base W417 built on a floor (29) (fig. 38). Within the north transept a grey and then a white mortar surface (fig. 39, BL I 28) may have been bedding layers for the relaying of flagstone floors.

A stilted apse (fig. 37), though an addition to the north transept, was probably constructed soon after the transept had been built and can be regarded as part of the original scheme. The interior width of the apse at its base was 11ft 8in (3.5m) and it was 10ft (3m) deep. The earliest surviving surface (floor or flagstone bedding) was of yellow mortar. When the chapel was later altered to a larger rectangular plan the apse was reduced so that new floors could be laid over it.

All four walls of the **crossing** have sleeper foundations. At the corner junctions substantial piers may be envisaged to support a lantern or tower. Since these have not survived, it is not possible to provide accurate measurements for the overall dimensions, although the area within them must have been approximately 26ft (7.8m) square. In trench BL V (fig. 33) wall 309, between the crossing and the presbytery, abutted the east-west walls 312 and 313, indicating that the transverse walls were inserted after the longitudinal nave walls had been built.

Early surfaces in the crossing appear to have been of mortar, although it seems likely that a flagstone floor had been laid and then later removed as in the north transept.

Later alterations masked much 12th-century detail in the area of the **south transept**. The original east wall of the transept W327 had a chapel apse W326 on its eastern side, presumably as part of the original layout of the church like that in the north transept. The apse had been strengthened with a roughly built buttress, not properly faced. Five courses of the apse foundation wall survived to show that the facing had been more carefully built than in many other walls.

The nave and west end (by R. M. Bryant)

The aisled **nave** was 125ft (37.5m) long internally. No evidence survived for the number of bays but if they were of a similar size to those at the east end then there would probably have been eight.

The walls and foundations west of the crossing were more heavily robbed than those to the east. The arcade between the nave and the north aisle was carried on a substantial sleeper wall W320 which was nearly 4ft (1.22m) deep where it survived unrobbed (fig. 40). It varied in width from 11ft (3.36m) near the crossing to 8ft (2.44m) near the

west end, and there was a significant change in alignment 27ft (8.24m) to the west of the crossing which may indicate the point at which work on the east end of the church reached a temporary halt, while the old church was demolished.

The wall foundations of the south arcade of the nave, W319, was only excavated at one point, about halfway down the nave in trench BM VII. At this point the nave was 24ft (7.32m) wide.

The north wall of the north aisle, W321, was even more heavily robbed than W320, but enough survived at the east end to indicate a similar construction. At the west end, however, the builders were confronted by a dense complex of Roman, Saxon and probably 11th-century walls and they seem to have abandoned the regular layered foundation in favour of a wider, roughly-laid foundation raft (fig. 33).

There is evidence of considerable levelling soon after the construction of the north aisle wall 321, but almost no floors or other layers associated with the abbey church have survived. A fragment of the nave floor was excavated just inside the west wall (BM IV 24), while in the north aisle there was a mortar bedding perhaps for a floor of flagstones (BN I 14).

The foundations at the west end of the church W324 were 10ft (3.05m) thick (figs. 41 and 42). Only one stone of the external face of the wall

41. The west end of the abbey church showing stone B, the only surviving facing stone in the west front, with courtyard layer outside west end running up to it

above ground level appeared to be in place (block B), with a series of 'courtyard' surfaces abutting it from the west. There is no dating evidence from these surfaces.

There is no surviving evidence of western doorways. The wall carried a wide, flat buttress (W334) on the line of the nave arcade and a clasping buttress (W335)at the north-west corner. It has been suggested that the foundations of the west wall may be of more than one phase. This interpretation appears to rely on the dating of a single chamfered block (stone A, trench BN VIII; figs 33, 42) to the 12th century, and the suggestion that stone A may had survived *in situ* on the line of an original 12th-century façade (Brown and McWhirr 1966, 249). The impression left by a robbed stone immediately north of stone A may indicate that there were two stones on the same line (Wilkinson 1983a). There is, however, no other indication of a break in the large area of the foundation exposed in the excavation that might betray this earlier façade. Furthermore, the block itself does not seem, from the surviving photographic evidence, to have any clearly 12th-century diagnostic features, and it could just as easily be late 11th century. Even if the block were of 12th-century date, it could be a damaged or reject block from the building work somewhere else on the site, simply re-used in the foundations.

The cloisters (by D. J. Wilkinson)
The excavations of 1964 were concentrated in the area of the east claustral range (fig. 43). They revealed the north transept of the church with its eastern chapel, the chapter house, an undercroft with perhaps the dormitory above, the east ambulatory of the cloisters and the east end of the buildings of the north range (Wacher 1965).

The east range of the cloisters including the north transept all used a common wall on the west side W354/333, which was also the outer wall of the cloister walk. This wall contained various mortars: pink, yellow and creamy white, but the varieties were sufficiently intermixed to represent essentially one build using different batches of mortar. The doorways were all rebuilt in the later medieval period, but many must mask earlier doorways (fig. 44). The foundations for W354 were 7ft 9in (2.31m) wide supporting a wall 7ft 1in (2.16m) wide, forming a continuous offset on the cloister side. The facing was generally of ashlar which was of better quality on the internal (east) face. The undercroft does not appear to have had an internal offset.

In contrast to the east range, the north range was apparently of two-room depth. The east range also continued further northwards and the structures located by St. Clair Baddeley in the course of excavations 'about 1930' (Reece 1962, 198) may have formed part of this range.

The 12th-century **chapter house** was rectangular in plan with the east end terminating in an apse W350; the maximum internal dimensions were 50ft (15m) by 25ft (7.5m). The rubble foundation walls of the apse thickened from 8ft (2.4m) to 14ft (4.2m) at

42. The west wall of the abbey church showing stone A in foreground (with small scale) and stone B at centre marked with ranging pole

its apex, but presumably supported a wall of even thickness of some 6 to 7ft (1.8 to 2.1m). In trench BJ XII, part of the rubble foundation is lined with ashlars indicating the internal curve of the apse (fig. 45). Also at the apex of the apse were some masonry fragments projecting eastwards, probably buttresses. This end of the chapter house had been so heavily robbed that it was impossible to recover the complete plan of either the early or subsequent periods. Evidence for its early flooring was fragmentary. Fig. 59 BH V 46 might represent the early floor; other deposits were apparently laid to level up the ground. The levelling material, which contained Roman rubbish, probably came from digging the chapter house wall foundations.

The northern wall of the chapter house W353 survived to a level of two courses above the offset, but only on the external face. The foundation was 2ft 9in (800mm) deep below the offset; although this represents nine courses, only the lower two or three were trench built.

The chapter house was separated from the undercroft by a narrow rectangular room, 'the **slype**' (fig. 43). It measured 26ft by 12ft (7.8 by 3.6m) internally. In the final years of the abbey, doorways existed at both the west and east ends but the west doorway at least, must have existed in the 12th century. The foundations of the walls were composed of limestone rubble with rough stone faces and were between 6ft 2in and 8ft 4in (1.85 and

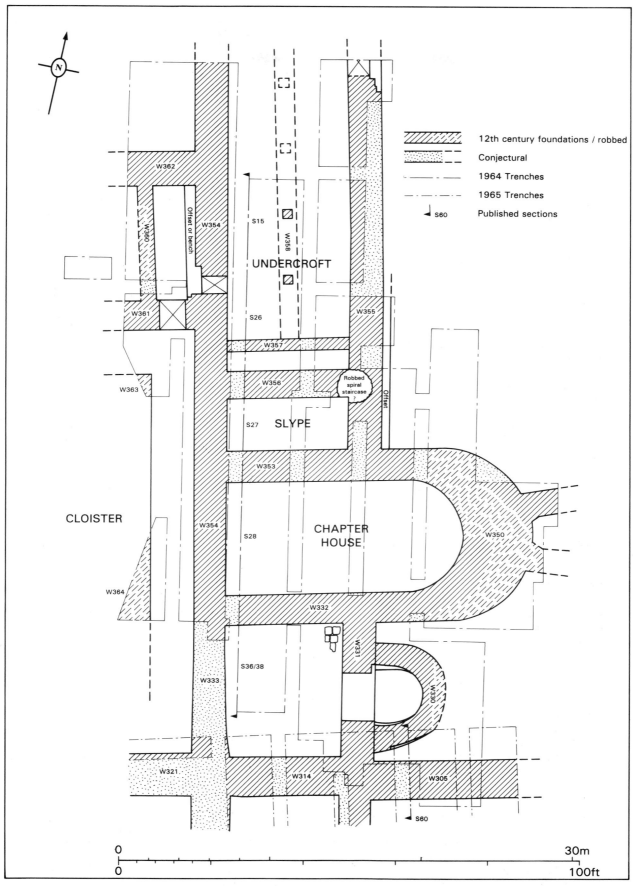

43. Plan of chapter house and east claustral range *c.* 1170

44. General view north-east of east cloister range during excavation, showing moulded door-jamb with remains of latest cloister floor still adjoining (trench BH ii)

2.5m) thick; the core of the western wall contained fragments of Roman brick/tile and Stonesfield slates. Where the wall survived above the level of the offset, it appears to have been composed mainly of rubble with a rough ashlar face. There is evidence for the ground being levelled-up by about 2ft (600mm) when the wall foundations were built (fig. 59, BH V 34, 35, 28). The material used probably derived from the construction trenches for the walls and it is therefore not surprising that these contained Roman debris. The earliest surviving floor is of hard and compact yellow concrete (BH V 27). The walls of this room each had very narrow offsets except at the west entrance, where the offset was *c.* 1ft 4in (400mm) wide: possibly a bookshelf or seat.

The undercroft and slype were separated by a narrow **passage** which was inserted in the southern end of the undercroft. Its northern wall 357 butted up to the east and west walls of the undercroft. W357 has the sleeper wall 358 (which supported the undercroft piers), butted up to it. Either the passage is an early modification of the initial plan, or W358 and its piers, along with W357, were later insertions. Although the east and west walls of the undercroft were over 7ft (2.1m) thick, W357 was only 2ft 9in (825mm) thick above its offsets. Up to three courses of the facing stones for W357 survived above nine irregular loose courses. The quality of the construction was very poor in comparison with that of nearby walls.

45. North transept, chapel, and chapter house, looking north-east

At the south end of the passage the earliest and only surviving floor was of yellow/brown mortar. At the north end there was no evidence for a floor, but the ground had been levelled up when the walls were built. The earliest floor may have been of flagstones. The floor levels generally were about 1ft (300mm) higher than in the undercroft proper. In the thickness of the wall at the south-east corner of the passage there was a robbed area, circular in shape and 7ft 6in (2.3m) in diameter, which may represent the position of a spiral staircase leading to the floor above the undercroft.

The **undercroft** (fig. 43), which may have had the warming room above (Wacher 1965, 107), was a large room in excess of 63ft (19m) and probably more than 70ft (21m) long and 22ft (6.6m) wide.

The western wall 354 was well-built with dressed facing stones and a rubble core, all well mortared. The core included fragments of Stonesfield slate and Roman brick/tile and was about 6ft 8in to 7ft (2 to 2.1m) wide above offset level. The eastern wall 355 was similar. The external facing seems to have been of finely dressed stones. The eastern wall 355 was partly bonded with W356 of the slype at foundation level. A sleeper wall 358, entirely trench-built of rubble, was about 4ft (1.2m) wide. It was between 2ft 3in and 2ft 6in (675 and 750mm) deep and of five courses. The wall supported plinths of which two survived (fig. 46), about 2ft (600mm) square, for the piers which carried the vaulted roof. The vault survived unaltered throughout the life of the abbey, as can be seen by the position of one of the collapsed arches (Wacher 1965, pl. XXXVIIa). Elsewhere, the undercroft was filled with the masonry of the fallen vaults, consisting of much mortar, many limestone slabs lying on edge, and a great deal of coarse limestone aggregate, carefully graded in size. This aggregate would seem to have been used as ballasting material over the vault, to provide added strength and also a level surface on which to lay the floor of the next storey. Similar material had been used to make up the floor of the north transept. A great deal of ash and charcoal had accumulated all over the floor of the undercroft in both this and later periods.

There was little evidence for early floors, although a fragment of pink mortar, perhaps the setting for flagstones, was found near W355 in trench BG IV. A slot in the north-west corner could be associated with the first period of use.

Access seems to have been through a doorway, in W355, opening to the east near the northern end of the undercroft, and through a doorway near the southern end of the undercroft. This southern doorway is at a higher level than the undercroft floor and a stone block was placed on the floor inside to allow for easy access. The southern doorway led into a narrow room which was equipped with a broad offset made of fine quality ashlar blocks about 2ft 6in (760mm) wide on its north side against wall 354. A channel, later lined with clay, ran down the middle of the floor. The offset might have supported the washing-basins of the *lavatoria*, with the channel taking away waste water.

ALTERATIONS TO THE TWELFTH-CENTURY ABBEY

Modifications to the 12th-century plan entailed removing old walls and building new; and the raising or replacing of floors. Frequently old floors of stone or tile were taken up and the materials reused either within the same room, or elsewhere. Few of the many alterations could be related one to the other. The dating evidence is so poor that there is little value in attempting to establish general building phases as minor repairs and alterations were probably almost continuous throughout the abbey's history. Coinage and pottery were of limited value in dating the alterations, which are described in the most likely chronological order.

Evidence for flooring was generally poor. Mortar floors frequently survive, although varying in quality and degree of survival. Their true nature and character were often difficult to determine, and many of the mortar 'floors' may have been bedding layers for floors of flagstones, glazed tile or wood, materials which could be reused in any refurbishment which took place.

The wall of the **north transept** chapel apse was levelled and a new buttressed wall 400 of undressed facing stones was constructed to form a rectangular chapel (fig. 57). W400 was nearly 6ft (1.8m) wide. There may have been three buttresses bonded onto the exterior, although details of the north buttress

46. General view of undercroft (trenches BG iii and BG iv) looking north, showing late medieval dividing walls 430, 431, and original moulded plinth

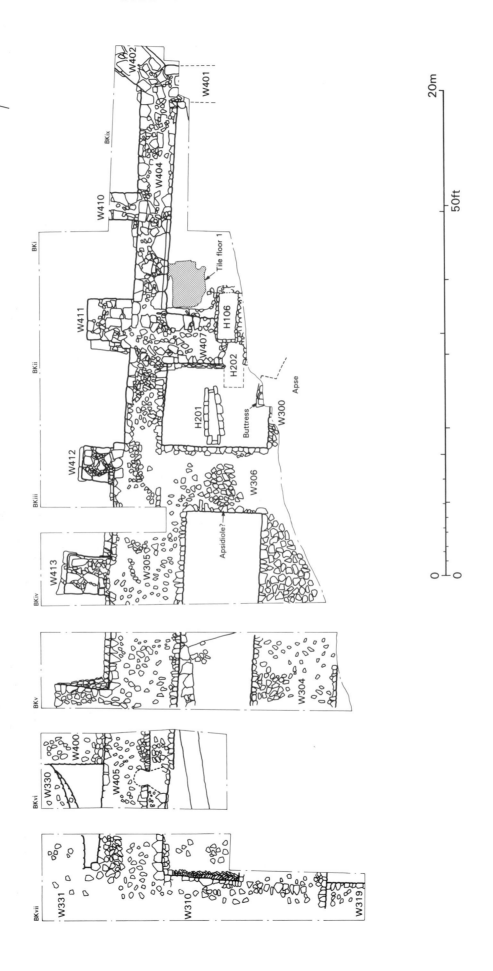

47. Plan of east end of north presbytery aisle and later eastern extension

were uncertain. The southern buttress, which also abutted the north wall of the north presbytery aisle, was larger than the central buttress. Five courses of W400 survived above offset level on the exterior.

Deliberate levelling with soil was carried out within the restructured chapel prior to the construction of a new white mortar floor. This floor contained tin-glazed ware (F 209) but this is probably intrusive. The latest layer pre-dating the rebuilding of the apse contained pottery datable to the 13th century. The new floor was subsequently replaced by another.

In the **undercroft**, three partitions W430, 431, 432 of rudimentary construction, were inserted (fig. 46). At the south end was a timber partition with flagstones butting up to it. Both the construction of the timber partition (fig. 32, BH IV 17) and the laying of the flagstones (BH IV 7) post-dated three earlier mortar floors (fig. 32, BH IV 22, 20, 18). Floor 22 contained pottery datable to the 13th century (F 200). These alterations are likely to have taken place around or soon after 1450.

A tomb, H59, (fig. 33) was inserted into the foundation of the south wall of the **south presbytery aisle** and was entered down steps. The construction of the tomb required the removal of much of the wall and its foundation, which was then lined with clay. The fill of the tomb contained early 14th-century Nash Hill floor tile.

If there was originally an apsidiole in the inner face of the east wall of the **north presbytery aisle**, this was now blocked. The date of the blocking must have preceded the date of the eastern extension and post-dates the mid 12th century.

The **eastern arm** of the church was extended from three to six bays; the presbytery now occupied four bays, with an ambulatory and eastern chapels in the two bays beyond (fig. 47). The ambulatory was thus comprised of the presbytery aisles with a cross wall behind the altar, providing access to the eastern chapels. The junction of the lengthened presbytery and the new eastern ambulatory was marked by a north-south sleeper wall 407. Wall 407 was later cut through for burial H106. A tile floor (Floor 1a) of early 14th-century Nash Hill type (below p. 142) was later laid across the top of the tomb. The tile floor sealed 14th-century pottery; however the tile floor had sunk 2in (50mm) below the level of the internal offset of W404, and had subsequently been patched, so the pottery may derive from the patching. Pottery in general suggests a date of late 13th to mid 14th century for the eastern extension (p. 100).

The construction of the north wall 404 of the eastern extension was generally of a higher quality than that of the 12th-century church, although only 4ft 6in (1.35m) wide (figs. 48, 49). The north wall 405 of the presbytery was rebuilt utilising the earlier foundations but was reduced in width above ground level to match the eastern extension. The top course of the external offset was of ashlar, with the internal offset at a higher level and carved out of one deep course of stone.

It seems likely that most of the superstructure to the east of the transept was rebuilt. The sleeper wall

48. North wall of north presbytery aisle looking west, tile floor 1 centre left, buttresses to right. Stone-lined burial H201 top left, burial H106 just below it

49. Eastern extension; 14th-century buttress bonded to wall 411 with tile floor 1

407 and the line dividing the ambulatory from the eastern chapels were matched externally by buttresses W411 and 410. Two further external buttresses W412 and 413 were probably added at the same time on the line of the original east end, and at the next bay to the west. The foundations for each of these buttresses were slightly different in size and shape. Further west, at the line of the next bay,

50. South transept, showing buttresses of various phases, looking south (trench BL xi). The vertical slab in the foreground may be refacing for the scar left after the removal of buttress 441

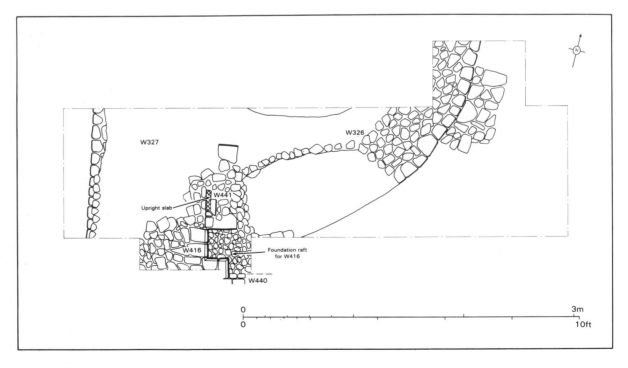

51. Plan of south transept (trench BL xi)

buttressing was provided by W400. The north eastern and south-eastern corners of the eastern extension were strengthened by angled buttresses, W402 and W403 (see fig. 33).

A roof boss with naturalistic foliage may have come from the presbytery vault (Brown and McWhirr 1966, plate XLb). The boss can be dated to the first quarter of the 14th century, a date which is compatible with that provided by the floor tiles and the pottery.

A north-south wall 401 was located joining the angled buttresses and this may have formed the eastern limit of the church. However, it should be remembered that many abbey churches, for example Dorchester, Walsingham, Thornton and Lilleshall, had extensions at the east end beyond the aisle terminals.

In the **south transept** (figs. 50, 51) the wall of the chapel apse was removed and the foundation was levelled off to the bottom five courses, presumably below floor or ground level. The east wall of the transept W416 was rebuilt with a buttress at the south-east corner. This required re-laying or extending a rubble raft foundation. Both the buttress and the remaining wall face of W416 were of large dressed blocks with a narrow chamfer 4.5in (100-120mm) deep at the top of the second course. Two feet (0.6m) to the north of the corner buttress is what appears to be a second buttress W441 projecting 1ft 8in (0.5m) from the face of W416. However, as the east face of this buttress had been robbed, it may originally have been of a size more comparable with those on the east side of the north transept chapel, which were c. 3ft 4in (1m) deep. Each side of W441 was faced with a large base block bearing a chamfer at the upper edge. This chamfer was a course below that of W416, and may suggest that the buttress and wall were not contemporary.

Buttress 441 was later taken down. A vertical slab, resting on a thin base-course that carries a hollow chamfer, may be part of the refacing of the scar left by the removal of W441.

Running east from the east face of the corner buttress is a well-built wall 440. The north face of this wall is butt-jointed against the buttress but at least one block within the wall is cut into the buttress to form a bond. The wall is regularly coursed but appears (fig. 50) to be of drystone construction. It is possible that this could be the south wall of the lady chapel that records suggest stood in this area (p. 17). However, the drystone construction makes it more likely to be a boundary wall. W440 is only about 2 ft (600mm) from the modern graveyard wall, and could represent its offset foundation.

There is no evidence for flooring within the area of the conjectured lady chapel. It is possible that post-Dissolution robbing may have destroyed all trace of floors. If the lady chapel was built in this area then presumably the apsidal chapel was levelled before the lady chapel was constructed.

In the **crossing**, ten successive floors in all were recorded. In addition to floors made of mortar, two were of red clay, BL V 18 (fig. 52). Resurfacing of the second, red clay, floor took place before a fine soil BL X 5 (fig. 52) began to accumulate between the stall foundations.

Choir stalls were constructed within the body of the crossing and were supported by parallel foundations built on the north and south sides of the crossing, the outer walls in each case overlapping the east-west sleeper walls (fig. 53). Three surviving courses of the northern foundation W418 (fig. 52) were almost completely built onto the main sleeper foundation W313. W418 was 3ft 1in (930mm) wide and overhung the sleeper by 4in (100mm). The southern foundation W421 was 2ft (600mm) wide and only overlapped the sleeper wall 312 by 6in (150mm). The stalls on these foundations would have been backed by screens, which would have closed off the crossing from the aisles and transepts behind.

The second row of foundations W419 and W420 lay inside the crossing and were built into shallow trenches. The inner northern foundation, W419 (fig. 54), was approximately 1ft 9in (530mm) wide and survived to a depth of 1ft 6in (450mm), while its southern counterpart W420 was 1ft 4in (400mm) wide and 1ft (300mm) deep.

To the east the stall foundation walls butted onto the sleeper wall 309 which divided the presbytery from the crossing (see fig. 33). To the west, the stalls were closed by a pair of L-shaped terminals constructed largely on top of the sleeper wall 316 between the crossing and the nave (figs. 55, 56). Much of the northern stall foundation W418 was robbed, including the point at which it returned on the west side. However, a small section did survive around the inner end of the northern terminal. At this point the stall foundation was c. 2ft (600mm) wide and survived as two courses with roughly dressed facing stones. About 4in (100mm) of wall rested on the sleeper while 1ft 8in (500mm) overhung on the west side. The outer face of the south return of W421 was totally robbed.

The inner face, the return of W419 and W420, survived on both the north and the south side, and each terminal was closed by a single row of stones. It may be assumed that there was access from the crossing to the nave through a screen erected between the terminals. A floor surface about 6ft (2m) wide survived at this point.

The way in which the foundation was used to support the stalls is not clear. The foundations were not symmetrically placed in the crossing, but the timber construction they supported probably was. It seems likely that planks were laid between the inner and outer foundations and that the fine soil (fig. 52, BL V 7 and BL X 5) accumulated beneath the boards. From the fine soil under the southern side came three silver coins dated to the late 15th century (p. 71). The soil was only 1-2in (37-50mm) thick, but presumably accumulated over a considerable period. The same soil under the north choir benches (fig. 52, BL V 7) contained sherds of pottery dated to the 15th or early 16th century (p. 101). The coins were dropped during the use of the

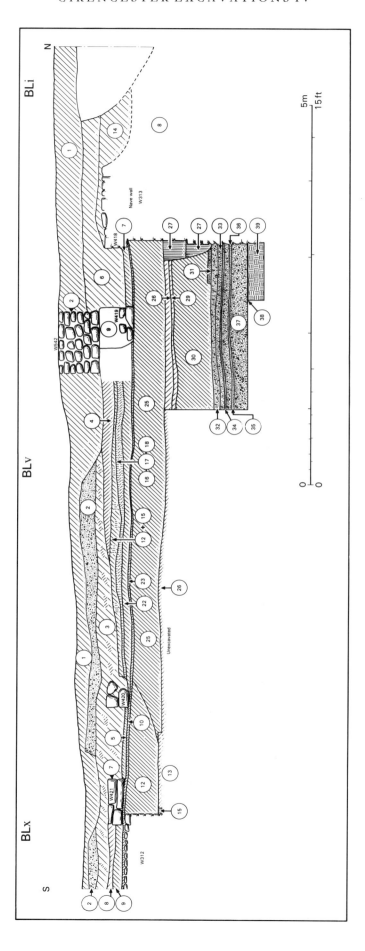

52. Section 71 through crossing (trench BL v, BL x); for position see figs. 33 and 53. See fig. 38 for continuation of this section

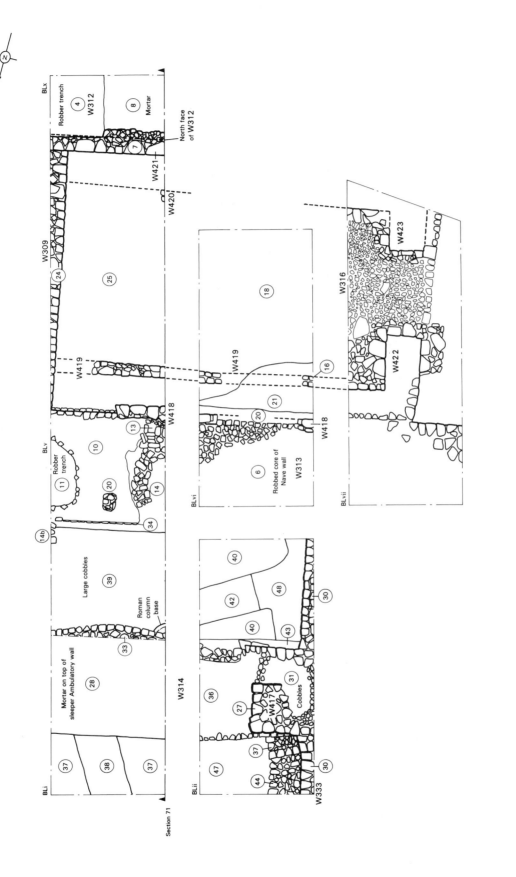

53. Crossing area: plan, showing foundations of choir benches

54. View north of crossing showing footings of choir seat foundations in foreground, nave sleeper wall 313 at centre (trench BL i and v)

55. View north of nave crossing showing west returns W422 and 423 of choir seating foundation set on sleeper crossing wall 316 (trench BL vii)

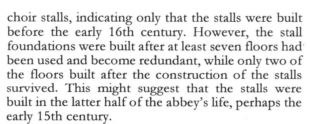

choir stalls, indicating only that the stalls were built before the early 16th century. However, the stall foundations were built after at least seven floors had been used and become redundant, while only two of the floors built after the construction of the stalls survived. This might suggest that the stalls were built in the latter half of the abbey's life, perhaps the early 15th century.

When Leland visited the abbey church in 1536 he wrote of the **nave** and presbytery: 'The Est part of the church shewith to be of a very old building. The west part from the transeptum is but new work to speke of' (Leland, *Itin.* **1**, 129). Since it is now clear that the presbytery was rebuilt in the early 14th century, the 'west part' was presumably of a later date. A large roof boss of late 15th-century style was found lying in the nave area (Brown and McWhirr 1966, 253). This boss and Leland's comments may indicate that the nave was rebuilt with a new vault towards the end of the 15th century. Any such reconstruction is unlikely to have begun before 1480, since William Worcestre would surely have mentioned the fact if building was in progress, or only recently finished, at the time of his visit (Evans 1993, 133).

The **west end** may have been rebuilt at the same time but, as has been indicated above (p. 49), the excavated foundations offer little evidence for such a rebuild. None of the surfaces that abut the surviving stone B in the west wall, including the latest (fig. 31, BN IV 10), contained any dating evidence.

56. As 55, view to south (trench BL vii)

The west end of the **chapter house** was considerably altered when rooms were inserted into the south-west and north-west corners of the original structure (fig. 57). This created a narrow passage leading from the cloister walk into the new smaller chapter house, flanked by small rooms or

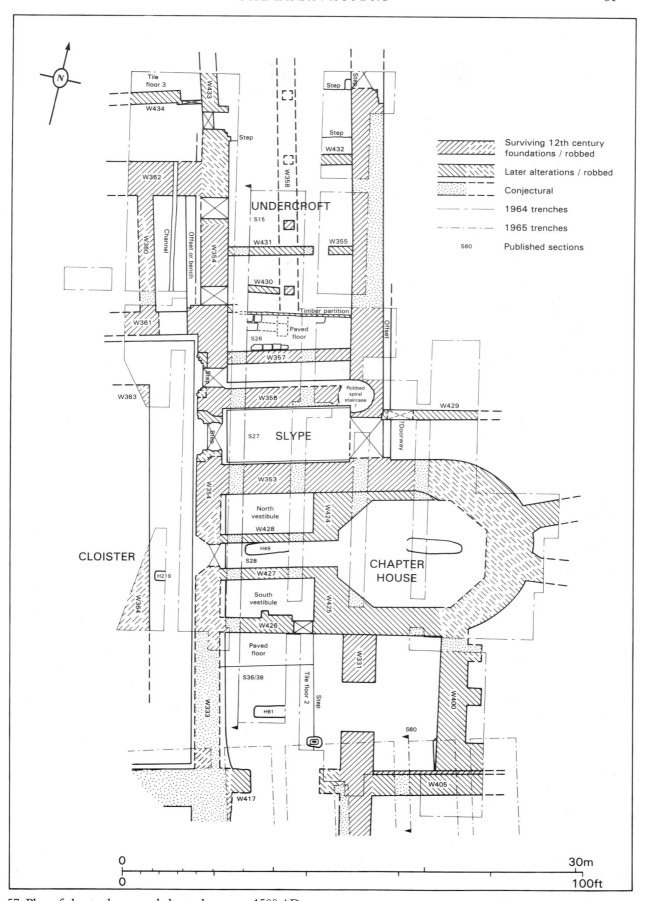

57. Plan of chapter house and claustral ranges *c.* 1500 AD

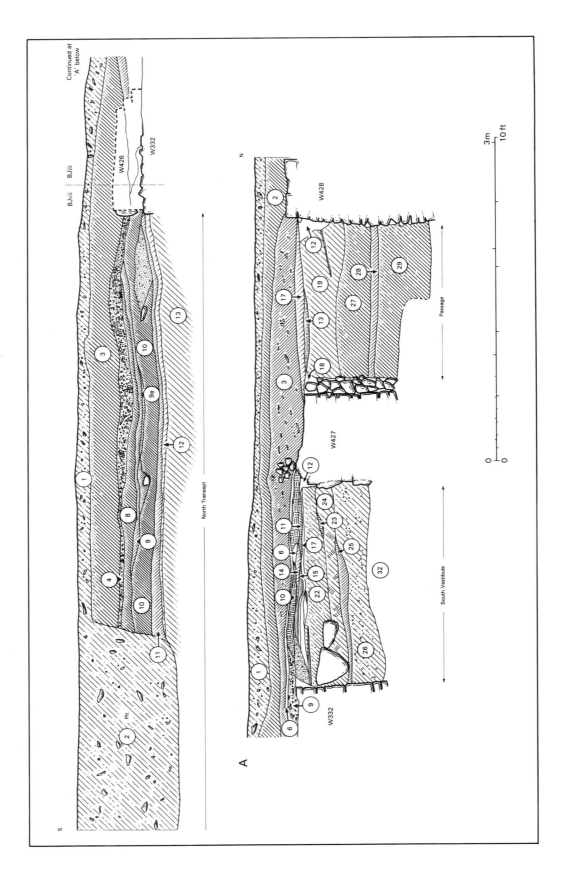

58. Section 36, 38 south-north from north transept through chapter house to undercroft (trenches BJ vii, BJ iii; see fig. 57), continued in fig. 59

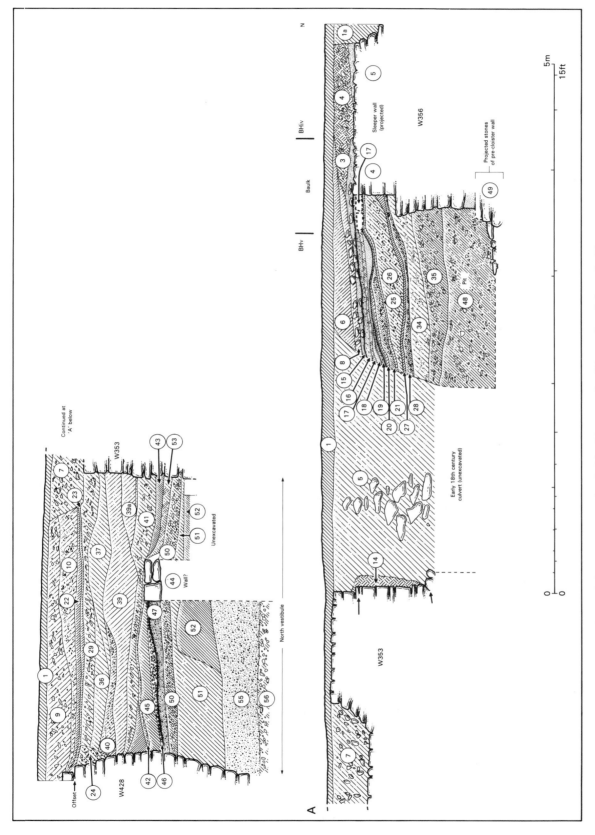

59 . Section 28, 27 south-north through east cloister range (trenches BH iv, BH v; see fig. 57), continued from fig. 58

vestibules. The new chapter house would appear to have been polygonal in plan, a transformation achieved by filling in the corners immediately east of the vestibules with solid platforms of masonry (W424, W425).

At the east end the apse appears to have been removed down to approximately one course above off-set level; there is no evidence for the new and probably thinner wall, which must have stood upon the old wall foundations.

The new plan may have been an irregular octagon (fig. 57). It is possible that six of the sides were of equal length with the east-west dimension being twice the length of the other sides. This would mean that all the vaulting ribs, except the central one between the pillars, would have been of the same length, thus creating vaulting panels of the same size and shape. They would have been based on 67.5, 67.5 and 45 degree triangles, with the whole vault of 12 panels resting on two columns. Such a layout would have reduced the thickness of the eastern wall to 4ft (1.2m) at a point where the thrust outwards would have been greatest. Even with thinner walls there would be a need for buttressing. Also alterations within the chapter house had necessitated the widening of the north wall 353 and the narrowing of the south wall, so the foundations of the 12th-century chapter house buttresses would no longer be symmetrically placed in relation to the new layout.

The new wall 426 on the south side of the south vestibule stood on the old wall foundation. It was narrower than its predecessor, but three offsets survived, giving the impression of steps. In the centre of the north side of the wall a square stone base or plinth had been inserted with its top surface between the levels of the lowest and middle offsets. The south face of W426 followed the original line of the 12th-century wall (fig. 58). The plinth may have supported a statue or some other free-standing ornament. Three courses of W426 survived, but the wall did not extend as far north as W425. There may have been a doorway here, although there is no evidence for door jambs. There must have been a point of entry into the vestibule and access from the north transept seems likely. There is some supporting evidence for a doorway in this wall in the north transept where there is a change of level from the east side to a tile floor on the west. This step is aligned on the east side of the hypothetical doorway (fig. 60).

The north wall 353 of the north vestibule, originally the north wall of the original chapter house, appears to have followed the same line as its predecessor. The north wall of the south vestibule W427 survived to a depth of 3ft (900mm) with eight foundation courses (fig. 58). For wall 428, there were 14 foundation courses to a depth of 4ft 6in (1.35m) with two dressed courses surviving. The top course was of very finely dressed facing stone of which four blocks survived on the west side of the trench. The wall at this point was 1ft 10in (550mm) wide. Although no finely dressed blocks survive on the foundation of W427, the foundation width of 2ft 6in

60. General view looking north across north transept tile floor 2 and step; entrance from north transept to chapter house vestibule

(840mm) would have been adequate to support a finely dressed wall similar to W428. One can only speculate as to whether the walls were solid to the roof or if, as seems more probable, they consisted of pierced stone screens.

A new doorway would have been built at the east end of the passage leading into the new chapter house. At this point there was a stone foundation aligned with W425 and W424 and probably bonded with them at a lower course to serve as a tie between the two. This foundation had curved edges with a core of graded stones. It showed signs of wear, but was probably overlain by a mortar or other floor. It was not laid throughout the whole length of the passage so it was not a floor surface. It doubtless supported the jambs of an arched doorway.

It is difficult to relate floor levels with the alterations and to make use of pottery within them for dating purposes. Evidence for flooring both within the passage and in the vestibules is poor. The earliest surviving floor was BJ III 17 with layer 15 as a replacement. Above this there appears to have been levelling associated with the construction of walls 427 and 428. The pottery from the levelling has been dated to the 14th century or later. A stone and mortar surface appears to post-date the construction of walls 427 and 428. Associated with this surface was a row of faced stones parallel, but opposed to wall 427 about 1ft 6in (450mm) to the south of it. This kerb perhaps formed a shallow drain or gully along the north side of the south vestibule, or could represent a support for book presses. Subsequently a white mortar floor provided the base for a tiled floor (CTD 31). A single tile may have been a stray or the only survivor of a relaid floor.

The pottery from contexts in the north vestibule was of little help in dating the alterations to the chapter house. The fill of a hearth, and of postholes, all post-dating the alterations, produced a single sherd of pottery (F200). Floors post-dating the construction of wall 427 contained pottery which need not be later than the 13th century.

Several contexts associated with the alterations produced late medieval pottery sherds and some early 16th-century wares (below, p. 101). This material should perhaps be regarded as intrusive, in view of the architectural evidence. Quantities of ornamental masonry were found in the debris overlying the latest surviving floor of the chapter house. Most of the fragments were in Perpendicular style; their counterparts can be seen in the parish church. Many of the decorated pieces had been gilded or painted and the workmanship was of a high standard (Wacher 1965, 108). Polygonal chapter houses were usually 13th to 14th century in date and the added vestibules may have been book rooms (Evans 1993, 121).

There were alterations at the east end of the **slype**. The foundation width of the eastern wall of the undercroft range W355 ranged from 6ft 6in-6ft 9in (1.98-2.06m) In BH IX, however, the wall width above offset level was only 5ft (1.5m) leaving a broad offset of 1ft 11in (580mm) on the outside. It seems strange that such a broad offset was left when it is noted that there was a stairwell only 1ft 4in or 1ft 8in (400 or 500mm) behind the face of the wall. The wall face at this point was composed of seven well dressed, but badly weathered, facing stones. It may be that this face was not the 12th-century original. The four facing stones on the south side of the stairwell were of very finely dressed stone and were less weathered. One bore a mason's mark in the form of a five-pointed star. Again these stones to the south of the stairwell do not appear to be part of the original 12th-century building as they match the width of the undercroft wall at this point 4ft 2in (1.25m). The wall was certainly reduced in width above offset level, and the presence of four dressed stones facing south would suggest a doorway. There was insufficient evidence to determine the number of occasions on which the wall had been refaced, or if the doorway was a replacement. Certainly at the time of the dissolution there was still access from the slype into the eastern ambulatory of the cloisters.

A new wall 429 was built eastwards from the north side of the slype, bonded into the north jamb of the doorway (fig. 57). The lower coursing of undressed stones was erratic, but with an offset, while most of the stones in the top surviving course were large and finely dressed. The blocks were longer on the north side (five blocks in 11ft 6in (3.5m)) than on the southern side (nine blocks in the same distance)(fig. 61).

61. General view looking south of cloister area, robbed foundations of chapter house centre left, robbed base of stair, bottom right

The westernmost facing stone on the north side seems to have been reused. Its topmost exterior edge had a chamfer moulding for all its length, with an additional and perhaps later rebate cut into the chamfer. It is possible that there was a doorway or step at this point. Traces of a flagstone floor were found to the north of the wall.

In common with much of the rest of the site, many of the floors yielded only early pottery which may be due to the fact that the later floors had been robbed or that the surviving pottery was residual. Mortar floors in the slype may be contemporary with the use of the doorway although as they were the earliest surviving surfaces, it seems more likely that a later concrete floor was contemporary with the later alterations. In either case a *terminus post quem* is provided by pottery dating to the 12th or 13th centuries. It seems likely that both the doorway and W429 were significantly later than this.

At the junction of the east **cloister** range and the north range, the latest alterations comprised walls 434 and 433 (figs. 62, 63, 64). W434 replaced an earlier wall 451 with a splayed entrance. The wall W362, apparently the original 12th-century wall, had been robbed. There were other walls in this complex area which have never been satisfactorily phased; some could date to the pre-abbey phase. There was a floor of re-used 14th-century tiles (floor 3, below p. 143).

62. General view of east cloister range looking south (trenches BG, BH) showing undercroft; balustrade of Abbey House on right

63. View of east cloister range looking west; garden wall on extreme right; tile floor 3 next to late medieval wall 434 with entrance (trench BG v)

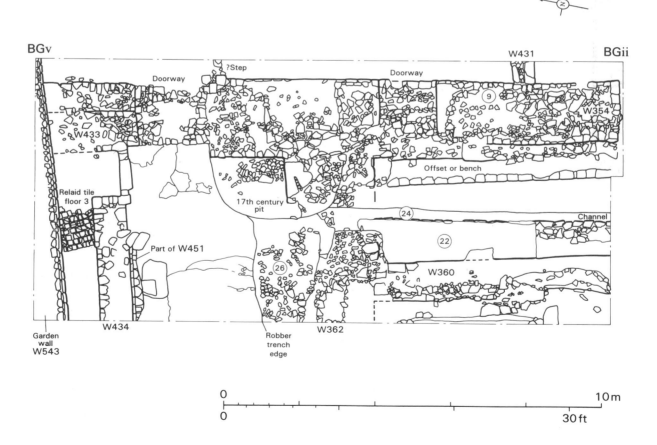

64. Plan of features in north area of east cloister range

THE DESTRUCTION OF THE ABBEY BUILDINGS AND POST-DISSOLUTION FEATURES

D. J. Wilkinson

In 1539 the abbey of Cirencester was dissolved. The Commissioners were instructed that all conventual buildings were to be pulled down, though some buildings of a practical character were allowed to remain (Evans 1993, 134). In May 1540 the site of the abbey, and its lands, were leased for 21 years to Roger Basing. By July 1541 the lead (the king's perquisite) had been stripped from the abbey church and Lady Chapel; Sir Anthony Hungerford and Robert Strange were buying and carrying away building materials (Evans 1993, 135). They maintained a complaint against Roger Basing that they had bought the 'Churche Steplee and Surplues howses off the late monasterye of Cyrcetour', and that as custodian of the site he prevented them from taking away 'the Stones Tymber and Stuff of the seyd church steplee and surplues howses' (P.R.O. E 321/17/48, cited by Reece 1962, 201-2). It has been suggested that some stone was re-used at no. 33 Gloucester Street (Clifton-Taylor 1984, 17).

In January 1565 the reversion of the abbey site was bought from Elizabeth I by Richard Master. Ruins still survived in the 1570s when they were seen by Camden (Evans 1993, 135). Much must have been cleared when the new mansion was built in the Elizabethan period (Bigland, **1**, 1791, 344). When Kip drew the house *c.* 1700 (figs. 65 and 66) nothing remained of the church and claustral buildings.

The documents thus suggest that demolition began after 1541 and was almost complete by the 1570s. However, the pottery from robber trenches and rubble deposits suggests that the destruction was carried out over a period of time, perhaps as much as one hundred years. It is also apparent that the destruction involved the removal not only of standing structures but also of features below

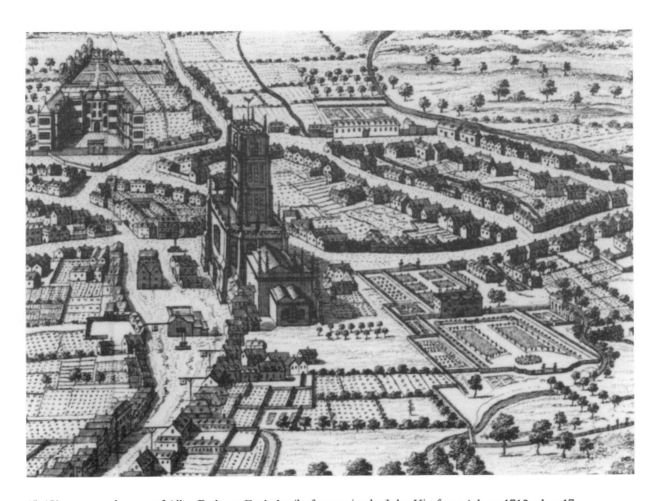

65. 'Cirencester: the seat of Allen Bathurst Esq'; detail of engraving by John Kip from Atkyns 1712, plate 17

ground. The early date of many of the surviving surfaces suggests that the latest floor surfaces, often of flagstones, had been removed. The presbytery walls were robbed to depths of over 4ft (1.2m) from the then ground surface; the robbing can be dated to the latter part of the 16th century. In the chapter house and presbytery, the robbing could be as late as the 17th century, although it still predates the dumping of rubble deposits. This may also be the case in the area extending from the north presbytery aisle west to the north nave aisle (phase 4a).

However, sometimes rubble was deposited prior to the robbing of walls. This process (phase 4b) seems to be concentrated in the area of the south side of the chapter house and eastern extension to the presbytery. Some of these deposits provide 16th century dates, others 17th century.

In attempting to provide overall dating for the deposition of rubble and thereby for the tearing down of the abbey buildings one has to balance the possibility of residuality in the single main phase of destruction with the possibility of redeposition and disturbance of rubble deposits. However, much pottery is later than the mid 16th century; most of the pottery in destruction deposits had been discarded by the mid 17th century (p. 101).

In general, destructive activity was at its peak near the late 16th to early 17th centuries. The site may have been partially cleared in the 16th century, perhaps to comply with royal conditions for the land grants or to honour contracts for the sale of materials from the abbey. Redeposition of rubble may have taken place as a preliminary to 17th-century garden landscaping (phase 5), perhaps as late as *c.* 1630.

66. 'The Abbey: the Seat of Thomas Master Esq' by Kip, from Atkyns 1712, plate 18

It is clear that the stonework content of the rubble deposits represents only a small fraction of that originally required to build the abbey. What stone remained included a fairly high proportion of mouldings, due no doubt to their complex shape which would have made their reuse difficult. The good quality ashlar would have been highly prized for re-use and it is this type of stone, originally the most prolific, which was conspicuous by its absence.

In the south-west area of the site there was a stone structure and drain which went out of use in the 18th century (phase 6b). This building is of interest because it occupied the area south of the abbey, north of the church, which in the late medieval period was used as a parish burial ground, but in post-dissolution times was evidently a dwelling .

As depicted by Kip, the mansion called The Abbey, built for the Master family, was probably square with five bays north-south with a projecting three storey porch and two bay windows on the entrance front facing Dollar Street. The Elizabethen house survived until the 1770s when it was demolished and a new house built, apparently on the same foundations, but with its principal aspect across a newly landscaped park and lake to the north-east. Demolition of this latest house in 1964 was in progress during the excavations but there was no opportunity to investigate the area prior to the building of the Abbey Flats.

A number of features were found which accord with the formal garden depicted by Kip (figs. 8b, 65, 66). Walls 541, 542 and 543 are on the lines of the sunken garden shown by Kip to the east of The Abbey, and there was a culvert running east-west approximately on the line of the central walkway of the garden. Pottery in the culvert backfill (its robbing?) was compatible with a deposition c. 1710. Two other linear features either side of the culvert may be remnants of a slightly earlier layout. Figure 8b thus shows the excavated elements of the formal garden, although the inner north wall of the garden seems to be missing.

A rubbish pit dating to the mid 18th century (phase 6a, BP I 4, fig. 8b) was situated in the property to the south of The Abbey grounds, between the grounds and the church. A group of linear features, lying in or near the small formal garden drawn by Kip to the south of The Abbey, were backfilled at some time in the 18th century. These may be bedding trenches for vegetables or herbs (fig. 9a).

A number of other rubbish pits date to the 19th century, when the formal garden had apparently fallen into decay, judging by the 1795 map (Anon 1795).

THE FINDS

THE MEDIEVAL AND LATER COINS

R. Reece and N. Mayhew; edited by J. F. Rhodes

1. Penny of William I, BMC type vii, North 847, 1083-1086; [Wareham], moneyer Ægelric, as identified by F. Elmore Jones (Jones 1966)(65 BK V 21, phase 2).
2. Penny of John/Henry III, short cross type vb, North 970, 1205-1218; Winchester, moneyer Miles (BJ VII 8).
3. Penny of Edward II, Fox type xva, North 1066, *c.* 1320; Bury St. Edmunds (BP I 27, phase 3c).
4. Penny of Edward III, 4th coinage brokage, 1351-1355 (BV I 3).
5. Halfpenny of Henry VI, annulet issue, North type 1434, 1422-1427; London (BJ XIV 2).
6. Clipped penny of Edward IV; probably York, Archbishop Neville, 1465-1476 (65 BK VII 2).
7. Penny of Henry VI; York, Archbishop Kemp, 1425-1452 (BL X 5, phase 3e).
8. Penny of Edward III/IV (BL X 5, phase 3e).

9. Farthing of Henry VII, initial mark for 1490-1504 (BL X 5, phase 3e).
10. Farthing of Charles I, royal 'Richmond' type, 1625-1634 (BP IX +).
11-12. Two farthings of Charles I, rose type, 1636-1644 (BJ VIII 1, BM II 1).
13. Tin farthing of Charles II, 1684 (BG VII +).
14. Farthing of Charles II/William and Mary (BN III 1).
15. Farthing of William III, 1697 (BG V 8).
16. Halfpenny of George III, 1773 (BJ XIV 2).
17. Coin weight for a rose-noble of Edward IV, after 1464-1470 (BL IV 7).

Nos 7, 8 and 9 in this list were from soil accumulated below the choir stalls. These three coins are unfortunately now missing so their identification cannot be checked.

RECKONING COUNTERS

R. Reece and N. Mayhew, edited by J. F. Rhodes

1. English counter, obv. bust as Edward II Fox type xv, rev. key as Berry pl. 3.8 but flanked by lis and with border I0I0s, *c.* 1325 (BP III 6).
2. Counter of Dauphiné, Barnard type 58, 1483-1500 (BP +).
3. French counter, Barnard type 68, 15th century (65 BK IX 2).
4. Low Countries counter, Barnard type 7, 1487-1507 (BG V 6).
5. Nuremberg counter, Barnard type 8, 16th century (BL V 6).

6. Nuremberg counter, Barnard type 8/9, pierced (BJ XIV 2).
7. Nuremberg counter, Barnard type 9 (BN VI +).
8. Nuremberg counter, Barnard type 18 (BL VI 4).
9-13. Five Nuremberg counters, Barnard type 82 (BN V 1, BM I +, BM I 26, BL IV 9, BL X 4).
14. Nuremberg counter, Barnard type 84 (BH X 3).
15. Nuremberg counter, Barnard type 85 (BL II 10).

OBJECTS OF SILVER AND COPPER ALLOY

D. J. Wilkinson

with contributions by

R. Brownsword, N. Griffiths, C. M. Heighway, D. R. Hook and E. E. H. Pitt

Objects not stated to be silver are copper alloy.

JEWELLERY (fig. 67)

1. Silver pin with faceted head; the head has been cast separately then joined to drawn or worked shaft. Probably Roman. BN VIII 24, mid to late 16th-century context.
2. Ring-headed pin. The lower half of the ring is enamelled, a central spot flanked by drop-shaped blobs; the upper half is covered with a thin silver band which is ribbed all round. Although now yellow the enamel was probably red when new. BN V 32, from the fill of a late Anglo-Saxon robber trench (Brown 1976, 19, fig. 3.1, no. 1).

This pin belongs to the group of ring-headed pins known as ibex-headed pins (Fowler 1964, 153). There are a few enamelled examples, though none seems to be decorated with a silver band in the same way as this one (Brown 1976, 19). Ring-headed pins may be examples of Roman metalwork types which continued in use through the 5th to 6th centuries in Britain (Pretty 1975, 54) though this hypothesis has never been confirmed. A similar pin was found at St Oswald's Priory, Gloucester (Heighway and Bryant forthcoming). Another came from 1973 excavations in Cirencester (McWhirr 1986, fig. 78, no. 10) (CMH).

3. Pin with large decorative head in the form of a rope knot, the knot formed by interlacing four parallel twisted wires. 65 BK III 8, late 16th to early 17th century, but probably earlier.
4. Pin with large spherical head. The head is formed separately from two domed pieces of metal filled with light grey solder. Length 68mm when straight. BV II 1, 17th-century context.
5. Annular brooch or buckle with pin. BL X 5, 15th to early 16th-century context.
6. Small silver ring with very narrow band, Roman, cross-hatching on band and two small lugs. BL II 28, mid 12th to 13th-century context.
7. Broken finger ring; surface decorated as a twisted cable with deep grooves between strands, and the whole surface gilded. BV III 5, 13th to 15th-century context.

Other items of jewellery included a small silver penannular ring with flared terminals from a late 14th-century context; a fragment of a mercury-gilded silver object with the gilding set into spiral grooves and on the circular edge; an unstratified copper alloy mount with incised concentric rings.

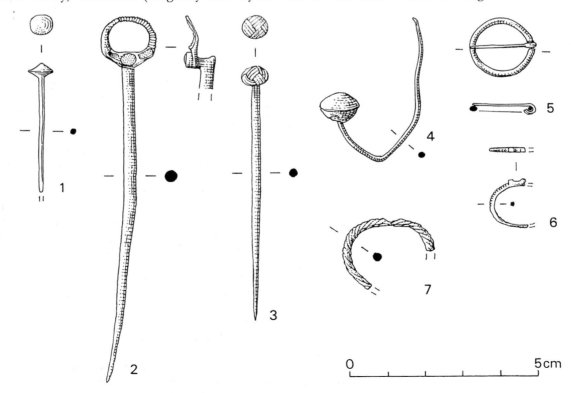

67. Copper alloy and silver small finds, 1:1; nos. 1, 6 silver; others copper alloy; 2 with enamel

BUCKLES AND BELT FITTINGS (fig. 68)

8. Strap end, hinged to buckle, both decorated with two parallel lines of fine dots. The cast buckle is trefoil-shaped with bevelled foils and knops. The strap end was formed from a continuous strip of sheet metal and pierced by three spherical-headed rivets. BV III 1, 17th-century context.

9. D-shaped buckle with sword-shaped tongue. D shape made from rectangular strip of metal with small groove for tongue - straight sided - oval cross-section bar attached to strip by two round rivets. 65 BK VIII 8, H101, tomb of Walter of Cheltenham, early to mid 14th-century context.

10. Sub-rectangular buckle cast with moulded pin-rest, plain pin. BP I 19, mid 16th to mid 17th-century context.

11. Double-oval buckle, cast, with 'cast-in' decoration in deep relief, of trailing foliage. BG/H/J, unstratified but probably 16th century.

12. Double-oval buckle cast with central lobed projections and lateral knops, remains of iron pin/tongue in position. Black japan coating. BL II 9, early 18th-century context, but probably 14th or 15th century.

13. Double-oval buckle with cast pin-rest and lateral knops. Pin/tongue missing. Object not very well finished-off after casting. Remains of continuous black japan coating over surface. BM I 26, mid to late 17th-century context.

14. Double-oval buckle with some cast-in decoration on outer edge and lateral knops. The pin/tongue is missing. It has extensive remains of black japan coating. BJ IX 1, early 18th-century context.

15. Double-oval buckle with central lobed decoration. Pin/tongue missing. BJ III 1, mid 18th-century context.

16. Buckle-pin with raised lateral notches, a form usually seen on medieval, frequently monastic, large annular brooches/buckles (NG). BJ IV 2, 18th-century context.

17. Buckle plate. Part of two corroded iron rivets survive in position. 65 BK VII 2, mid to late 16th-century context, but probably earlier.

18. Probable buckle-plate, now unfolded: lower drawing shows original form; four rivet holes with two corroded iron rivets in position; the centre of the plate has a slot. BJ XIV 1, 18th-century context, but probably 16th century.

Objects not illustrated, mostly from post-medieval contexts, include:- a D-shaped buckle with missing tongue, a double-oval buckle with cast-in decoration, a buckle fragment, two strapend plates, a small decorative belt-mount; also a cast belt-chape, decorated with radiating lines, from an early to mid 12th-century context.

DRESS ACCESSORIES (fig. 69)

19. Triangular/heart-shaped badge, bevelled edges and shallow scored zig-zag decorative lines on front, possibly a love token. BH VI 5, early 17th-century context, but perhaps 16th century.

20. Circular, slightly domed mount with central hole, fixed by two rivets. BL X 5, 15th to early 16th-century context.

21. Decorative mount, cut from sheet metal in quatrefoil form with iron rivet heads surviving in the centre of each circular foil. BH X 3, mid to late 16th-century context.

22. Openwork belt-mount, with slot for suspension and side ring; probably 16th to 17th century (NG). BH V 5, mid to late 18th-century context.

23. Hook-and-eye fastening. 65 BK VII 2, mid to late 16th-century context.

24. Eye, part of a conventional hook-and-eye fastener used on clothing. 64 BK IV 35, associated with burial H59; possibly 13th to 14th century.

25. Ring-tie formed by twisting together ends of small piece of wire. BJ VIII 1, early 18th-century context, but probably earlier.

26. Pair of small circular mounts with central holes. BJ VIII 19, 14th-century context.

27. Chain of open-ended 'S' links. The terminal swivel-link has notches cut into the outer band of the ring. BJ XV 1, 18th-century context, but probably earlier.

28. Length of chain, composed of open-ended 'S' links, probably about 40 links, surviving length c. 31.7mm. BJ IX 2, late 17th to early 18th-century context.

29. Two fragments of chain; each link comprises a triple loop of a single strand of wire. 16 links survive in total. BV III 15, late 12th-century context.

Unillustrated was a thong-guide of silver-coated brass, from a 16th to 17th-century context.

Lace tags

30. Slightly tapering tube formed by bending metal sheet into cylinder, straight join now open; probably a large lace-tag or 'point'; also referred to as 'lace-chapes'. BP VIII , unstratified.

A total of 137 lace tags, 'points', were found on the site in 41 contexts. The distribution pattern of lace tags follows closely that for pins, with the greatest concentration in the area of the choir crossing. The lace tags were made from sheet metal rolled or folded so as to enclose the lace and varied in length from 18-28mm. Points are known to have been used from the mid 18th century (Egan and Pritchard 1991, 281) and could be used either on clothing such as jerkins, hose and jackets or as shoe laces. Their frequent occurrence with pins (as on this site) has led to the suggestion that they were used as pin protectors. It is more likely, however, that pins and lace tags were both made by pinners (Clay 1981, 137).

31. Pin formed from twisted wire with a small loop. BJ VII 8, 14th or 15th-century context.

THIMBLES (fig. 69)

32. Open-ended tailor's thimble, decorated with four irregular bands of large indentations. BM IV 5, 18th-century context.

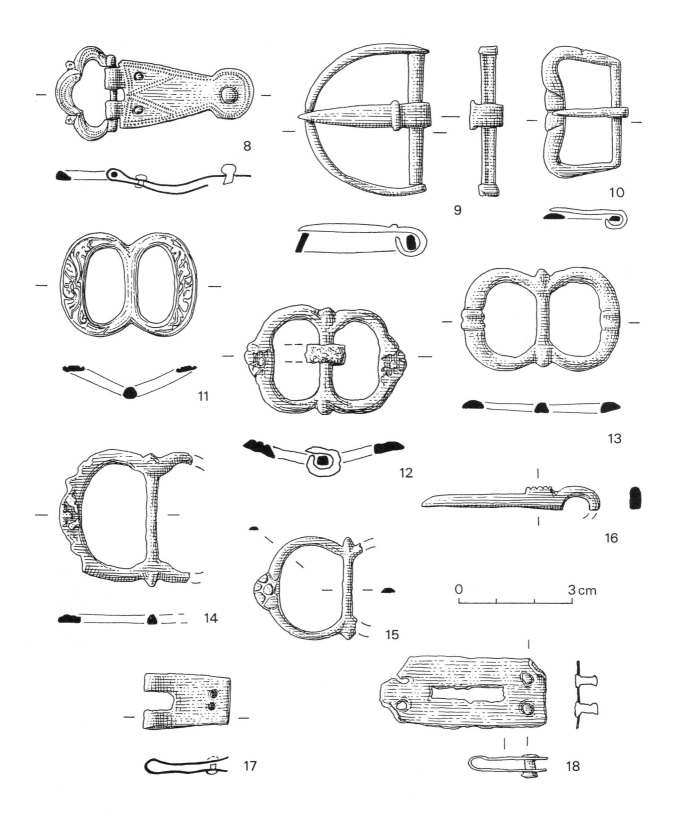

68. Copper alloy small finds, 1:1

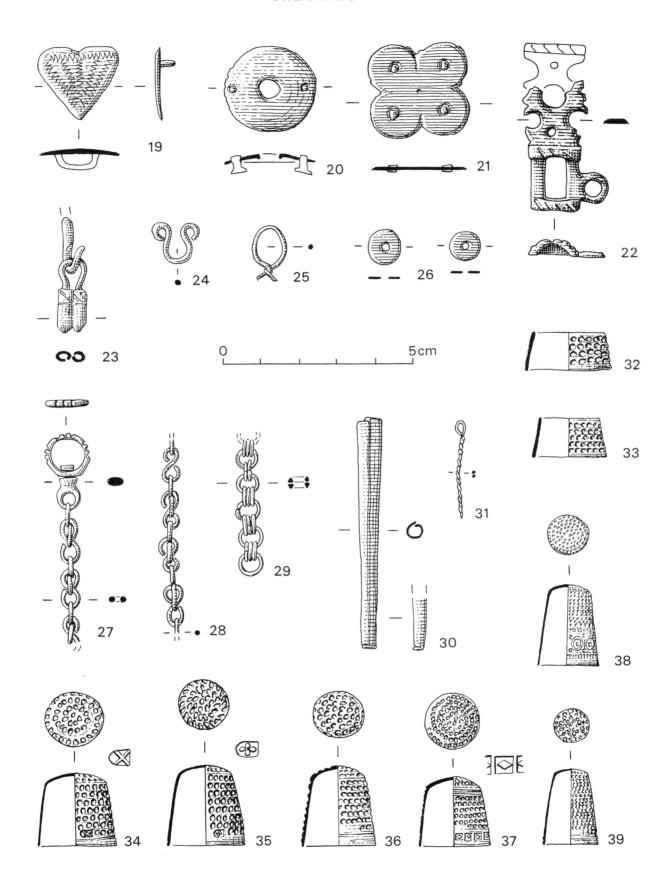

69. Copper alloy small finds, 1:1; details of stamps of nos. 34, 35, 37 at 2:1

33.   Open-ended tailor's thimble, decorated with four irregular bands of sub-rectangular indentations above incised line. BM IV 1, 18th-century context.

34.   Thimble with spiral of relatively large indentations over entire surface, above an incised line around the base. BJ III 8, early 16th-century context.

35. Thimble decorated with continuous spiral of indentations, terminating in a clover-leaf maker's mark. BJ VIII 10, late 16th to early 17th-century context, but probably earlier.

36.   Thimble decorated with a spiral of large indentations, above two incised lines around the base. BH V 13, mid to late 16th-century context, but probably earlier.

37.   Thimble decorated with indentations arranged

spirally in two zones on top and body. In addition the base has a decorative lower band. BH III 1, 17th to 18th-century context.

38.   Thimble. The upper zone has ten bands of indentations while the lower zone has a band of concentric rings, with finely engraved lines within the rings and pairs of dots dividing each group of rings. The band of concentric rings lies within cross-hatched bands and there is a plain band at the base of the thimble. BJ XIII 1, early to mid 18th-century context, but probably earlier.

39.   Slim thimble decorated with spiral of fine indentations. BG V 8, early 18th-century context.

There were four other thimbles all from post-medieval contexts.

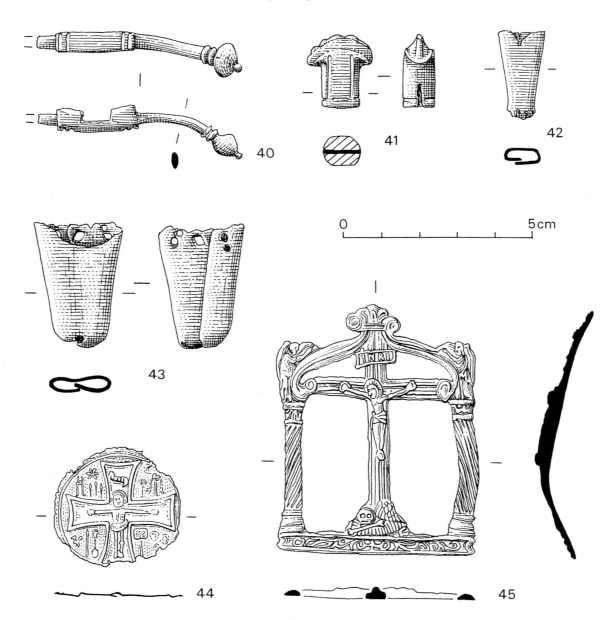

70. Copper alloy small finds, 1:1

PINS

A total of 154 pins were recovered from 39 contexts (on site BG 18 pins from 12 contexts, BH 11 from 2, BJ 26 from 11, BL 64 from 3, BM 11 from 3, BN 2 from 1 and site BP 22 pins from 7 contexts). Site BL yielded 22 pins from BL V 7 and 41 from BL X 5, contexts related to the choir crossing stalls, and probably deposited in the 15th to early 16th century. The technique of manufacture of the head in all cases was to twist a length of wire around the top of the shaft and either to leave it untreated, or to round and smooth it off. The length of the shaft varied from 22-32mm. Pins were used to fasten veils and head-dresses (Egan and Pritchard 1991, 217) which poses the question as to why so many are in an abbey of canons.

WEAPONS AND KNIFE SHEATHS (fig. 70)

40. Quillon-block and one quillon of a dagger, probably 16th century (NG); central boss with two cylindrical arms, one broken and the other bent, but complete with acorn type finial. BN V +, from topsoil.
41. Knife end-cap, cast solid, irregular hexagonal cross-section with crescent-shaped end, rectangular channel for iron tang of knife contains remains of iron corrosion. BL V 7, 15th to early 16th-century context.
42. Small plain chape, formed by folding over a thin sheet of metal then cutting notches out of one end and squashing that end in. Lap join and squashed end held together with solder. Possibly from a knife sheath. BJ XIV 2, late 16th to early 17th-century context.
43. Plain chape formed from sheet folded over and soldered. Five holes are punched through the back (around the join). Possibly from a knife sheath. BJ XV 1, 18th-century context, but probably earlier.

The unillustrated objects include what seems to be a copper-alloy knife blade: the XRF shows a very high tin content (speculum metal) and small amounts of arsenic and lead; from an 18th-century context.

RELIGIOUS ITEMS (fig. 70)

44. Pilgrim's badge. Circular thin sheet with repoussé decoration, including central crucifix and the emblems of Christ's Passion in each of the quarters. BL X 5, 15th to early 16th-century context.
45. Part of a pax. An ogee arch surmounts columns with twisted flutes each side which in turn stand on a common decorated base. The centre is filled by a crucifix above which there is the inscription INRI. The columns are surmounted by angels and there is a skull and bone amongst grass at the base of the crucifix. Three small lumps of metal on back of badge, possibly for attachment. BG V 15, late 16th to early 17th-century context, but probably earlier.

BOOK CLASPS (fig. 71)

46. Book clasp made from two wide plates. One end is bent to form a shallow hook to clasp hinge, the other end has seven decorative notches. Three rivets survive to hold the smaller back plate. A fourth hole in the front plate is decorative. BL X 5, 15th to early 16th-century context.
47. Book clasp, one end narrowed and bent back to form a shallow hook, the other splayed with a large central and two small flanking decorative notches. Long sides partly bevelled and each with two small notches. Three rivets were used to fix back plate. Central hole is surrounded by finely engraved concentric rings and three punched holes in triangle. BL VII 15, 15th to early 16th-century context.
48. Book clasp, roughly made from a rectangular plate with a hook at one end and decorative notches in the opposite edge. There are fine engraved lines at right angles to the edges and several real and some decorative rivet holes. BL V 7, late 15th to early16th-century context.
49. Book clasp, made from a rectangular plate with one end narrowed and bent back to form a shallow hook, the other splayed by cutting three notches into the edge. Three rivets hold back plate. Central motif of punched hole surrounded by incised ring. BL X 5, 15th to early 16th-century context.
50. Book clasp, considerably worked from a rectangular plate. Small shallow hook at one end extending from a wider segment with fine engraved zig-zag ornament. The other end is wider and has three decorative holes, engraved lines and hatching as well as two sharp and two shallow notches cut into the end. Rivets still hold the back plate. BL X 5, 15th to early 16th-century context.
51. Book clasp. Made from two sheet metal plates riveted together in three places. Top plate has one end narrowed and bent back to form a hook, the other end with a broad splay and decoratively shaped edge. Otherwise plain with slightly bevelled edges. BL VI 4. Mid-late 16th-century context, but probably 15th century.
52. Book clasp with remains of leather. Made from a rectangular plate. One end narrowed and turned over to form a shallow hook, the other end splayed with notches cut into the edge. Three rivets still remain to hold the back plate. Front plate decorated with punched hole surrounded by two concentric rings, chamfered edges and two darts opposite each other along the edge. BL V 7, 15th to early 16th-century context.
53. Book clasp, made from a rectangular plate with one end narrowed and bent back to form a shallow hook, the other splayed with three notches in the edge. There is a decorative circle and dot inscribed into the centre of the plate. The side edges are bevelled. Three rivets fasten the plates together. BL V 6, mid 16th-century context, but probably 15th century.
54. Miniature book clasp or hooked tag. Narrow end with hook and splayed end with notches. Length 18 mm, width 7 mm. BG V 3, 18th-century context, but probably earlier.

Another bookclasp is unillustrated and came from a 15th to early 16th-century context.

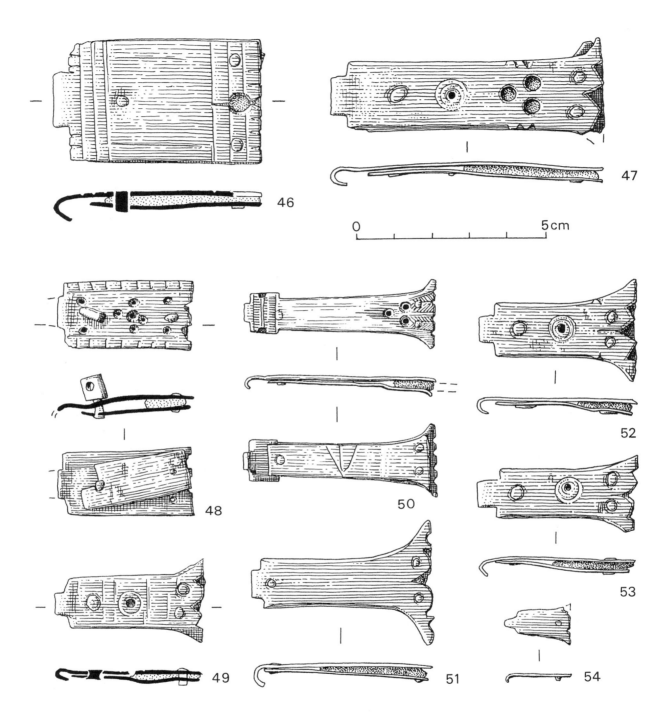

71. Copper alloy small finds, 1:1; nos 46-53 with leather

HOUSEHOLD ITEMS

Not illustrated: a possible bucket handle, half a rumbler bell, decorated, from an 18th-century context, and four metal buttons, two from 18th-century contexts, two unstratified.

Candlesticks (fig. 72)

55. Fragment of Limoges enamel from the base of a tripod pricket candlestick, metal with high copper content, trailing plant design outlined in gilded copper relief infilled mainly with blue enamel with some white, yellow and green in trefoil terminals. 13th century; analysed below, sample C200b. BJ XV 2, 17th-century context.

56. Turned candlestick with rilling and mouldings. The base is made separately and has broken away leaving a small fragment of sleeve. Analysed below, C196a; 16th century. BN IV +, from topsoil.

57. Cast bar, sub-rectangular in cross-section, two curves form a cusp; possibly part of one leg of a tripod candle-holder (NG). BJ XII 2, late 16th-century context.

58. Candlestick base, diameter 137-163 mm. Analysed below, sample C199b, 16th century. BN V, 18th-century context.

59. Candlestick base, diameter 115-125 mm. Analysed below, sample C198b; 16th century. BM II 7, early 17th-century context.

Another candlestick stem is discussed below: sample no. C197a.

Door knocker (fig. 73)

60. Fragment of mask; remains of nose and eye together with part of cheek and forehead, probably of a lion. It probably once included a ring to act as a door knocker; its composition is discussed below (sample K2). BN V 2, 18th-century context, but associated with 13th-century pottery. Possibly Roman: see below.

Spigot (fig. 73)

61. Cockerel cut from thick sheet; part of spigot tap. Circle-and-dot eye, with T-shaped stamp mark on body. Analysed below, sample T5. BP I 6, 18th-century context, but probably late medieval.

Plates (fig. 73)

62. Fragment from the rim of a large plate or dish. BP V 7, probably 17th-century.

63. Small fragment probably from the rim of a plate or dish. BM I 20, early to mid 17th-century context. Three other plate rim fragments were found.

Bell (fig. 73)

64. Fragment of thick cast sheet with slight carination. Possibly from a bell but the alloy composition would throw doubt on this interpretation; see analysis below, sample U1. BN V 1, 18th-century context.

Utensils (fig. 73)

65. Strainer. Thin rectangular sheet with holes punched through, rough edges of punched holes left upstanding, area of sheet 10.1 sq.cm. BL X 5, 15th to early 16th-century context.

66. Fragment of spoon with part of bowl and handle. BJ III 1, mid 18th-century context.

Scales (fig. 73)

67. Balance arms from scales; pair of flattened arms attached to a central shaft, holes at the ends of the arms and at the fulcrum. BP VIII, unstratified.

68. Pan from folding balance cut from very thin sheet metal with three holes for threads or chains around outer edge. 65 BK VII 2, mid to late 16th-century context, but probably earlier.

69. Balance pan of very thin sheet metal with five holes, three of them original, for attachment. Diameter 40mm. BJ XIV 2, late 16th to early 17th-century context, but probably earlier.

Furniture (fig. 74)

70. Part of the hasp from a lock; bent: Roman (NG). BL V 25, 11th or 12th-century context.

71. Drawer-pull, 17th to early 18th century (NG). BP I 4, mid 18th-century context.

72. One of four probable furniture studs. The heads are decorated with three grooves that form six-armed stars. Pins of each stud vary in length but all are roughly square in cross section. Head of each stud is gilded. BJ VIII 2, 16th-century context, probably disturbed early 18th century.

73. Mount for leather or textile. BJ VII 4, mid to late 16th-century context, but probably 14th or 15th century.

74. Fragment of very thin copper alloy sheet gilded and decorated with foliage repoussé work. Roughly triangular with hole punched from non-gilded side at apex of triangle; angled ridge along base of triangle. BP V 5, 18th-century context, but probably earlier.

Rings or annular brooches

75. Annular brooch; pin pissing. BJ XIV 2, late 16th to early 17th-century context but probably earlier.

76. Annular brooch with deep band. Diameter 22 mm. BJ VIII 11, 15th-century context.

Five other plain rings are not illustrated.

Miscellaneous (fig. 74)

77. Thick rectangular plate with centrally-placed hole and slightly bevelled edges, width 40 mm, 3 mm thick, at least 35 mm long. 65 BK I 12, from fill of tomb H106, 14th-century context.

78. Fork with two prongs springing from a finely worked arm. BM IV 3, 18th-century context.

79. Rectangular strip of sheet metal, one side gilded. Decoration along edges of strip in the form of three concentric rings, punched from gilded side, also two rivet holes punched through from gilded side. 65 BK IV 2, early to mid 18th-century context, but probably earlier.

80. Unidentified fragment with tang. Incised decoration on convex side of angled end. XRF

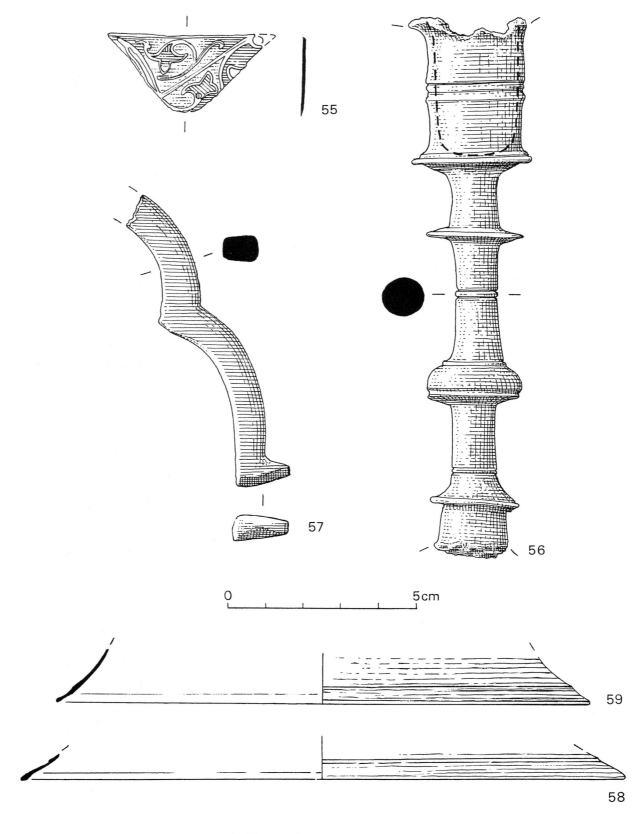

72. Copper alloy small finds, 1:1; no. 55 with enamel

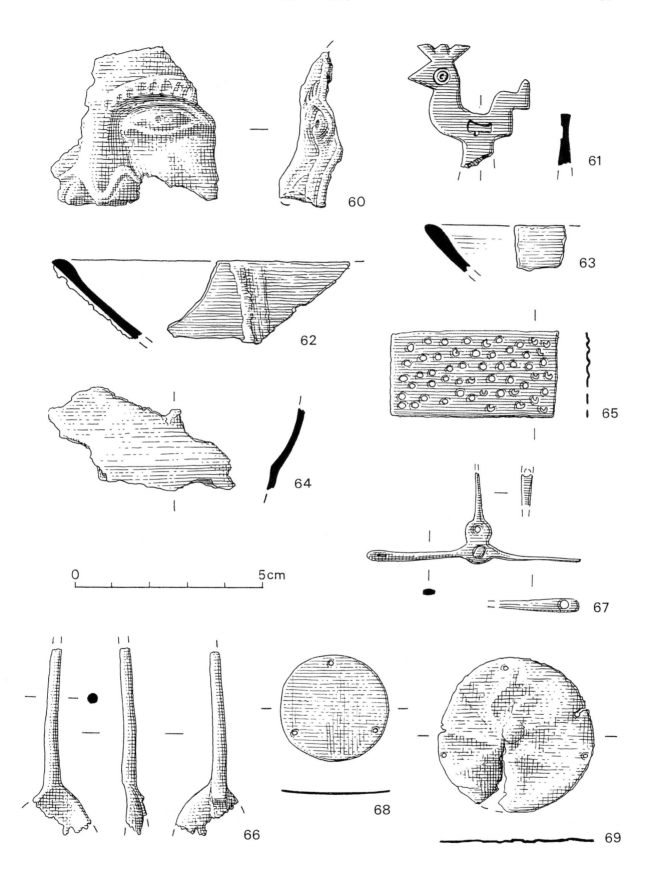

73. Copper alloy small finds, 1:1

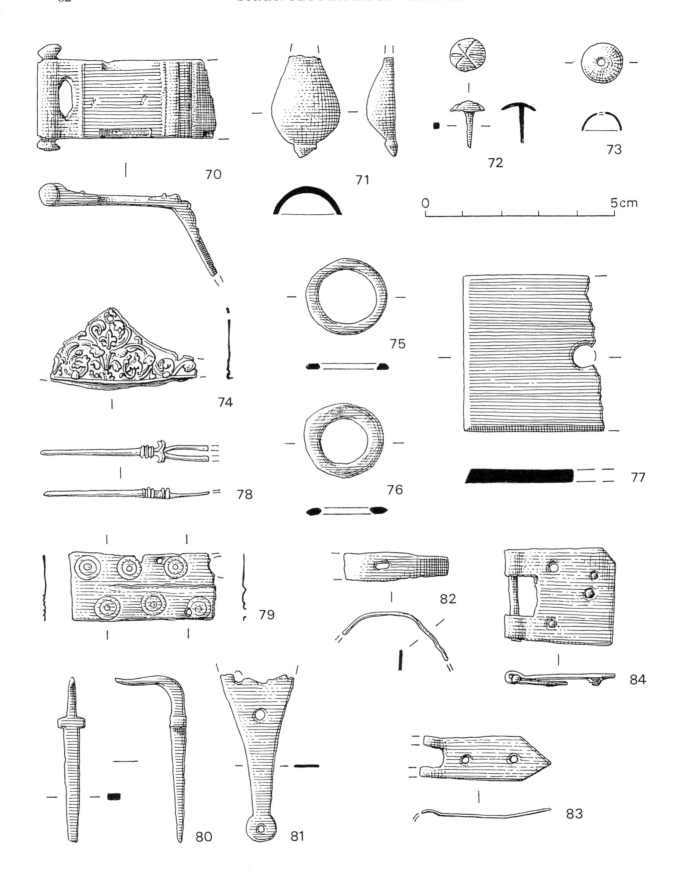

74. Copper alloy small finds, 1:1

analysis indicated a tin coating on either a copper or tin bronze base. BM V 15, 16th-century context.

81. Fragment of thin sheet, broken at one end but tapering with a circular lobe terminal at the other end, two surviving central fastening holes. BN I 5, late 17th-century context.

82. Bent strip of varying width with small rectangular slot. BJ VIII 2, 16th-century context, but probably earlier.

83. Possible hinge with two rivet holes (NG). BH VI 2, early 18th-century context, but probably 14th century.

84. Hinge with four rivet holes (NG). BL V 7, 15th to early 16th-century context.

Also present were the following miscellaneous items: a gilded strip, a variety of strap bindings, a disc, wire loops, various other binding-strips of sheet fragments, tubes.

ANALYSIS OF CAST COPPER ALLOY OBJECTS

by R. Brownsword, D.R. Hook and E.E.H. Pitt

Introduction

A number of cast copper alloy items were examined at the Corinium Museum by two of the authors, contributing to research being carried out at Coventry (Lanchester) Polytechnic in 1982 on the copper-based casting alloys used in the medieval and Tudor periods.

Sampling and analytical technique

Small amounts of metal (10-20 mg) were taken by drilling or filing as seemed most appropriate from positions unlikely to interfere with future study or display of the objects. The samples were mounted on Mylar film in the laboratory and secured with an adhesive tape known to be low in metallic impurities. The mounted samples were analysed by X-ray fluorescence spectrometry using a chromium target tube. The analysis was carried out qualitatively/ semi-quantitatively by recording the X-ray spectra. This was followed by quantitative analysis using fixed angle counting in conjunction with appropriate standards. The results are contained in the Table below.

Discussion of the objects and their analyses (figs. 72, 73)

No. 56 sample no. C196a

At the end remote from the socket, there is the stub of the stem of metal with a small wedge or spacer between the ring and stem. Although the ring has an alloy composition similar to that of the stem it is not thought that the ring is the remaining part of the original candlestick base. The size of the socket and the scale of the decoration of the stem suggest that it is the upper part of a tall candlestick, made in more than one part. A similar candlestick (C122a - from a private collection) with slight differences of detail in the stem decoration has been analysed in the laboratory and its composition is very similar to C196a.

No. 59 sample no. C198b and No. 58 sample no. C199b

These fragments both come from the bell-shaped bases of candlesticks of broadly the same type as sample C122a. The machined detail of the rim suggests that the fragments were similarly produced and finished; their alloy compositions are similar to those of C196a and C122a.

Sample no. C197a (not illustrated)

It is clear that this is part of the lower end of a candlestick stem the fragment is too small to discern the form. The alloy composition is different from the others (C196a, 198b, 199b); they are probably English although the possibility of French origin cannot at present be eliminated. C197a is probably an example of an English alloy having a low zinc content, as has one used for a candlestick stem at Gloucester Museum (C202a). Sixteenth-century dates are suggested on the basis of style and alloy composition for all the fragments so far discussed.

No. 55 sample no. C200b

This item is very different from the other fragments in that it shows traces of enamelling. The composition of the metal also contrasts markedly, being nearly pure copper. This fragment has come from the triangular side of the base of a tripod pricket candlestick of the Limoges type, made in that region in the 13th century. Several Limoges enamelled candlesticks have been analysed and each is made from copper containing a small amount of lead and little else (eg. C188b), as is the case with the present fragment.

No. 60 sample no. K2

This fragment appears to be part of a lion mask and it is likely it formed part of a door knocker; a lion mask with a ring in the jaws was the most common type of door-knocker (cf Werner 1977, 144). The alloy composition of the fragment is that of a heavily leaded bronze with, apart from copper, lead and tin, remarkably low levels of other elements usually found in this type of alloy. The low nickel content in particular suggests a relatively early date (pre 15th century). Certain early medieval cooking pots, of the type with a spherical body-form and legs of circular cross-section, have similar alloy compositions to this mask fragment. The lion mask knocker published by Werner (1977, 144) has also been shown to be made of a highly leaded bronze with low impurity levels and the mask analyses are compared in the Table. The mask analysed by Werner was dated to the 2nd-3rd centuries AD and so the present fragment might be

Roman.   A very different alloy was used in the manufacture of a medieval monkey mask knocker in the Museum of London (Table, K3).

No. 61. sample no. T5

The cockerel almost certainly formed part of a tap on a spigot. At the bird's 'feet', there is a fracture at the point at which it would have been attached to the conical plug of the tap. There are complete examples of late medieval cockerel spigots in the Ashmolean Museum, Oxford, and the Museum of London. In alloy composition, the closest analogy is with a spigot (sample T1), without the tap handle, in the National Museum of Wales; its composition and that of the present fragment are compared in the Table.

No. 64 sample no. U1

It has been suggested that this fragment came from a bell but the alloy composition would throw doubt on this interpretation. Medieval bell-metal contained more tin (15-20%) and much less lead than the present fragment. The alloy composition is fairly close to that of the mask fragment, the only serious variance being in respect of the arsenic content. This is one of the more difficult elements to determine accurately when high lead alloys are analysed, as is the case in this instance. It is not impossible that this too may be Roman in origin but an early medieval date is possible since there is a close alloy parallel in a cauldron of the type described above (CV105) in the Museum of London.

TABLE: ANALYSIS OF COPPER ALLOY OBJECTS
Italics indicate data from elsewhere.

Lab. no.	Cu	Zn	Sn	Pb	Ni	Fe	Sb	As	Ag%	Museum no.
C196a	76.2	8.81	2.92	9.37	0.38	0.41	1.37	0.49	0.07	No. 56
C122a	*76.9*	*6.24*	*4.05*	*10.0*	*0.32*	*0.96*	*0.84*	*0.68*	*0.02*	*Private collection*
C198b	75.4	5.93	3.52	11.5	0.39	0.82	1.57	0.83	0.04	No. 59
C199b	80.3	4.05	4.85	7.45	0.25	0.63	1.56	0.83	0.10	No. 58
C197a	91.4	2.94	3.63	0.15	0.24	0.24	0.66	0.64	0.10	p. 79 (not illustrated)
C202a	*85.0*	*2.20*	*9.16*	*2.19*	*0.12*	*0.53*	*0.24*	*0.42*	*0.13*	*GLOUC A36*
C200b	98.4	0.09	nd	1.14	0.07	0.12	0.14	0.12	0.02	No. 55
C188b	*97.8*	*0.09*	*0.01*	*1.48*	*0.07*	*0.06*	*0.39*	*0.09*	*0.05*	*M235/2*
K2	78.7	0.08	7.66	12.9	0.04	0.04	0.09	0.44	0.02	No. 60
284		*nd*	*7 c*	*20*	*0.02*	*0.05*	*0.09*	*0.05*	*0.05*	*BERLIN 26 (Werner 1977)*
K3	*85.7*	*11.1*	*0.67*	*1.62*	*0.28*	*0.21*	*0.05*	*0.32*	*0.02*	*LON 8074*
T5	78.4	14.1	1.24	5.16	0.33	0.68	nd	0.14	0.03	No. 61
T1	*77.1*	*10.2*	*3.45*	*5.86*	*0.45*	*1.92*	*0.03*	*0.92*	*0.15*	*WALES 31.7*
U1	77.1	0.08	8.06	14.3	0.04	0.05	0.23	0.09	0.02	No. 64
CV105	*77.4*	*0.09*	*8.02*	*14.2*	*0.05*	*0.06*	*0.22*	*0.05*	*0.01*	*LON*

IRON OBJECTS

D. J. Wilkinson

with contributions from N. Griffiths and C. M. Heighway

Items not illustrated will be found fully catalogued in the site archive.

Knives (fig. 75)

85. Knife with wooden handle with a long thin blade. Back in line with tang. Cutting edge forming sharp shoulder with tang. Four rivet holes in tang with three rivets still holding handle. X-radiograph shows maker's mark on blade and band holding handle to end of tang. BL V 6, early-mid 16th-century context.
86. Large knife blade, probably a carver. Back in line with tang. Cutting edge convex near tip of blade and forming a sharp shoulder with broad tang. Soft white metal band, either side of blade/tang junction shown by XRF analysis to be a tin-lead alloy (?solder). Two stamps forming a maker's mark visible near tang. BM I 26, mid-late 17th-century context, but probably 16th century.
87. Knife blade, possibly a presentoir. Cutting edge and thick back both faintly convex and each forming a shallow shoulder with the tang. Tang coated with a sheet of copper alloy. Radiograph shows heavily worked cutting edge. BH IV 1, 18th-century context.

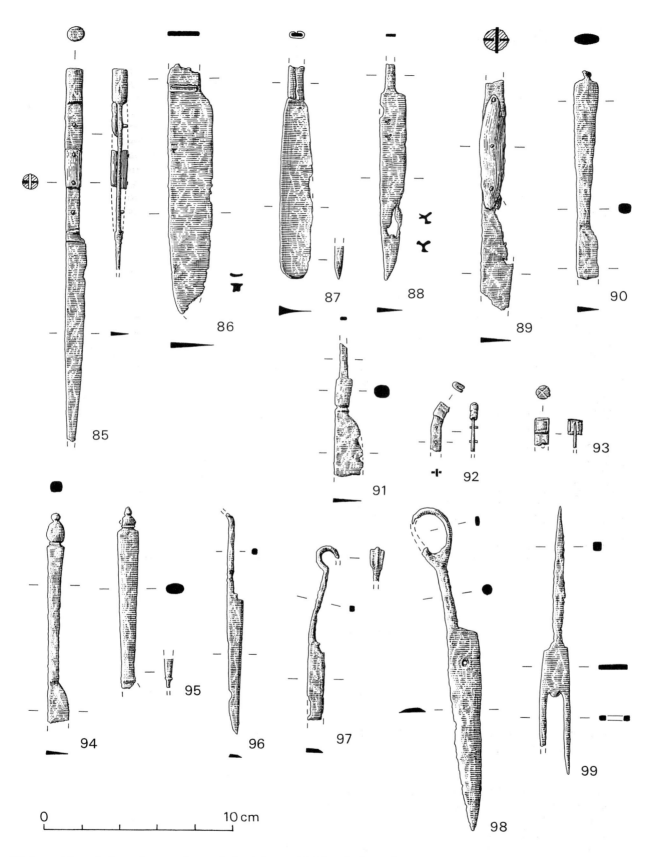

75. Iron objects; knives, shears, scissors, forks, 1:2, nos. 86, 88 maker's marks at 1:1.

88. Knife blade. Straight back forms shallow shoulder with narrow tang. Convex cutting edge forms shoulder with tang. Two maker's marks on blade. BH IX 1, 18th-century context, but probably earlier.

89. Knife. Back parallel with cutting edge and in line with tang. Very short, broad blade, perhaps broken. Cutting edge forming sharp shoulder with tang. Mineral replaced remains of wooden handle still fixed by three rivets. BN IV 7, mid 16th-early 17th-century, but probably earlier.

90. Knife with most of blade lost. Blade and handle in one piece. Handle in line with back, but forming neck with cutting edge. BM V 2, 18th-19th century context, but possibly 17th century.

91. Fragment of knife. Straight back in line with first section of iron handle. Narrow tang for socketed handle. Flower-shaped maker's mark on blade visible on radiograph but only partially revealed by cleaning. Collar bolster may originally have been silvered or tinned - too little to spot test. BJ XV 1, 18th-19th century context, but probably much earlier.

92. End of knife handle. A small copper-alloy cylinder is fixed to the end of an iron tang and provides a stop for the strips of wooden handle (now mineral replaced). These would have been fixed to each side of the tang with rivets. Similar to no. 93

although the copper-alloy stop is damaged and bent. BL V 7, 15th-early 16th-century context.

93. End of knife handle. A small copper-alloy cylinder is fixed to the end of an iron tang and provides a stop for the strips of wooden handle. These would have been semi-circular in section and fixed to the tang with rivets. The copper-alloy stop has two decorative grooves around its girth and a simple cross incised into the stop end. Similar to no. 92. BL V 7, 15th-early 16th-century context.

94. Knife (see no. 90) implement with acorn terminal at one end. BJ VII 1, 18th-century context, but probably earlier.

95. Knife handle with shaft tapering to chisel-like tip which is broken. Decorative acorn-type knob. BJ V 1, 18th-century context, but probably earlier.

34 knives or fragments of knives have not been illustrated; they are mostly from post-medieval or unstratified contexts.

Shears (fig. 75)

Apart from those illustrated here, there were four fragments of blades of shears, one from a 13th-century, three from 16th-century contexts.

96. Blade - probably half of shears. Narrow tang or

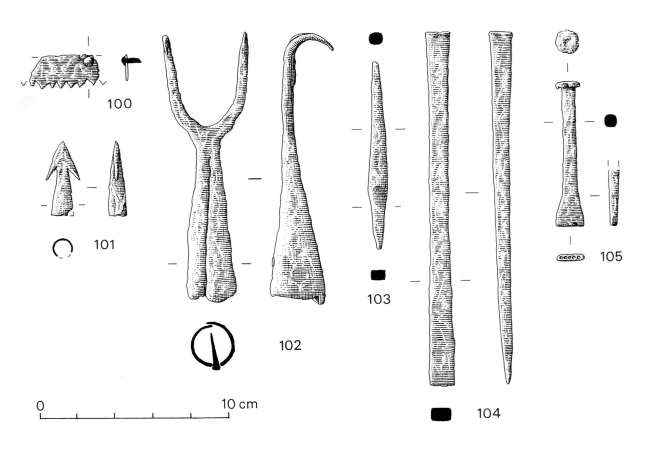

76. Iron objects: tools, weapons, 1:2

handle straight with back. Tang forms double angular shoulder with straight cutting edge. BJ VII 4, mid-late 16th-century context.

97. Half of a pair of shears. Handle loop and blade slightly damaged. BJ XV 1, 18th-century context, but probably earlier.

Scissors (fig. 75)

98. Half of a pair of scissors. Handle with loop and bevelled cutting edge. BH V 13, mid-late 16th-century context.

Forks (fig. 75)

99. Two pronged fork. Both prongs broken near tip. Long thin tang complete. Faint incised lines at junction between prongs and body. BJ XVII 1, 18th-century context.

A second two-pronged fork came from an 18th-century context (CMH).

Tools, Weapons (fig. 76)

100. Fragment of saw blade with serrated teeth. 64 BK I 18, mid to late 16th-century context.

101. Socketed arrowhead. Brazed seam inside and outside. BL V 7, 15th to early 16th-century context.

102. Flesh hook. Two curved prongs with socketed handle with seam. BJ XIII 3, late 17th to early 18th-century context, but probably 13th to 14th century.

103. Punch. One end square-sectioned point, the other end round-sectioned. BG III 3, mid to late 16th-century context.

104. Chisel. Rectangular cross-section at thick end and hammered on end. BH V 22, 15th-century context.

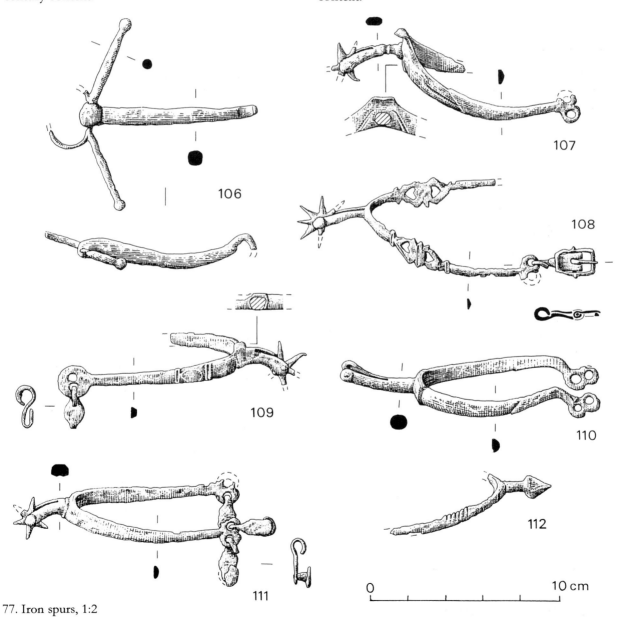

77. Iron spurs, 1:2

105. Punch with a row of five (possibly six) holes that would produce a line of circles. Hammering end has a small depression in the centre of it and has been heavily hammered. BL I 7, early 17th-century context.

Apart from the illustrated items, there were two billhook fragments, a sickle fragment, a mason's hammer and a drift, a possible awl, a spatula, a possible gouge bit, a chisel edge and a scoop. All these were in post-medieval or unstratified contexts.

Horse equipment (fig. 77)

106. Half a snaffle bit composed of one cheek piece and half of a mouth piece. BH IX 1, 18th-century context but associated with 14th and 16th-century material.

107. Rowel spur. One terminal is broken away and the rowel is damaged. Short decorated shank and double loop terminal. Rowel attached to spur by central pivot visible on one side. BN I 7, early-late 17th-century context.

108. Rowel spur. One terminal is broken and the whole is very corroded. Short straight shank. Arms have double decorative loops and remains of white metal (probably silver). Terminal has double loop with attached buckle. Rowel has eight prongs and is attached by a domed-head pivot. BM V 5, 17th to 18th-century context.

109. Rowel spur. One terminal broken away, with attachment at surviving terminal. Short thin plain shank. BH V 13, mid-late 16th-century context.

110. Rowel spur. Rowel missing. Short straight shank and double loop terminals. BJ I 2, 17th-century context.

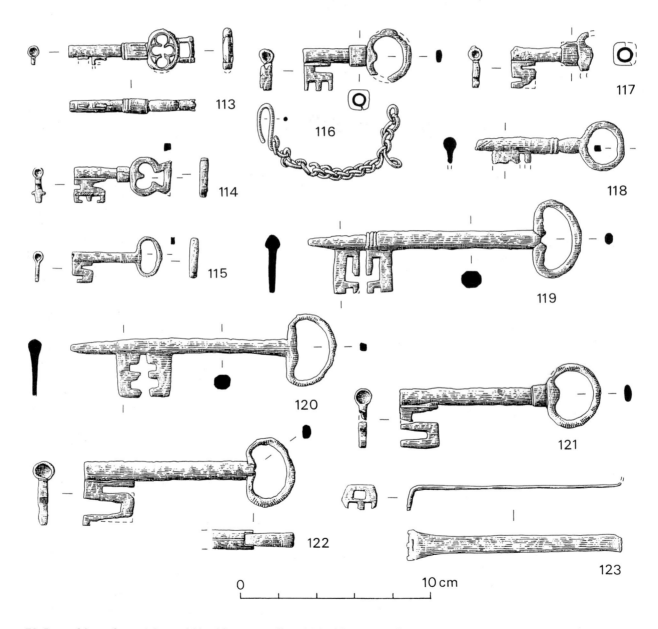

78. Iron objects: keys, 1:2; no. 113 with copper alloy; 116 with copper alloy chain

111. Small rowel spur. Very short shank. Double loop terminals, with stud attachments. Remains of white metal (probably silver) around junction of arms and rowel. BP VI 1, 18th-century context.

112. Prick spur. Plain conical prick. Broken terminals. Fragment of original surface surviving on arm of spur - spiral (?) groove possibly originally containing silver or tin wire - no white metal remaining. BV II 10, 13th to 14th-century context.

Another spur has not been illustrated and there were seven horseshoes (CMH).

Keys (fig. 78)

113. Small casket key. Shank hollow, cylinder completely brazed on internal surface with lap seam. Wards broken away. Wards brazed onto outer surface of shank. Openwork quatrefoil bow with additional rectangular frame. BG V 15, late 16th-early 17th-century context but probably 13th-14th century.

114. Small casket key with oval/trapezoid bow with three cusps. Hollow shank. Bow attached to shank by internal tang and external brazed collar. E-shaped ward brazed onto outer surface of the shank. Two thin lateral bars brazed onto either side of ward. BG, BH, BJ unstratified.

115. Small casket key with kidney-shaped bow. X-radiograph indicates that the shank is partly hollow. BJ III 6, early 16th-century context, but possibly 12th-14th century.

116. Casket key with copper-alloy chain. Hollow shank with short sleeve near oval bow. Oval bow attached to shank by internal tang and external square collar. Extensive brazing on surface - probably spillage from joins. Wards well defined. X-radiograph shows copper-alloy chain made of 'S'-shaped links linked with copper-alloy pin at end. On cleaning it was found that the chain was attached to the key only by means of massive corrosion. BJ III 6, early 16th-century context, but possibly 14th or 15th century. Found with 117 and 119.

117. Small casket key with broken bow. X-radiograph shows hollow shank with bow fitted with internal tang and external brazed collar. Wards brazed onto shank. BJ III 6, early 16th-century context, but possibly 14th or 15th century. Found with 116 and 119.

118. Small key. Solid shank with double waist near oval bow. Wards appear to have been manufactured with the rest of the key - no brazing lines visible. BJ VIII 23, 13th to 14th-century context.

119. Large key. Solid shank narrows just below the head and tapers to the point. The bit is symmetrical for use from either side of the door - the wards surround a central opening. The bow is D-shaped. BJ III 6, early 16th-century context, but possibly 14th or 15th century. Found with 116 and 117.

120. Large key. Solid shank tapering to a projecting point. The bit has symmetrical wards so that the key can be used from either side of the door - the wards surround a central opening. Kidney-shaped bow. BV

III 1, 18th-century context, but probably 15th century.

121. Key. Narrow hollow shank and near circular bow. Part of small solid bit survives. The shaft of the key is formed from a tube with a brazed joint. The ward was attached by brazing onto a small platform on the tube. The ring was attached by means of a smaller collar which was brazed over the tube. Radiograph also shows a solid plug extending from the ring down inside the tube. BG II 10, mid 17th to mid 18th-century context.

122. Key. Short pointed tang of bow brazed into shank. Designed to operate a lock with a central projecting pin over which the hollow cylindrical shank is placed. Wards brazed into rectangular recess cut into shank along its seam. BJ IV 3, 16th-century context, but probably 13th century.

123. Barrel-padlock lifter with three teeth and a square hole. BH IX 1, 18th-century context, but possibly 13th century.

There were ten other keys and two padlock lifters (CMH).

Lamp (fig. 79)

124. Hanging lamp. Shallow circular dish for oil or wax with curved strip handle. BP I 19, mid 16th-mid 17th-century context.

Buckles (fig. 79)

Other than those illustrated below there were 36 buckles of various kinds, mostly in post-medieval or unstratified contexts. A circular buckle with tongue was found with burial H49 on the pelvis. This would have been for a low belt, or possibly one of a pair for keeping up hose, similar to some found with late-medieval burials at St Oswald's Priory, Gloucester (Heighway and Bryant forthcoming). (CMH).

125. Circular buckle with short tongue. X-radiograph shows that it was probably plated with tin. BM VI 4, mid 17th-century context.

126. Two oval loops joined by a rivet, creating a swivel link. One small lateral knop. BM I 26, mid to late 17th-century context.

127. Small double-oval buckle inlaid with white metal (silver or tin). Inlay formed by hammering silver or tin wire into prepared groove. BG V 3, 17th-century context but typologically much earlier.

128. Buckle. Square frame with tongue. Small area of white metal (silver) remaining on one arm. BP V 4, 18th-century context.

Miscellaneous (figs. 79-80)

129. Decorative mount. Four large holes leave four loops linking the arms of a cross with a central dome-headed rivet. BJ VII 6, 15th to early 16th-century context.

130. Small cog. Six rounded teeth with a square hole in the centre of the cog. BJ VII 4, mid-late 16th-century context. Possibly part of a clock mechanism (NG).

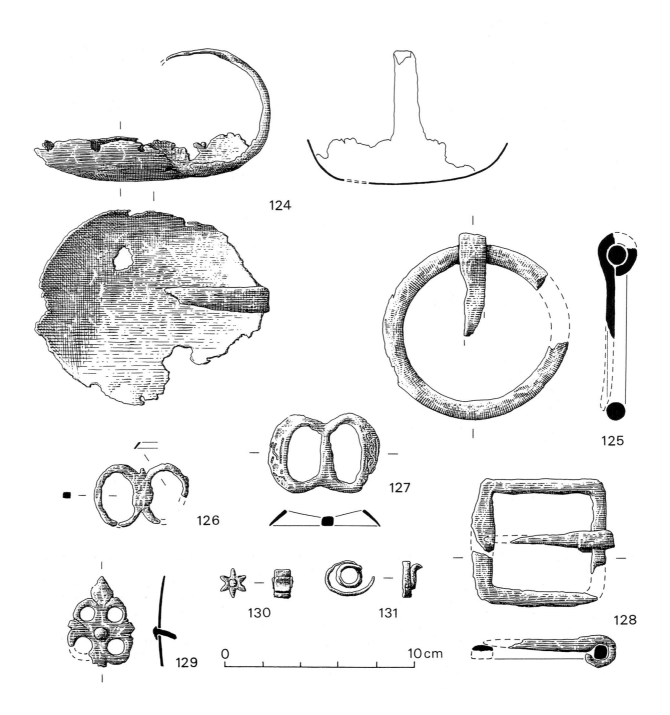

79. Iron objects, 1:2

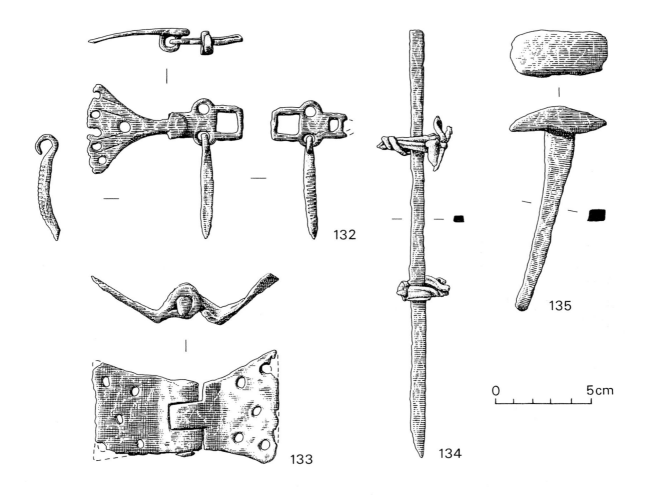

80. Iron objects, 1:1; no. 134 with lead

131. Spring-loop. BJ XIV 2, late 16th-century context, but possibly 14th-15th century. Possibly part of a clock mechanism (NG).

132. Three interlinked components. Mounting plate with attachment holes attached to a rod via a link with a buckle. Traces of silver on plate and rod. Horse furniture? BG V 2, late 16th to early 17th-century context, but probably earlier.

133. Two angled plates with five holes in each. Plates interlock and are held together with a central pin. BP

I 16, mid to late 17th-century context, but possibly 14th to 15th century.

134. Window bar. Lead cames are wrapped around the centre. Two blobs of solder remain at one end of each tie. BH IV 2, 17th-century context, but probably 14th or 15th century.

135. Large nail or bolt. Sub-rectangular domed head. Slightly curved shank with point missing. BV II 10, 13th to 14th-century context.

LEAD AND PEWTER OBJECTS

D. J. Wilkinson

with a contribution from G. Egan

Lead Seals (fig. 81)

136-8. Papal bulls, attached to letters, grants or indulgences issued by the Popes. The term bull, derived from these leaden seals or bullae, has been transferred to the document to which it was attached. The reverse of each bears an inscription SPA SPE over the conventional heads of St. Paul and St. Peter in pear-shaped aureoles with a Latin cross between. The obverse inscriptions in neo-Lombardic capitals record the names of the Popes, in this instance Popes

Honorius III, John XXII and Gregory XI. All three were in late 17th to 18th-century contexts, in an area of disturbance in the apse of the north transept chapel.

136. HONORIUS PP III date of accession 1216 (-1227) (cf Birch 1900, p 270, nos 21, 746-9). BJ XIII 3.

137. IOHANNES PP XXII date of accession 1316 (-1334) (Birch 1900, 283, nos 21, 854-66). BJ XIII 2.

138. GREGORIUS PP XI date of accession 1371 (-1378)(Birch 1900, 286, nos 21, 886-8). BJ XIII 3.

0   3cm

81. Lead seals, 1:1

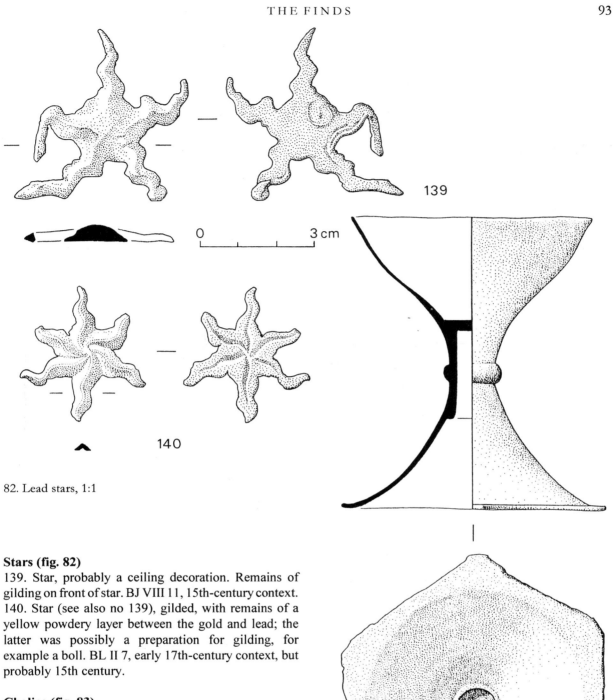

82. Lead stars, 1:1

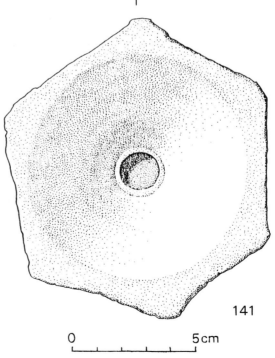

83. Pewter chalice 2:3

Stars (fig. 82)

139. Star, probably a ceiling decoration. Remains of gilding on front of star. BJ VIII 11, 15th-century context.
140. Star (see also no 139), gilded, with remains of a yellow powdery layer between the gold and lead; the latter was possibly a preparation for gilding, for example a boll. BL II 7, early 17th-century context, but probably 15th century.

Chalice (fig. 83)

141. Pewter chalice; the bowl tapers into the foot, which terminates in an irregular hexagon; simple band relief at neck. 64 BK IV 35, Burial H59, probably 14th century.

The lead or pewter objects also included: five lead discs, some of them probably weights, all in post-medieval contexts, a star similar to nos. 139-140 above, a washer, bars and handles, a tin spoon handle, a lead spoon in a 17th-century context, ballshot, fragment of pipe, a collection of 78 lead came fragments, predominantly from 16th to 17th-century destruction deposits, lumps, one from the repair of a pot, sheet, and a fragment of chalice stem from burial H49 (CMH).

LEAD CLOTH SEAL

G. Egan

142.   Cloth seal. BJ XV 1, unstratified. This incomplete two-disc seal would originally have been attached to a cloth as part of the alnage system of industrial control and taxation (Endrei and Egan 1982; Egan 1994). Despite the central hole, which was to accommodate a corresponding rivet on the missing disc, the surviving portion bears enough of the stamp to identify the county of origin and the approximate date. Around a crown over a portcullis is a Lombardic-letter legend, which, from the visible traces of the lower parts of the letters, appears to be consistent with ..AICOWORCES, indicating that it is a seal for a Worcestershire cloth. Alnage seals were supposed to be put on each newly-manufactured cloth after it had been examined by an officer of the Crown to establish that there were no deficiencies and that it conformed with the dimensions required by law. The cloth could not legally be sold without this seal, which guaranteed the quality and also acted as a receipt for the cloth tax of a few pence levied at the time of the examination. Faulty cloths were specially marked and sold as seconds, or, in extreme cases, destroyed. This cumbersome system probably never worked entirely satisfactorily. Evasion and fraud became more evident as the scale of production increased. After the end of the alnage in 1724, leaden seals continued to be used for a variety of labelling purposes in the textile industry.

Crown-over-portcullis cloth seals were in widespread use in the 16th century in several textile-manufacturing counties, mainly in the reign of Elizabeth I. More complete stamps show that the legend is an abbreviation of the Latin for 'seal of alnage of saleable cloths in the county of ....' *sigillum ulnagii pannorum venalium in comitatu*. The present seal was probably for a coarse woollen cloth (cf. Egan 1994, 53-4 no 105). Another Worcestershire seal,

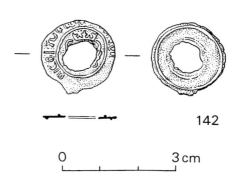

84. Lead cloth seal, 1:1

which has a different stamp with the legend in roman lettering, has been found in London (collection of Messrs R. and I. Smith). A number of cloth seals, including three for Gloucestershire, one of which is a portcullis issue, have been found at Kingsholm in Gloucester (Egan forthcoming). A portcullis-series seal for Gloucestershire with the legend (S VL)...(E)AL?I?CO?GLCT'S was excavated at the Capel House site in the City (Museum of London, Dept. of Urban Archaeology, CAP86, context 602/603/595, no. 21; for further portcullis seals, see Egan 1994, nos 41 - fig. 116, another Gloucestershire issue - 48-9, 107 and 114-5).

Different Gloucestershire seals found in London date to the reign of Edward VI and to the 17th century, and at least two mid 17th century seals for cloths exported from the county have been discovered in New York State in the U.S.A. (Rochester Science Centre collection at Rochester, N.Y.: pers. comm. Judy L Ozone); cf. Egan 1995, 318.

OBJECTS OF WORKED BONE

The bone objects included several knife handles or parts of handles, all in late or post-medieval contexts. A spindle-whorl may be Roman. A disc with a central hole came from a late 16th to early 17th-century context (CMH).

None of these objects is illustrated.

CLAY PIPES

D. J. Wilkinson and A. Peacey

Stamps (figs. 85-6)

1, 2.   Small barrel-shaped bowl with flat heel and milled rim, dated 1600-40. Stamp on heel reads 'I R', origin unknown. BM II 7, early 17th-century context; BN I 1, mid to late 18th-century context (Peacey 1979, fig. 11, no. 131).

3, 4, 5.   Stamp on heel reads 'P C'. Oswald (1975, plate III, no. 4) illustrates a similar example from Stony Stratford, Bucks, stating that similar and duplicate marks come mainly from London on pipes dated *c.* 1620-40. The pipe maker is probably Peter Cornish. BJ IX/XIII unstratified; BM II 5, early 18th-century context; BN I 5, late 17th-century context.

6. Bowl of 1600-40, with flat heel, stamped with a Tudor rose. BN I 5, late 17th-century context.

7, 8. Heel stamp of 'R B', also recorded from Gloucester, Bristol and many other sites in West Country. Generally attributed to Richard Berri(y)man working in Bristol 1619-52 (Peacey 1979, fig. 11, no. 132). BJ XV 1, 18th-century context; BN I 1, 18th-century context.

9. Heel stamp 'A N' on a pipe dated 1630-1660. Examples recorded locally from Stroud, Gloucester, Hereford and Bristol (Peacey 1979, fig. 11, no. 135).

Origin unknown. BN V 2, 18th-century context.

10. 'W C' on heel, origin unknown. BP III 1, 18th-century context.

11. Stem stamped 'GILES CHAPE LINE', a maker working at Ashton Keynes. Died 1739. (Peacey 1979, fig. 11, no. 118). BJ VIII 2, 16th-century deposit, but disturbed early 18th century.

12. Stamp on stem 'THO WI DOS', also recorded from Chalford, and Marlborough his place of work c. 1710-30 (Atkinson 1965, 93; and Peacey 1979, fig. 11, no. 119). BP II 3, early 18th-century context.

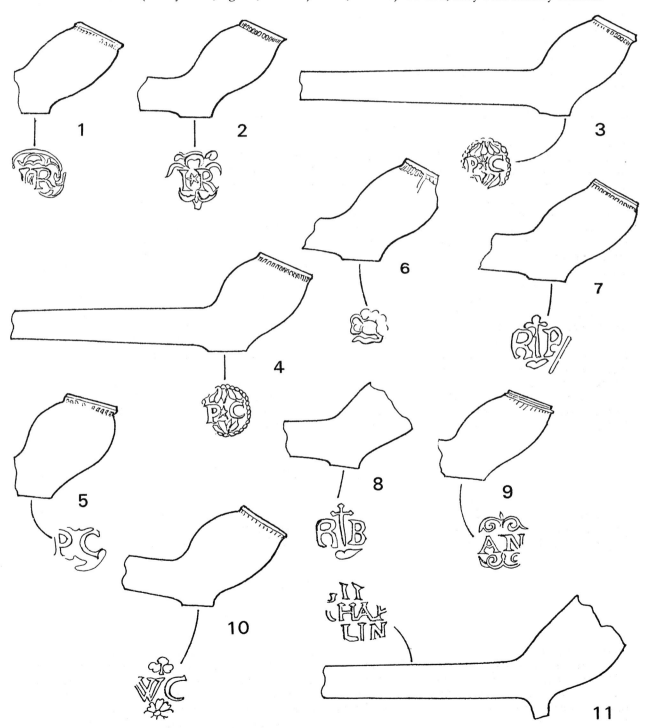

85. Clay pipes and stamps, 1:1

13, 14. Stem stamp 'ED HIGG ENS'. Prolific maker, with stamps recorded from sites throughout Gloucestershire. Pipes stamped by Ed Higgens are equally plentiful at Salisbury and Cirencester, and are undoubtedly from identical dies. Atkinson (1980, 69), on present evidence, believes it likely that Ed Higgens worked at Cirencester in the late 17th century and moved to Salisbury when he was married in 1698, carrying on his business there until at least 1710. Alternatively he had pipeworks in both towns and moved about from one to the other. 64 BK IV 4, early 18th-century context; BM II 6, early 18th-century context; BJ XVII 1, 18th-century context; BG, BH, or BJ unstratified.

15. Stem stamp semi-legible 'SAM ACTO BRON'. Recorded from Ross and Gloucester (AP). BP I 4, mid 18th-century context.

16. Stamp on stem 'RICH MATH EWS GLO', with other examples from Gloucester, Stroud, Ross, Frocester, and Selsley (Peacey 1979, fig. 3, no. 29), recording the maker Richard Mathews of Gloucester. The stem stamp is a typical Broseley-style rectangular mark of the 18th century. BP I 4, mid 18th century.

17. Bowl decorated with a human figure in relief, with outstretched arms, smoking a pipe. BP I 4, mid 18th-century context.

Unstamped bowls (not illustrated)

18. Small overhung bowl with flat heel and milled rim, dated 1600-1640. BM II 6, early 18th-century context.

19. Bowl with spur, dated 1690-1720. BG VII 4, late 17th to early 18th-century context.

20-25. Globular shaped bowls with spur, dated 1700-1750. BG VII 2, early 18th-century context, two examples; BH IX 1, 18th-century context; BP I 4, mid to late 18th-century context; 64 BK II 1, 18th-century context; BG, BH or BJ unstratified.

26-8. Bowls with spur, dated 1730-1800. BN I 2, late 18th-century context; BP I 4, mid 18th-century context, two examples.

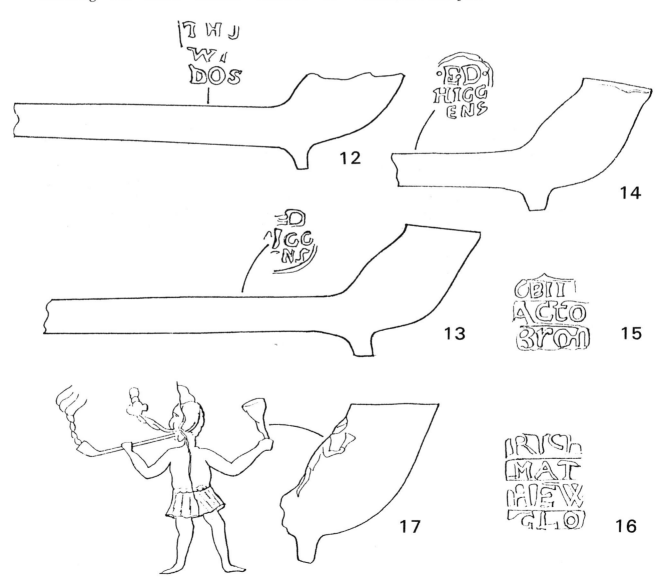

86. Clay pipes and stamps, 1:1

POST-MEDIEVAL VESSEL GLASS

D. J. Wilkinson

Other than a few small fragments, all the vessel glass (total 40 fragments) was found to be within the phase 6a pit. Many of the bottles were for wine and can be dated on typological grounds to the first half of the 18th century, a period during which there was considerable change in the shape of the most common bottle types being used.

The pit group is not completely closed, but the majority of the vessel glass was deposited by 1760. Other than one anomaly the date of deposition is compatible with those allotted on typological grounds to the clay pipes found from the same pit.

There is one neck fragment and two bases from onion bottles, typical of those in use *c.* 1715. There are at least 15 bases of Mallet-type bottles (Green 1977, 95-101), although a few could be early examples of equal cylinder bottles. These are datable to *c.* 1730-1760. There are about ten neck fragments mostly from Mallet-type bottles. The bottle fragments are pale or dark olive green. All the bases have concavities or 'kick-ups' and nearly half the fragments display considerable iridescence.

PORTABLE OBJECTS OF STONE

D. J. Wilkinson

with a contribution from T. C. Darvill

Two hones of micaceous schist, one perforated at one end, were from post-medieval contexts but might be medieval. Another hone fragment came from a late 17th-century context. A fourth fragment of a possible hone had a decorative terminal with sub-square section and carved knob; this was from a late 17th-early-18th century context, but was probably 13th century. A spindle whorl was unstratified. A crystal detached from its setting was probably earlier than its mid-late 16th-century context; a small pink bead was from an 18th-century context.

Two pieces of worked flint were in fresh condition with little recent damage. They presumably derived from prehistoric activity in the vicinity of the site. Neither piece can be assigned firmly to a particular period or cultural tradition (TCD).

THE POTTERY

C. A. Ireland

Editor's note: this report is as written in 1989 and is presented here as it has not been superseded by further work on medieval pottery in the Cirencester area.

INTRODUCTION

There was a very high incidence of residual finds, including pottery; large, contemporary groups of material were few, making it impracticable to examine the pottery in terms of 'key groups'. No attempt has been made to use the pottery, therefore, to establish detail about the site and its inhabitants by spatial analysis. The pottery is also of limited value in providing dating. Most assemblages, particularly in the early medieval period, are composed of 'locally' produced domestic wares, whose production period is little understood. Independent dating for this material, from coins or other finds, is almost wholly lacking, and dating therefore rests largely upon the stratigraphic position of the context, or on associated pottery types for which parallels can be found on non-local sites. There is also a problem with long-lived pottery industries represented only by featureless sherds, or with regional products for which parallels could not be found.

The abbey is the first and largest post-Roman site to have been excavated in Cirencester in its own right. With the exception of St John's Hospital there are no other comparable sites with published pottery evidence (Vince 1982, 202-7). The factors outlined above limit the archaeological uses of the pottery and were understood when pottery analysis began. However, because the emphasis in Cirencester has so often been towards researching the Roman town, it was important to establish the basis for a post-Roman type-fabric series for Cirencester, and to examine the sources of supply.

METHODOLOGY

The pottery was sorted into fabric types, determined by the inclusions visible in the fired clay using a x10 hand lens. Each fabric was allocated a number in sequence from 200. Saxon, medieval and post-medieval fabrics thus occur in the same numerical sequence. Table 1 provides a complete list of the post-Roman type-fabric series for Cirencester to date. A reference collection of sherds of each fabric, together with fabric descriptions, is housed in the Corinium Museum.

The pottery was recorded on a context by context basis, giving details of vessel types recognised, and the quantity of sherds present; percentages based upon sherd counts have been used to represent proportions of fabrics and vessel types. It should however be borne in mind that as was usual in the early 1960s, some pottery sherds, particularly the post-medieval sherds, may have been discarded on site.

In order to assess the pottery evidence chronologically, assemblages from the phases have been used to determine proportions of fabrics and vessel types at different periods. The phases are not in all cases independently determined stratigraphically and by no means all contexts were assigned to a phase. In some cases contexts have been grouped together as phases even though they may not be strictly contemporary. For example, the construction of the abbey took a considerable period of time, but all the contexts attributable to that event have been put together. This procedure is clearly not wholly satisfactory, but it does provide a framework for establishing a chronological sequence of pottery types. The assemblages from each phase are examined chronologically, together with tables depicting basic information about the fabrics and vessel types present (Tables 2-9). The sequence of fabrics is then examined in some detail.

The following abbreviations are used in the tables:

CP	cooking pots
E	early
F	fabric number
HM	hand-made
L	late
M	mid
SP	spouted pitcher
TF	type-fabric
TP	tripod pitchers
V	very
WF	wheel-finished/hand-rotated
WT	wheel-thrown
U/S	unstratified

STRATIFIED POTTERY ASSEMBLAGES FROM DEFINED PHASES

Residual material is noted only where this adds to the range of sources and vessel types.

PHASE 1 PRE-ABBEY CONSTRUCTION

Phase 1a   The Anglo-Saxon period

The structures and associated levels attributed to the Anglo-Saxon period produced no contemporary pottery. Four residual sherds recovered from the general area of Saxon activity (BN, BT and BV) may belong to early to mid Anglo-Saxon hand-made cooking pots (grouped under F255). One or two could be late Roman oddities. Only one sherd could be paralleled with any certainty with grass-tempered sherds from the amphitheatre (Wacher 1976, 16).

Phase lb   The post-conquest pre-abbey period (Table 2)

Pottery was recovered from three sources: robber trenches for the earlier Anglo-Saxon features; a deposit of black soil containing burials in area BP; and a series of features attributed to a pre-abbey structure in the area of the subsequent undercroft (BG and BH; fig. 32). The total of pottery was small (81 sherds). Some contamination from later robbing was evident.

The most common fabric was a coarse limestone-tempered ware (F202, 86.4%), producing hand-made baggy cooking pots with flaring rims. Club rim vessels were present in the robber trenches. A second coarse fabric tempered with limestone gravel and some flint was present in contexts associated with the phase 1b structure beneath the undercroft (F231). Residual sherds of this fabric were present in construction layers for the abbey in the same area. Hand-made vessels, including a cooking pot sherd and fragments of a possible beehive base were represented. A single, non-local, wheel-thrown glazed pitcher sherd was present in a robber trench in area BV (F254).

A large quantity of F202 occurred in layers associated with the construction of the abbey (phase 2). It seems likely that a proportion of this material is residual from earlier features. Several stamped sherds indicate the presence of spouted pitchers, and there were two fragments from lamps. It has not been possible to isolate residual cooking pots since no typological development for these vessels could be discerned. A second non-local wheel-thrown glazed pitcher fabric was recognised residually (F247).

PHASE 2   THE ABBEY CONSTRUCTION (Table 3)

The construction of the 12th-century abbey was in progress from *c.* 1130, or earlier, to *c.* 1176. The pottery evidence for this phase has been taken from a variety of contexts: wall foundations and floors. A coin of 1083-1086 was present (p.71, no. 1).

These features produced a relatively large assemblage of pottery (462 sherds), some of which may be residual. F202 predominated (89%), with hand-made baggy cooking pots forming the bulk of the assemblage (78%). A small proportion of straight-sided club-rim vessels were present (1%), a dish or bowl, sherds from unglazed pitchers (8.2%) and two lamps. Several glazed sherds and a handle in the same fabric were present, indicating, perhaps, the production of tripod pitchers by this industry in the 12th century. Examples of rims and handles from these vessels were present in much later contexts (fig. 88, nos. 30-2).

The small proportion of the assemblage occupied by other fabrics mainly derived from one other source. Hand-made tripod pitchers from the Minety industry in the Forest of Bradon in north Wiltshire were represented by small undiagnostic sherds (F200, 3.2%). Evidence from excavations in Gloucester shows that these vessels were produced from the early 12th to the mid 13th centuries (Vince 1983a, 126) with typological changes in the late 12th century. The lack of featured sherds has made it difficult to identify residual 12th-century material. A rim from a bowl or curfew in the same fabric was recovered; such vessels were more common in 13th-century contexts.

Non-local industries were poorly represented: 2 sherds from a sand-tempered tripod pitcher (F221), and a single cooking pot rim (F240).

PHASE 3   USE OF THE ABBEY

As might be expected there was very little pottery from deposits laid down during the abbey's lifetime. Pottery mainly occurred where alterations had been made. Even where stratified pottery occurred, the quantities were small. A few sherds were associated with major structural alterations, for example, the eastern extension built between the late 13th and mid 14th centuries.

A certain amount of pottery, mostly residual in post-destruction deposits, could be dated by analogy to between the 13th and early 16th centuries. Two areas of the site produced a larger proportion of this material, BG and BH (the area of the undercroft) and BV, BT and BP (outside the west front of the abbey). In the latter area, pits, ditches and courtyard surfaces attributed to a courtyard produced pottery of the 12th century to the middle of the 13th century. Later features were not well sealed; it has therefore not been possible to illustrate with confidence the ceramic sequence between the 13th and mid 16th centuries. The pottery included here has been selected for two reasons: firstly, the contexts form part of a recognisable archaeological event, and, secondly, there was a reasonable amount of pottery to examine.

The stratified material is grouped as follows:

Phase 3a: first half of the 13th century: pits, robbing, a 'courtyard' and L-shaped ditch outside the west front of the abbey;

Phase 3b: second half of the 13th century: re-flooring in the undercroft;

Phase 3c: late 13th and 14th centuries: construction of an extension to the north transept chapel, the construction of a new east end to the abbey and buttresses, the fills of tombs in the new east extension, the fill of a tomb in the south transept, a cobbled area outside the west front (BP I 27) containing a coin of *c.* 1320, and alterations in the east claustral range;

Phase 3d: 14th or 15th century: a pit outside the west front (BP I 19);

Phase 3e: 15th to first half of 16th century: repairs to and relaying of floors, occupation on floor surfaces prior to the abbey destruction; the build-up of soils below the choir stalls containing coins dated to the end of the 15th century, and alterations to the chapter house.

Phase 3a First half of 13th century (Table 4)

The assemblage was dominated by hand-made cooking pots in F202 (70%). It seems likely that most of this material was contemporary, although residual quantities of this fabric were present in most contexts up to the latest post-destruction contexts. Sherds in the same fabric from glazed, hand-made tripod pitchers were present, in addition to a bowl (or curfew) and a 'beehive base'. The quantity of Minety wares (F200) was relatively large (23%). Sherds from hand-made tripod pitchers, including slashed handles and an example of a pulled spout, were common (19%). Several sherds from other vessels were present, including hand-made cooking pots (fig. 89, 41), a globular vessel, similar to a 'ginger jar' (fig. 89, 40), and a bowl (or curfew). Non-local wares were better represented than in the 12th-century assemblage. A non-local hand-made tripod pitcher (source unknown) was represented by a single sherd (F270). Jugs are first apparent in this assemblage (5.7%): hand-made vessels in Ham Green ware from the Bristol area (F206, 2%); wheel-thrown vessels in Developed Stamford ware (F268); a possible North French import (A. Vince pers. comm., F265); and a sherd from a jug of unknown source (F233). Alternative sources for cooking pots were poorly represented: a single sherd of Bath Fabric A (F240).

Phase 3b Second half of 13th century (Table 5)

The small quantity of hand-made cooking pots in F202 suggests that this industry had declined by this time. Sherds from thick-walled bowls (or curfews?) and hand-made jugs were present in the same fabric indicating an attempt to compete with vessels from the Minety industry (F200). Sherds of Minety hand-made tripod pitchers were present but may be residual, since sherds from wheel-thrown jugs and jars from this industry formed a small proportion of the assemblage. There were also examples of the large bowls/handled pans in F200 and together with those in F202 this vessel type dominated the assemblage (74%). Including material from subsequent phases, this vessel type cropped up primarily in the area of the undercroft, a factor which may provide a clue to its function (fig. 90, 57-9).

Several sherds representing glazed jugs imported from further afield were also included in this assemblage. Elaborately decorated jugs from Brill (Bucks) were clearly common at this period: post-destruction deposits, including a large pit group, contained examples of a type current in the second half of the 13th century (fig. 91, 70a-b), including more complete fragments of the vessels found in phase 3b. A large heavy jug base from an unknown source (F223) and sherds from undecorated jugs (F219; ?F269) from Nash Hill (Wilts) were present, with further examples in post-destruction deposits in the same area. Fabrics which only occurred as residual sherds of glazed jugs, and for which sources could not be located probably also belong to this date (F221, F232, F235).

Phase 3c Late 13th and 14th centuries (Table 5)

The quantity of pottery stratified in this phase was small (c. 67 sherds), and no conclusions can be drawn from it. It is likely that many of the sherds were residual, except for a few new fabrics and vessel types. A single sherd of a Worcester-type jug (F239) occurred in the foundation trench for W400 (north transept chapel). Sherds from a tomb in the eastern extension and a cobbled area outside the west front were from tall dark green Brill jugs including a possible triple-decker form. Other jug fabrics were F219 and F233, also glazed overall to appear dark green.

The most common fabric was wheel-thrown Minety ware (F200) with large jars predominating. A single fragment from a bung-hole cistern was noted.

Phase 3d 14th or 15th century (Table 5)

A pit outside the west front of the abbey (BP I 19) cut through floor layers in a building overlying a cobbled area containing a 14th-century coin and sherd. The pit contained a complete profile of a small bung-hole cistern in Minety ware (F200, fig. 89, 53), in addition to sherds from wheel-thrown jars and fragments of ridge tile in the same fabric.

Other contexts of this general date included vessels in Minety ware (F200): wheel-thrown jars; jugs and ridge tile. There were a few sherds from non-local industries including a Malvernian jug sherd (F204) and sherds from Bristol-Redcliffe jugs (F262, fig. 91, 72). A sherd from a Tudor Green cup was also present (F220).

Residual material in post-destruction contexts adds little to the range of sources illustrated by the 'stratified' material. A single stoneware beaker rim from Siegburg (F253; Beckmann 1974, 189, fig. 17, 131-6) was the only example of a continental import which could be dated to this period. Two residual wheel-thrown cooking pot rims from the Malvernian industry (F204) are probably of 14th or 15th century date (Vince 1977a). Additional sherds of Bristol-Redcliffe jugs were recognised (F262) in addition to a compartmental inkwell or condiment set from the same source, in post-destruction contexts (fig. 91, 73).

Phase 3e Latest use of the abbey (Table 6)

Unfortunately the dissolution of the abbey in 1539 did not provide a secure *terminus post quem* for the latest contexts associated with the use of the abbey. The destruction of the buildings began in 1541 and was complete by 1565 though there were still some ruins in the 1570s (Evans 1993, 135). Some evidence that the buildings were open to rubbish accumulation after the Dissolution is perhaps indicated by the occurrence of fragments of ridge tile in 'occupation material' on floor surfaces, and the presence of pottery types in late abbey contexts which would generally be dated to after the mid 16th century. The rubble layers which cover the site cannot, therefore, be seen as a contemporary sealing layer belonging to a 'destruction phase'.

The latest contexts of the abbey include relaid floors, repairs to flooring and soil which had built up on flooring. These contexts might span a considerable period of time, from the late 15th to the mid 16th centuries. Pottery evidence indicates that the remodelling of the chapter house took place in the latest phase of the life of the abbey.

The quantity of stratified pottery was too small to provide a representative sample of pottery types supplied to the abbey during the first half of the 16th century. Most of the pottery dated to this period was recovered from post-destruction layers.

Soil below the choir stalls in the crossing produced a small money box in a ?local fabric (F250) and a Cistercian ware cup rim (F244). Coins from the same deposit suggest that this small group of sherds belongs to the late 15th or early 16th century.

Elsewhere deposits on floor surfaces produced sherds of late Minety wares (F200), including wheel-thrown jars and jugs; sherds from Tudor Green cups (F220); Cistercian ware cups (F208); and a sherd from a French flask (F248; Hurst 1966, Type I). Associated with new flooring were sherds of Minety ware jars and conical bowls (F200); Cistercian ware cups (F244; F208); an earthenware copy of a Raeren stoneware drinking jug (F224); sherds of jars or bowls from a local earthenware industry at Ashton Keynes, not far from Minety (F201); sherds from Frechen stoneware drinking jugs (F216) and a sherd from a tin-glazed drug jar (F209). The last two fabrics are generally suggestive of a mid to late 16th century date, indicating perhaps that the abbey buildings were not covered over until then. Incorporated into new walling and floors in the remodelled chapter house were sherds of a range of fabrics datable to the first half of the 16th century or later. Domestic wares were represented by wheel-thrown jars, jugs and a lid in Minety ware (F200), and jar and bowl sherds in Ashton Keynes ware (F201). The remaining sherds all came from vessels used for drinking: Tudor Green (F220) and Cistercian ware cups (F208; F244) and Rhenish drinking jugs (F225; F216).

PHASE 4   DEMOLITION AND ROBBING: 16TH AND 17TH CENTURIES (TABLE 7)

The demolition of the abbey appears to have taken place over a period of time. It has not been possible to determine the point at which the demolition of above ground structures was completed. The archaeological evidence points to a haphazard and continuous process of robbing from the mid 16th until well into the 17th century.

Phase 4a   Robbing pre-dating primary rubble deposits

The pottery assemblage from the earliest robbing contexts was small; three fabrics predominated: F201, F208, and F216. Sherds of late Minety wares, including jugs and a pipkin lid were present (F200). Contemporary domestic red earthenwares were provided by the industry at Ashton Keynes (F201): mainly jars and bowls with odd sherds from flanged dishes. A possible hybrid fabric between the Minety

industry and that at Ashton Keynes is represented by sherds from a pipkin and bowl (F230). Non-local wares were predominantly represented by Cistercian-type cups (F208; F244), F208 being more common (a fluted base in F208 may belong to a figurine). Continental imports were dominated by table wares from Frechen (F216) providing drinking jugs and bottles. Decorated tin-glazed 'Albarello' sherds were also present (F209) including a vessel of possible Mediterranean origin (Biek and Gillies n.d.).

Phase 4b   Primary rubble deposits

The pottery from these disparate contexts was examined as a single assemblage. The pottery included residual material from elsewhere on the site or indeed the town; it demonstrates that rubble was deposited up to the 17th century. One or two contexts produced sherds of fabrics of the late 17th to 18th centuries and these are considered intrusions.

The largest quantity of ridge tile (fig. 98) was recovered from these demolition deposits (F200; F201; F202). A range of late Minety products was recovered (F200). It is possible that this industry had ceased production during the early 16th century. The quantity of Ashton Keynes products was greater in this phase and included a variety of bowl forms, including curving walled bowls with flanged rims, bowls with grooved rims and heavily moulded rims of bowls or jars. A dripping pan was noted. There were also table wares, including chafing dishes, jugs and tankards, and flanged dishes, or plates with chevron stamping on the rim. Internally glazed jars may represent cooking jars and pipkins. Several jug and bowl sherds were present in the hybrid fabric F230.

Non-local imports were dominated by sherds of handled cups in F208, including examples of straight-sided corrugated mugs. A small quantity of cups in Tudor Green (F220) and a Cistercian ware (F244) was present, but may be residual. Odd sherds from other non-local industries were present: Malvernian jugs (F204); a Herefordshire border jug sherd (F224); a horizontal handled bowl from the Surrey-Hampshire border industry (F222); a small manganese speckled drinking vessel in tin-glazed ware (F209); and a dimpled, handled black-glazed vessel from East Anglia (F242).

Continental imports include odd sherds from a variety of sources - F225, F228, and F248 - but the majority of sherds were from Frechen vessels and include drinking jugs and 'Bellarmine' bottles (F216).

PHASE 5   THE FORMAL GARDEN: 17TH-18TH CENTURIES (TABLE 8)

Formal gardens were probably laid out during the 17th century. Archaeological evidence included flower beds; gravel paths and drives; walls, and drainage features (phase 5a). The excavation of flower beds had resulted in the redeposition of rubble layers (phase 5b) and there was a small number of rubbish pits (phase 5c).

A similar pattern is repeated of three predominant fabrics (F201; F208; F216). It seems likely that a proportion of this material is residual, particularly the Frechen jugs (F216) and the Cistercian cups (F208). It is difficult to establish with any certainty what proportion of the Ashton Keynes domestic earthenwares were contemporary (F201). Despite the evidence for gardening activity, the quantity of Ashton Keynes flower pot sherds was very small. Several sherds in a variety of fabrics (F252) were present in the later features associated with the stone culvert in area BP I. None was decorated, and most would appear to have been produced at Ashton Keynes.

Non-local industries were represented by isolated sherds. Domestic earthenwares were present in tiny amounts: single sherds of Surrey-Hampshire ware bowls (F222), Malvernian jars (F204), and several sherds from Herefordshire Border ware bowls (F224). A small quantity of tin-glazed wares, possibly derived from Bristol (D. Dawson, pers. comm.) and London, include small, handled, chamber pots, painted plates, and drug jars decorated with blue, purple and yellow paint (F209). A small earthenware ointment pot with a thick white slip may be a regional imitation of a tin-glazed vessel (F267). A single sherd of a Fulham stoneware tankard was present (F263); three further sherds occurred unstratified.

The range of the occasional sherds of Staffordshire wares suggests that gardening, or the disturbance of the garden area, continued into the mid 18th century: F238, F213, F236 and F215.

Imported wares included a costrel fragment from the Iberian peninsula (F227) and sherds from Westerwald tankards (F217).

PHASE 6   18TH-CENTURY FEATURES (TABLE 9)

Phase 6a Pit BP I 4

This modest assemblage represents the largest group of contemporary material found in a single deposit in the post-medieval period from the site. The Staffordshire wares suggest a date in the middle of the 18th century, confirmed by contemporary finds of vessel glass and clay pipes (see p. 97, p. 94). A maximum of 40 vessels are represented, although mostly by incomplete fragments.

Of interest is a group of red earthenwares from Ashton Keynes (F201), including a large jug, two flanged conical bowls, a thumbed bowl rim and a tankard base. The firing of the domestic vessels is perhaps significant when identifying contemporary 18th-century wares from less well-dated deposits. The vessels are oxidised throughout with a clear glaze on the interior (earlier vessels were commonly reduced, wholly or partially). A straight-sided bowl with grooved rim was also present, a type which appears in Gloucester in the 18th century (Vince 1983a, 132). A shallow internally glazed bowl in an inclusionless earthenware (F260) is probably also a

local product, and it is possible that this may be a variant of F201.

Regional imports can be divided primarily into two groups: tin-glazed wares, probably from Bristol and London, and Staffordshire wares. Only a single example of a tin-glazed blue-painted plate was recovered, the remaining items comprising two chamber pots with handles, an ointment pot and a painted drug jar. The Staffordshire wares are predominantly table wares, and include several turned white salt-glazed slop bowls with spouts (F215), a coffee pot lid and a bowl or cup with incised, blue-filled decoration. Two slip-decorated moulded plates (F213) were present, a white slip-coated stoneware tankard (F261) and a brownware teapot rim (F257). One sherd from a deep internally black-glazed bowl (F256), the bases of two iron-streaked chamber pots with well scoured interiors and a tankard fragment were present (F236). A single sherd from a Nottingham Stoneware tankard was noted (F249).

The only continental import from the pit came in the form of a straight-sided Westerwald tankard (F217).

Phase 6b   Stone structure and culvert in area BP I

A number of features in trench BP I point to there having been a building associated with a stone culvert which ceased to be in use in the 18th century. Eighteenth-century pottery filled the disused features. As with previous assemblages most of this material must be seen as rubbish accumulation, including a fair proportion of fabrics current in the late 15th to 17th centuries (F200; F220; F208; F216; F244; F224; F204; and probably fragments of F201). Two sherds of flowerpots (F252) were present. A small fragment of a saucer in ?Chinese Porcelain (F218) occurred in the sealing layer below many of the features, but may be intrusive. Two fragments of Staffordshire ware tankards occurred in the brick drain (F238 and F215).

Phase 6c   Later rubble spreads

A large quantity of pottery was recovered from a spread of rubble in the area of the chapter house. This included a range of residual material from early medieval to the 18th century and later. The latest material included a small fragment of a Chinese Porcelain saucer (F218), a moulded plate rim, soup plate rim and bowl sherd in white salt-glazed stoneware (F215); a brown streaked tankard (F236); a slip-decorated cup (F241); a Willow Pattern transfer-printed plate rim (F214) and a drainage pipe of 18th-century type in a coarse Ashton Keynes fabric (F201).

Phase 6d   Stony layer

A stony layer, BP I 8, contained fragments of vessels from the phase 6a pit in addition to a sherd from a Wedgewood black basalt machined coffee pot (F258) and a cream-coloured stoneware bowl (F259), dated to the late 18th century.

CHRONOLOGICAL SEQUENCE OF FABRICS AND TYPOLOGICAL DEVELOPMENTS

ANGLO-SAXON FABRICS

Hand-made pottery attributed to the early to mid Anglo-Saxon period *F255*

Each sherd described below represents an individual fabric (sources unknown), but because of the rarity of such material all the sherds have been grouped together under a single fabric number until further examples of the fabrics are forthcoming.

i) base sherd of a cooking pot with reduced light grey interior and blackened, burnished exterior. The fabric contains some white mica, clay or grog inclusions and a scattering of burnt-out organic material (BN IV 38, a late Roman, or later silt layer).

ii) neck sherd of a baggy cooking pot, with reduced dark brown fabric containing mica, dark organic inclusions and rare brown ?sandstone inclusions (BN IV 36, pit robbing walls of Saxon building and Roman drain: Keely 1986, 228).

iii) body sherd of a cooking pot in a reduced grey-brown fabric containing mica, scattered platelets of shell, sub-angular milky quartz and rare sandstone (BT I 4, 12th century context).

iv) An unidentifiable body sherd, of which the outer surface has been completely worn away and the inner surface smoothed. The fabric is dark brown-black fine-grained sandy ware with a slightly abrasive feel. There are moderate to common grass/chaff voids up to 5mm long. There are also sparse mixed sub-angular quartz grains up to 1.5mm. Rare mica and a single yellow brown sandstone inclusion of *c.* 3mm were also present (BP IV 5, medieval context in area of Saxon church; description by Janet Keely).

The fabric of this sherd was identical to two of the four grass-tempered sherds from excavations in the amphitheatre in 1962-3 (Wacher 1976, 16).

FABRICS PRESENT FROM THE LATE 11TH CENTURY

'Local' products

A coarse limestone gravel and flint-tempered ware *F231*

This fabric has a lower iron content than F202, oxidised yellowish-brown with darker brown surfaces. The fabric was uncommon: 18 sherds including one or two dubious identifications. Of these, 6 sherds were stratified in features associated with a post-conquest structure beneath the undercroft of the Abbey, including acute-angled base fragments which may indicate a 'Beehive base'. All vessels were hand-made and rim fragments, where present, indicate an upright, slightly infolded rim (fig. 87, 1). A similar fabric (positive identification has not been confirmed) was noted on sites in north Wiltshire: Swindon, Old Town, Toothill, and Cricklade (unpublished at time of writing).

A coarse limestone-tempered ware *F202*

An iron-rich fabric tempered with coarse oolitic limestone fragments, rare quartz and iron ore lumps. The ware is fired to a dark reddish-brown to black and generally poorly finished. A detailed description based on thin-section analysis is published by Vince (1982, 203). Sixty-five percent of all sherds which could be attributed to the medieval period occurred in F202, 30% of the total sherds recovered from the excavations. The earliest stratified examples occurred in a post-conquest structure beneath the undercroft of the Abbey, in robbing features post-dating the Anglo-Saxon structures, and in graveyard soil accumulations during the post-conquest period (phase 1b). The bulk of material, however, came from large assemblages of sherds deposited in disturbed layers associated with the construction of the abbey in the early 12th century (phase 2). The quantity of this material suggests it derives from late 11th-century occupation. It is unclear as to whether cooking pots in this fabric were supplied to the abbey continuously throughout the 12th and into the 13th century.

Most of the sherds recovered belonged to hand-made cooking pots, almost entirely of globular, baggy shape with rolled back or everted rims. In many examples it was possible to determine that rims were added as a strip of clay to the neck of the vessel and smoothed, sometimes rather crudely, together. In some examples a pronounced wiped groove was present on the top of the rim (e.g. fig. 87, 9). A selection of the range of rim forms is given on fig. 87, 2-17. Within the large assemblage in abbey construction levels only *c.* 1% of the total cooking pot sherds could be attributed to straight-sided club-rimmed vessels (fig. 87, 18-21). Cooking pot sherds continued to be found in all medieval contexts, but it is unclear how long the production of these vessels continued and at what point it ceased.

A variety of other vessels was recovered, although in much smaller quantities than cooking pots. Several stamped sherds were recovered (fig. 88, 23-5), a handled rim (fig. 88, 22) and a proportion of internally leached body sherds, indicating the production of stamped spouted pitchers during the late 11th and early 12th centuries. Only a single example of a shallow dish was noted (fig. 88, 29) and a possible socket from a handled bowl (fig. 88, 26). The large hook-rimmed bowls found in some quantity on the St John's Hospital site were entirely absent (Vince 1982). Two fragments from crudely formed lamps (or possibly, lids) were noted (fig. 88, 27).

In the 12th-century construction layers (phase 2) several sherds of hand-made vessels with a thick yellowish-green glaze were noted, indicating the production of hand-made tripod pitchers. Residual sherds from later medieval and post-medieval contexts illustrate the appearance of these vessels (fig. 88, 28, 30-2). Some confusion is possible here with products of the Minety kilns (F200, see below), although the coarseness of the inclusions and the presence of iron ore helps to distinguish them. Sherds from these vessels were uncommon, but do indicate an attempt to update the range of products.

In 13th-century contexts sherds of thick perforated walled vessels in a very coarse fabric were noted, and where profiles can be established from residual material, it seems that curfews were produced (fig. 88, 33). The interior of no. 33 does show signs of heat damage, but similar vessels in F200 suggest that the vessels may have been large pans. Associated with these vessels and typical medieval jugs were sherds of hand-made jugs in a very sparsely glazed, oxidised fabric (fig. 88, 34). Again such vessels were uncommon, and are the latest vessel types in F202 noted on the site. Crudely knife-trimmed ridge-tile fragments were recovered from post-Dissolution contexts, and were probably produced during the 13th century. The neckless, everted rim jars noted at St John's Hospital were not present here (Vince 1982).

Regional Imports

A glazed wheel-thrown ware   F247
This fabric is iron-free with abundant quartz sand tempering giving a granular feel. The sherds are covered with a thick pale green glaze that appears crazed. The source has not been confirmed but it resembles Stamford products. Only two sherds were recognised, both residual, including a tiny rim fragment from a wheel-thrown pitcher (not illustrated).

A glazed wheel-thrown ware   F254
This fabric is finer than F247 and the external glaze yellowish green. Three sherds were recovered in total, one of which was stratified in a robber trench of the Saxon church in BV III. The remaining sherds were residual in later medieval contexts. It seems likely that the source of this fabric is Stamford (not illustrated).

FABRICS PRESENT FROM THE EARLY 12TH CENTURY

Local products

Minety Ware   F200
This fabric is characterised by fine oolitic limestone tempering. A detailed description based on thin-section analysis is published by Vince (1982). Minety is situated in the Forest of Bradon in north Wiltshire and is only about 8 miles from Cirencester. No kiln sites have been located, only waste dumps. Those excavated in 1971 (Musty 1973, 79-88) contained material of the late medieval period and of the latest phase of production. Alan Vince has traced the extent of trade in the products of the industry in the Severn Valley, South Wales and the west coast of Ireland (Vince 1985, 56). The stratified sequence in Gloucester provides a useful control for the present site where stratified material has no independent dating evidence and where a large proportion of material is residual (Vince 1983a, 126-30).

The earliest stratified sherds occurred in the construction layers of the abbey (phase 2). This suggests that the Minety industry was in production by the mid 12th century. Fifteen sherds were stratified in these contexts and include externally glazed sherds from hand-made vessels, some with combed decoration. It seems likely that these sherds belonged to tripod pitchers, rather than Selsley Common-type cooking pots. Tripod pitcher sherds occurred in contexts well into the late medieval period, but it is known from Gloucester that the production of these vessels died out in the mid 13th century. Few diagnostic examples were recovered here. No early tubular spouts were noted, or complex handles (fig. 88, 35-9).

A rim of a thick-walled curfew, or pan, was found in a construction context (phase 2), but the majority of examples of these vessels were residual in the area of the undercroft or outside the west front of the abbey. Stratified fragments were associated with jugs of the mid to late 13th century (fig. 90, 57-9).

Very few hand-made cooking pot sherds were identified with any certainty. A rim of a Selsley Common type came from a 13th-century context outside the west front (fig. 89, 41), associated with a globular vessel similar to a 'ginger jar' (fig. 89, 40). This vessel had slashed decoration and was designed to take a lid (phase 3a).

Sherds stratified in contexts between the mid 13th and early 16th centuries indicate that production and firing methods had been refined by the late 13th century. Wheel-thrown jugs of various sizes with strap or rod handles were produced with thin walls and a very sparse use of glaze. The firing produced pale pinkish buff surfaces with pale grey cores, as opposed to the 12th to mid 13th-century material which was predominantly reduced with a more generous covering of glaze. Large wheel-thrown jars with everted neck-less rims glazed on the rim top were presumably used for cooking and storage (fig. 89, 42-3). These jars were sometimes given tripod feet, opposing strap handles and a bung-hole, although examples of these vessels were rare here (phase 3d). Sherds from jars occurred in 14th-century tomb fills (phase 3c) and in silts over late flooring before the Dissolution (phase 3e).

At some point during the 15th century the range of vessels was expanded. The kiln dump in Minety produced many of the vessel types found in the latest pre-Dissolution and immediate post-Dissolution contexts here (phases 3e and 4a) (Musty 1973): pipkins with lids, tall, thin bung-hole cisterns, flange rim conical bowls, dripping pans with side mounted handles, bottles, a ?money box, and a tiny ?chafing dish (figs. 89-90, 44-56, 60-5). The occurrence of these vessels would appear to be rare outside the immediate locality, although bowl sherds have been found in Gloucester in late 15th-century contexts (Vince 1983a, 130) and jars in Oxford at a similar period (Mellor 1980b).

It is unclear when production ceased, but it seems likely that this was during the early 16th century when the production began at Ashton Keynes of red domestic earthenwares. A sand and oolitic limestone-tempered fabric (F230) may represent an overlap between the two industries.

Regional imports

Bath Fabric 'A'   F240
This fabric is characterised by the polished quartz grains in the fired clay, presenting a glittery appearance. A full description of this fabric is published by Vince (1979b, 27). Four sherds were recovered in total, one of which was stratified in a context associated with the construction of the abbey (phase 2) (fig. 91, 66) and a second in an early medieval pit outside the west front of the abbey (phase 3a) (fig. 91, 67). The remaining sherds were residual. This fabric is a very common component of 12th to 13th-century assemblages on rural sites in north and west Wiltshire and in the Severn Valley. Its source of production has not been located but seems likely to be in the south-west Wilts/Avon area.

A sand-tempered ware F221
This fabric is comparable with Oxford fabric AG (Haldon and Mellor 1977, 117-8). Three sherds were recognised on the present site: two recovered from 12th-century construction contexts (phase 2) represent hand-made tripod pitchers with external lead glaze. The third residual sherd belonged to a jug of probable late 13th to 14th-century date and was coated with a white slip beneath a copper rich glaze. Jugs in this fabric were common during this period at Newbury and a source in the Kennet Valley is suggested (Alan Vince pers. comm.).

FABRICS PRESENT FROM THE EARLY 13TH CENTURY

Regional imports

Developed Stamford Ware   F268
Three sherds belonging to wheel-thrown, glazed jugs were recovered. Two, including the rim and part of a pulled spout were stratified with early 13th-century wares outside the west front of the abbey (phase 3a) (fig. 91, 68), the third sherd was residual in a late abbey context.

Ham Green Ware F206
Nineteen sherds were identified, generally occurring in two areas of the site: in the area of the undercroft, and outside the west front of the abbey (BG IV and BV III), the majority of these being in residual groups of medieval sherds of the 13th and 14th centuries. An example of a rim and thumbed base were stratified in the bedding for the western 'courtyard' (phase 3a) (fig. 91, 69). Evidence from Gloucester has shown that the production of these vessels began during the first half of the 13th century (Vince 1979a, 176).

A sand-tempered ware F270
This off-white fabric is tempered with well assorted sand and contains cream coloured clay pellets. The interior of the two examples recovered are discoloured black, the exteriors covered by a clear lead glaze; one sherd is decorated with applied elongated clay pads. As in the case of F206 the examples came from BG IV and BV III.

Continental imports

An imported ware F265
Two sherds in an iron poor fabric with mica and rounded quartz may belong to jugs from northern France (Alan Vince pers. comm.). They are very thinly potted and have an external thin lead glaze. Both were stratified in medieval contexts outside the west front of the abbey (phase 3a) and were associated with other early to mid 13th-century wares.

FABRICS PRESENT FROM THE MID 13TH CENTURY

Regional imports

Brill-type wares F207
The excavations produced a total of 136 sherds, probably representing around 29 individual vessels or less. The majority of sherds belonged to elaborately decorated squat jugs which were in production during the second half of the 13th century (Mellor 1980b, 176). Sherds from a highly decorated jug were recovered from repairs to flooring in the undercroft (phase 3b), and sherds from the same vessel were residual within a post-Dissolution robbing pit in the same area (fig. 91, 70) (BG IV, BH VI). This vessel has a direct parallel with a vessel found in phase BIII at the Hamel, Oxford (Mellor 1980b, fig. 15, 28), dated to the mid 13th century. Several sherds clearly belonged to tall, thin jugs of later date with an overall olive green glaze. One example stratified in the fill of a 14th-century tomb in the eastern extension (phase 3c) may have belonged to a jug of triple-decker type (M. Mellor, pers. comm.).

Worcester jugs F239
Six sherds from wheel-thrown jugs were recovered, most of which displayed the decorative features described by Barton (1967). A single jug sherd was stratified in the construction trench for the new eastern extension of the north transept chapel (phase 3c). Four sherds were recovered from the uppermost layers of area BT I and may be residual, the remaining sherd was residual in an 18th-century rubble layer. Excavations in Gloucester have shown that these jugs were present during the first half of the 13th century (Vince 1979a, 176 - TF 90), although they predominated in the mid 13th century in Hereford (Vince 1985, 53-4).

FABRICS PRESENT FROM THE LATE 13TH CENTURY

Regional imports

Nash Hill Wares F219
A large proportion of the glazed, decorated floor tiles from the abbey were produced by the industry at

Nash Hill, near Lacock, north-west Wiltshire (see pp. 143-4) in the 14th century. This industry also supplied decorated jugs (fig. 91, 71), ridge tiles and other roof furniture. A fragment of a chimney louvre was residual in an 15th-century rubble layer. All the sherds from jugs were recovered from area BG, the area of the undercroft, and most were derived from post-Dissolution activity in this area, with the exception of a single sherd which was stratified in a pit in room 20. Seventy-three sherds from jugs were recovered, possibly representing a maximum of about 23 vessels, probably far less.

A jug fabric F269
The source of this fabric has not been identified, but the typological features of the 26 sherds recovered have much in common with the products of the Nash Hill kilns (McCarthy 1974, fig. 19), also the products of the Laverstock kilns in south Wiltshire (Musty, Algar and Ewence 1969). The majority of sherds were recovered from the area of the undercroft including 4 sherds found within repairs to flooring pre-dating the erection of a partition (phase 3b). Other examples were present in contexts outside the west front of the abbey (fig. 91, 74-5).

A jug fabric F233
This sand-tempered fabric as yet has no provenance. Ten sherds were identified including a rim with applied bands in a sand-free clay. All examples have a rich copper green glaze (fig. 91, 76). Sherds were recovered from a 14th-century rubble layer in the undercroft, a medieval pit in area BP V, and a medieval ditch in area BT I. It seems likely that this fabric was produced into the 14th century.

A jug fabric F223
The 11 sherds noted may belong to the same vessel; all were recovered from the area of the undercroft, including several stratified in repairs to flooring (phase 3b). The source is unknown. The heavy thumbed base fragments suggest a large, tall jug.

A jug fabric F232
Two sherds were attributed to this fabric, the source of which remains unknown. Both sherds belonged to possibly hand-made vessels and were externally glazed, one having applied clay pellet decoration, the other decorated with finger nail marks, combing and an applied clay strip. One sherd was associated with wares of late 13th-century date, or later, outside the west front. However, the method of manufacture may indicate an earlier date.

A jug fabric F234
Two sherds belonging to a jug strap handle were found in a post-Dissolution context in the area of the undercroft containing many other wares of this date (phase 4a). The source is unknown, but may be local.

A jug fabric F235
Four sherds were recovered from a post-Dissolution pit in the area of the undercroft (phase 4a) and

probably belong to the same vessel, which was a small jug with an internal copper-coloured glaze. The fabric of the vessel is pale pink and extremely powdery, but it would seem that this may be the result of the action of fire, since the context was associated with a hearth.

FABRICS PRESENT FROM THE 14TH CENTURY

Regional imports

Bristol wares F262
Apart from a single example of a slashed strap handle found in area BT I, the remaining examples of the fabric (seven sherds) were recovered from site BP. The majority of sherds belonged to jugs with external glaze (fig. 91, 72). However, an example of an inkwell set (or possibly a condiment set) was recovered from a rubble layer in area BP II probably laid down at the time of the Dissolution or earlier (fig. 91, 73). Other examples of this type of vessel from the same industry have been noted from Bristol itself (D. Dawson pers. comm.) and from a late medieval context in Gloucester (Ireland 1984, TF 92, fig. 61, 144).

Malvernian glazed ware F204
A single cooking pot sherd from this industry was recovered at St John's Hospital (Vince 1982, F203), but no further examples were noted at the abbey. Floor tiles were produced during the late medieval period (see p. 146). The earliest stratified example of a Malvernian vessel here was a single glazed wheel-thrown jug sherd in area BP II, associated with later medieval jug sherds and a sherd of Tudor Green (F220). The majority of Malvernian products on the site could be dated by analogy to the 15th to early 17th centuries, although few sherds were stratified in useful contexts. Two rims from 14th/15th-century cooking pots were noted (fig. 93, 115). The majority of vessels represented were small jugs with sparse patches of copper-flecked glaze and tall, narrow-mouthed jars with cordons or thumbed strips around the neck (fig. 93, 118-121), which can be dated between the late 15th and early 17th centuries (Vince 1977a, 285-6). Two examples of chafing dishes were noted (fig. 93, 116-7), recognisable by the rims, although a number of internally glazed 'bowl' sherds may belong to vessels of the same type current in the late 16th to early 17th centuries. A single vertical-handled vessel with grooved girth was noted (fig. 93, 122), unparalleled elsewhere (A. Vince pers. comm.) and may represent a handled cooking vessel, or possibly a chamber pot? A total of 51 sherds were recovered, most from post-Dissolution contexts.

Continental imports

Early Siegburg stoneware F253
A very small fragment of the rim of a beaker of 14th to 15th-century type (Beckmann 1974, 189, fig. 17, 131-6) was residual in a post-destruction rubble layer.

FABRICS PRESENT FROM THE 15TH CENTURY

Local products

A local fabric F250

The presence of oolitic limestone in this fabric suggests a local origin, possibly related to fabric 230 although the iron content may be higher. Sherds from a very thin-walled money box with a frilled base were recovered from soil below and behind the choir stalls (phase 3e). Further sherds from the same vessel were recovered from the post-Dissolution rubble layer which covered this area. Associated was a sherd from a Cistercian ware handled cup (F244), and coin evidence suggests that F250 was in production in the late 15th or early 16th century. A sherd from a jug base was found in a residual context.

Regional Imports

Tudor Green wares F220

Sherds from Tudor Green handled cups were present within contexts associated with the latest use of the abbey (phase 3e), but more precise dating was not possible, these contexts possibly belonging to a period between the 15th and mid 16th centuries. A sherd from a lobed cup with internal yellow glaze was recovered from late 'occupation' silts on the floor of the chapter house; three sherds from cups also were included in an 'organic' layer deposited prior to the laying of the latest floor in a room in the east claustral range. In both instances associated sherds were from late Minety wares (F200). Five sherds from cups were included in primary rubble deposits post-dating the Dissolution. The majority, however, were residual in later robbing and rubble deposits and gardening contexts. Seven sherds were rather thick-walled for cups and may belong to jugs. A single sherd displayed knife-cut glazed perforations and may have come from a money box or chafing dish, and may belong to the more general group of Surrey border wares produced between the 16th and 17th centuries (F222).

A Cistercian ware F244

The fabric of this ware is characteristically inclusionless and fired to a chocolate brown, although overfired examples were noted. A clear glaze was used and several examples bear applied decoration in the form of white clay pads and strips. The single sherd associated with F250 in the choir stall silts (phase 3e) suggests a late 15th-century beginning for the ware. Several sherds were recovered from floors laid late in the life of the abbey and represent handled cups with incurving rims (fig. 94, 129). The majority of examples were recovered from post-Dissolution contexts, notably rubble layers. Other vessel types include 'posset pots' with inset rims and opposing handles and the lids to cover them. Two examples of lids had white applied decoration (fig. 94, 124, 127), no. 127 having the clay

knob broken off and sharpened as if to indicate its replacement by a knob of another material. A portion of a three-handled cup of Brears Type 8 (Brears 1971) was recovered from the rubble layer above the choir stalls in the crossing and may be derived from the earlier context below (fig. 94, 126). A fluted base from a salt cup or goblet was residual in a gardening context. None of the later straight-sided, corrugated cups noted in the other Cistercian wares fabric (F208) were noted in F244, possibly suggesting a relatively short-lived production of this typical Cistercian ware.

Continental imports

Imported, unglazed stoneware flasks F248

Four sherds, including the rim and neck, from flattened flasks in a hard, cream fabric correspond to Hurst's Type I flasks dated to the late 15th to early 16th centuries (Hurst 1966, 55). Only one of these sherds was stratified in a pre-destruction context (phase 3e).

FABRICS PRESENT FROM THE 16TH CENTURY

Local products

Early Ashton Keynes/late Minety variant F230

This fabric combines the sandy texture of Ashton Keynes wares and the oolitic limestone tempering of Minety wares. The firing is similar to late Minety products as is the use of decoration and the application of glaze. Thirteen sherds were recognised (some with less oolitic limestone than others) indicating that the products were not an important component of post-medieval assemblages. A single bowl or jar sherd was stratified in a pre-destruction context (phase 3e). Most sherds were residual with odd examples in post-destruction robbing and rubble. Products were confined to domestic items, including conical bowls with decorated flanged rims (fig. 93, 113), jugs, jars and pipkins.

Ashton Keynes wares F201

The kilns at Ashton Keynes were only a few miles from Minety where pottery was produced between the early 12th and the early 16th centuries. It is possible that there may have been some overlap of production between these two industries (see F230). Ashton Keynes products are first found in stratified contexts in the early 16th century in Gloucester (Vince 1983a, 132) indicating that there may have been continuity in the trade links established by the Minety industry. On the present site very few sherds were recovered from pre-destruction contexts (phase 3e). A sherd from a conical bowl was associated with a late floor in the north aisle crossing. A bowl sherd was associated with the disuse of the undercroft. Contexts robbing the buildings prior to the deposition of rubble (phase 4a) produced a range of vessel types, including jugs, conical flange-rim bowls, jars and curving walled bowls. The range is expanded in contexts attributed to primary rubble deposits (phase 4b) which would appear to have been laid down between the mid 16th and early 17th centuries or later, and includes complex rimmed bowls, dripping pans, chafing dishes, drinking vessels including tankards, and a variety of smaller bowls, and jars or pipkins. It would appear that a consistent repertoire was produced between the 16th and 18th centuries. Eighteenth century contexts produced, in addition, large flanged plates with roller-stamp decoration on the rim, chamber-pot fragments and shallow bowls with straight sides. The 18th-century pit (phase 6a) demonstrates that a certain degree of proficiency in manufacture and an evenness of firing and glaze application may be used to distinguish later from earlier products. Many of the vessels from the earlier features were fired with a reduced core and oxidised surface beneath an unevenly applied lead glaze, which could appear greenish. Vessels from contexts between the mid 16th and late 17th centuries displayed a variety of techniques, including the use of reduction to produce a dark green, almost black glaze, and the use of iron specks in the glaze to produce a streaked effect. The 18th-century vessels were predominantly oxidised with a well fitting clear glaze. Decorative motifs throughout the period of production were used on jugs, flanged bowls and plates and the sides of jars and bowls and include chevron stamping, combing, roller stamping, thumbed strips and incised lines. Tile fragments, flower pots, a drainage pipe and stove tile fragments were recovered from 18th-century and later contexts.

Regional imports

A Cistercian ware F208

This fabric is characterised by inclusions of quartz, iron ore and sandstones, producing a generally 'lumpy' feel. Most vessels were very finely potted, the inclusions often protruding through the surfaces into the glaze. When fired normally the fabric appears brick red, but when overfired a virtual stoneware was produced to the colour of dark purple or grey. The glaze was applied very thickly, often running towards the bases of vessels which often showed signs of saggar firing by the adhering sand grains.

This fabric was one of the most common recorded in post-medieval contexts (333 sherds), although it was probably only produced between the early 16th and mid 17th centuries. The earliest sherds were recovered from pre-destruction contexts (phase 3e), including relaid floors and occupation or disuse silts on floor surfaces. The vessels represented are handled cups of Cistercian ware type including waisted, bulbous forms with opposing handles, and posset pot types with inset rims for lids. A fluted splayed base, possibly from a figurine or goblet, was recovered from a robbing context post-dating demolition (phase 4c) (fig. 94, 130). Sherds from primary rubble deposits indicate the production of straight-sided corrugated tankards or cups during the 16th and into the 17th centuries (fig. 94, 131-3). The

fabric also occurs in Gloucester (Vince 1983a, TF 60) but the source remains unidentified.

Herefordshire Border wares   F224

The fabric is characteristically inclusionless with a high mica content, fired mainly to an orange red. Two phases of production of this industry were represented here: copies of Raeren stoneware drinking jugs with frilled bases and olive glaze, dated to the 16th century (fig. 94, 135-6), and later kitchen wares, represented by internally glazed bowl sherds produced in the 17th and 18th centuries (fig. 94, 137). Five sherds from copies of stoneware jugs were noted, including a base fragment stratified in a late abbey floor dated to after *c.* 1500. Sherds stratified at the East Gate site in Gloucester (Vince 1983a, 134, fig. 81, nos. 128, 139) were dated to the late 16th century. Seven sherds from later bowls were noted. A sherd from an internally glazed bowl was present in a primary destruction context of the abbey (phase 4b) and may be intrusive; other sherds occurred in robbing contexts and later gardening features.

Continental imports

French flasks F248 (not illustrated)

Six sherds of flat, round flasks in a grey stoneware fabric with reddish brown gloss were noted representing examples of Hurst's Type II flasks dated to the 16th century (Hurst 1966). A single sherd was stratified in a late abbey context (phase 3e) and one in a robbing context. Other sherds were residual in later contexts.

Saintonge ware F245 (not illustrated)

A single example of a chafing dish rim with comb-stamped decoration and splashes of copper-green glaze dated to the early 16th century (Hurst 1974, 233-47) was residual in a culvert associated with gardening activity (phase 5).

Raeren stoneware F225

Surprisingly, only a single sherd from a typical drinking jug was stratified in a context associated with the alterations to the chapter house (phase 3e). The majority of examples were recovered from post-destruction rubble and robbing features, or were residual in later garden features. With the exception of a large flat-based ribbed jug which possibly had an applied face mask (fig. 95, 164) and an unglazed cordoned jug neck, all other sherds belonged to typical squat drinking jugs with frilled bases (fig. 95, 161-3).

Cologne stoneware F228

Three vessels were recovered representing two globular drinking jugs and a straight-sided tankard, dated to the mid 16th century. The drinking jugs provide examples of two types of typical decoration: twining roses and rose leaves (fig. 95, 165) and sprigs of oak leaves (fig. 95, 166). The tankard was a tiny fragment displaying a figure of Eve facing left. The earliest stratified example (no. 165) was present in a primary rubble deposit (phase 4b) with joining sherds in redeposited rubble caused by later robbing and gardening activity. No. 166 was present in a robbing feature post-dating primary rubble contexts (phase 4c).

Frechen stoneware F216

Sherds of typical Frechen drinking jugs were extremely common in contexts post-dating the destruction of the abbey in roughly equal amounts to sherds of Ashton Keynes earthenwares (F201) and Cistercian ware cups (F208) suggesting use into the 17th century. However, several sherds did occur in late contexts (phase 3e), including levelling for a floor in the north transept, silts built up on floor surfaces and alterations to the chapter house. Sherds from 'Bellarmine' type bottles were relatively uncommon, but examples were present in robbing and rubble deposits post-dating the abbey destruction (phases 4a-b). A large jug or bottle with applied roses was residual in a post-destruction context (fig. 95, 168).

Siegburg stoneware F253

A single fragment of a tall, straight-sided tankard in an unglazed, off-white stoneware dated to the late 16th century, was residual in a gardening context (phase 5) (fig. 95, 179). The sherd displays applique decoration in the form of an urn and foliage.

Tin-glazed ware F209 (not illustrated)

The earliest tin-glazed wares on the site were sherds from thin-walled highly decorated 'Albarellos', ten of which were recognised (detailed descriptions are in the archive). One of these occurred in a late floor laid in the north transept chapel. This was a small fragment with blue painted decoration and may be intrusive. Burnt sherds were recovered from a pit associated with a hearth in the area of the undercroft which may pre-date the demolition of the abbey. These sherds were analysed and the tin-glazing confirmed (Biek and Gillies n.d.). Other sherds were recovered from post-destruction contexts, including robbing features and rubble deposits, some of which may represent continental imports. Two small fragments with cobalt blue glaze may represent examples of 'flower vases' from the south Netherlands, dated to the early 16th century, although neither was stratified in a contemporary context. Two tiny sherds in a white powdery fabric similar to that used in tin-glazed wares, but with a bright green glaze (F266), may represent fragments of an 'Albarello', but were residual in garden contexts.

FABRICS PRESENT FROM THE EARLY 17TH CENTURY

Regional products

Surrey-Hampshire border ware F222

Fourteen sherds in total does not imply a major source of kitchen wares, but rather a trickle of products from this industry. The majority of sherds belong to bowls. Where profiles were present two forms are indicated: a flanged rim deep bowl (fig. 94, 142), and a bead rimmed bowl with horizontally applied handle (fig. 94, 141). This vessel was the earliest stratified example in phase 4b. A single example of a tripod pipkin was noted, but was not stratified in a contemporary context. Comparable vessels were recovered from an early to mid 17th-century pit at St Ebbe's, Oxford (Mellor and Oakley 1984, 187, fig. 16, 5-9) and the keep of Farnham Castle in Surrey dated to the Civil War period (Moorhouse 1971, fig. 2). An onion-shaped knob of a chafing dish was also noted residually in topsoils. A similar example is recorded at Basing House, Hants (Moorhouse 1970, 46, fig. 10, 23) dated to the second quarter of the 17th century.

Table wares are represented by four sherds from ribbed barrel-shaped mugs, contemporary with similar mugs in tin-glazed ware (fig. 94, 143-4) and Fulham stoneware (fig. 94, 148-9). These examples display a mottled brown glaze in imitation of stoneware (Haslam 1975, 173). None of these sherds was usefully stratified.

A marbled ware F226

A single rim of a cup or tankard in a marbled red and white clay with dark brown glaze (fig. 94, 134) was stratified in a post-destruction context.

A sandy black-glazed ware F242

This sandy red earthenware with black glaze is a common component of 17th-century assemblages in East Anglia. Ten sherds were identified mainly belonging to tall, ribbed, handled tankards, with one example of a two-handled cup base with impressed dimples (fig. 94, 138). The earliest stratified examples occurred in primary rubble deposits (phase 4b), including no. 138, with examples in robbing features and later contexts associated with gardening activity.

A fine sandy earthenware F251 (not illustrated)

Several sherds were singled out from the bulk of Ashton Keynes earthenware due to the fine-grained texture and inclusion free fabric. The fabric is not dissimilar to products from Donyatt, Somerset and represent internally glazed jar sherds, including a rim with top-mounted bucket handle, one of which was stratified in a primary rubble deposit (phase 4b).

Imported wares

Merida wares F227

This characteristically laminated micaceous fabric was only represented by three sherds including a bowl rim (fig. 95, 177), a ?lid (fig. 95, 178), and the side of a barrel-shaped heavily knife-trimmed costrel (fig. 95, 176). No. 177 was stratified in a post-destruction pit while nos. 176 and 178 were found in contexts associated with garden activity.

Martincamp flasks F229

A single sherd of a Type III flask (Hurst 1966, 57) in a dark red ware was stratified in a post-destruction context.

FABRICS PRESENT FROM THE LATE 17TH AND EARLY 18TH CENTURIES

Local products

Flowerpots F252 (not illustrated)
All flowerpot sherds were grouped together under a separate number, although on examination almost all were found to have been produced in the Ashton Keynes fabric. A single unglazed base in a micaceous fabric may have come from Cranham in Gloucestershire. All examples were from plain flowerpots with bulbous rims, often painted with a white slip band. A shallow curving walled bowl was also noted. Sherds were recovered exclusively from four areas of the site (65 BK, BM, BN and BP), and despite ample evidence for gardening activity were not numerous (17 sherds), the majority found in garden soils (phases 5-6) and redeposited rubble.

Regional import

Tin-glazed wares   F209
It is possible that some of the decorated Albarello sherds from post-destruction contexts may have been produced in London (see above p. 109). It has not been possible to attribute provenance with certainty. The earliest stratified example of English tin-glazed wares occurred in post-destruction rubble (phase 4b) in the form of fragments of a manganese purple speckled globular jug and handle (not illustrated). However, tin-glazed wares were not much in evidence until contexts associated with gardening, redeposited rubble layers and 18th-century rubbish pits where a range of products was noted. The source of many of these products is likely to be Bristol with some examples from London (D. Dawson pers. comm.). A single example of a late 17th-century white barrel-shaped mug (fig. 94, 144) was residual in a late 17th or early 18th-century context. A bottle rim imitating a stoneware form was unstratified. The remaining vessel types belong to a period between the late 17th and mid 18th centuries and include squat 'drug jars' decorated with blue, mauve and yellow paint (fig. 94, 145; fig. 97, 191); small ointment pots (fig. 97, 192); lead glazed backed decorated plates; flat blue painted plates (fig. 97, 201); chamber pots in a variety of sizes (fig. 94, 147; fig. 97, 190) with one or two examples with blue painted decoration; small bowls probably imitating Chinese Porcelain tea bowls including examples with imitation Chinese blue and white decoration (fig. 94, 146); and a single example of a flanged ?coffee or tea pot lid.

Staffordshire wares

Moulded slip-ware plates   F213
These wares were relatively uncommon mainly occurring as rubbish survivals in garden soils, with the exception of vessels recovered from the phase 6a pit (fig. 97, 202-3).

Wheel-thrown slip decorated plates F212
Only two sherds were noted, one example in a rubble context (fig. 94, 159), the other in topsoil.

Slip decorated hollow wares F241
Very few sherds were recognised and many of these very tiny fragments. It seems possible that some of these were derived from Bristol (Barton 1961). Many of the fragments appear to have belonged to handled drinking vessels or chamber pots. A small globular vessel with upright rim (fig. 94, 158) can be paralleled with a similar example at the Albion Square kiln site, Stoke-on-Trent (Celoria and Kelly 1973, no. 154). Examples were stratified in redeposited rubble deposits and garden soils.

Black-glazed wares F238
Sherds of this ware were fairly numerous compared to other Staffordshire products (29 sherds) and mainly belonged to tall, handled cups, or tygs (fig. 94, 155-7), including two examples with white painted slip decoration. Thicker body sherds may belong to chamber pots. A single example of a bowl or plate rim occurred in the 18th-century pit, BP I 4. Other stratified examples occurred in rubble deposits (phase 4b), robbing features (phase 4c), garden features (phase 5) and 18th-century pits (phase 6).

Iron streaked wares F236
Sherds of these wares were more numerous than other Staffordshire products (54 sherds) representing two vessel types in equal numbers: tankards with ribbed sides (fig. 94, 150-l) and round-bellied chamber pots (fig. 97, 196). Sherds of tankards were recovered from robbing features which post-dated primary rubble deposits (phase 4c) and a redeposited rubble context, possibly associated with garden activity (phase 5), but the majority of sherds came from topsoils. The phase 6a pit produced two chamber pot bases and a tankard rim.

Early Staffordshire stonewares F261
Six sherds were noted of which five belonged to cylindrical tankards. One example of a white slipped vessel with brown dipped rim (fig. 94, 153) was residual in a late 18th-century robbing trench, while a base and rim were present in the mid 18th-century phase 6a pit (fig. 97, 199). A turned bowl or drinking vessel with iron brown slip was residual in topsoils.

Other regional wares

Nottingham stonewares F249
This ware was uncommon (5 sherds) and occurred largely as residual material in topsoils with the exception of a bowl rim and tankard sherds in the phase 6a pit. The remaining sherds represent fragments of a tankard with rouletted decoration, a drinking cup and a possible bowl.

Fulham stoneware   F263
Four sherds from ribbed barrel-shaped tankards of types current *c.* 1680 (C Green pers. comm.) to the

early 18th century (fig. 94, 148-9). Two were present in garden contexts, the remaining residual in topsoils.

Continental imports

Westerwald stoneware F217
Nineteen sherds were recovered representing two drinking vessel forms: globular drinking jugs (two sherds) and cylindrical tankards. Few were stratified usefully, occurring mainly in topsoils and late 18th-century redeposited rubble, although two sherds from tankards occurred in the phase 6a pit (fig. 97, 193). Decorative features on tankards include blue painted 'clubs', painted diamonds, blue stripes, a 'GR' crest, incised fleur de lys, and blue chequer pattern. A sherd from a globular vessel was decorated with vertical ribbons of moulded circles and diamonds painted with blue and purple.

FABRICS PRESENT FROM THE LATE 18TH CENTURY

'Local' products

An inclusionless earthenware F260
It seems likely that this fabric represents a refined inclusionless variant of Ashton Keynes ware (F201). Four sherds were recognised representing three vessels. A shallow bowl, internally glazed with brown gloss on the exterior was present in the phase 6a pit (fig. 96, 187) with an adjoining sherd in later phase 6d; other sherds were present in garden soils.

Regional products

A micaceous earthenware with iron F267
This red earthenware is highly micaceous with characteristic tempering of black iron ore specks, but the source is unknown. A single vessel was recovered from garden soil (phase 5): a small ointment jar with a white underglaze slip perhaps in imitation of tin-glazed wares (fig. 94, 139).

Staffordshire white salt-glazed stoneware F215
All sherds (18 in total) belonged to a variety of table wares including three examples of moulded plates with decorative rims; bowls with turned bases, including one example with 'scratch blue' decoration (fig. 97, 197); several examples of 'slop bowls' with pulled or moulded spouts (fig. 97, 194-5); and a lid from a tea or coffee pot (fig. 96, 187). A single sherd from a jug may be a 19th-century intrusion in topsoil. A group of these vessels was recovered from the phase 6a pit including the 'scratch blue' vessel, while other sherds occurred in redeposited rubble dated to the late 18th century and include a sherd from a tankard with chevron rouletting and moulded plate rims.

Staffordshire black glazed kitchen wares F256
A single sherd from a black-glazed deep bowl was recovered from the phase 6a pit.

Staffordshire brown-bodied wares F257
A single rim of a small jar or coffee or tea pot was stratified in pit BP I 4 (fig. 97, 188).

An unidentified ?London stoneware F237
The base of a ribbed tankard with white slip and band of brown paint on base was residual in topsoils.

FABRICS PRESENT FROM THE LATE 18TH CENTURY

Regional products

Cream ware F211
A single sherd from a plate was present in topsoil.

Wedgewood Basalt ware F258
A single fragment of a machine turned ?coffee pot was stratified in late 18th-century phase 6d.

Cream bodied ironstone wares F259
A single sherd from a kitchen bowl was stratified in late 18th-century phase 6d.

Transfer printed ware F214
Four sherds from plates were recognised, all decorated with the ubiquitous willow pattern, stratified in late rubble spreads and robbing features.

Imported wares

Chinese porcelain F218
Three small fragments were noted all representing tea-wares; a small cup with painted blue flower (fig. 95, 180) was unstratified in topsoil. Fragments of ?saucers were recovered from a structure in area BP I and a late rubble spread (BJ XIV 2).

DISCUSSION

THE ANGLO-SAXON POTTERY

The four sherds described above (F255) would appear to be the only pottery of this period to have been recovered so far from within the town walls. Several sherds of hand-made, grass-tempered pottery were recovered during excavations in the amphitheatre (Wacher 1976, 16); a small, stamped accessory vessel was found with a burial at Barton Farm (Brown 1976, 32, fig. 3.3), dated to the 6th century; and a scatter of sherds was recovered during the construction of the Cirencester ring-road in 1982 and included a fragment from a stamped vessel in addition to plain domestic pottery in sand-tempered, chaff-tempered and quartzite-tempered fabrics. The recognition of pottery of this period at the abbey may suggest some form of post-Roman occupation, perhaps the ditch noted above (p. 7).

Late Anglo-Saxon wares were not present as a defined group on the site. The hiatus, in ceramic terms, between the early to mid Anglo-Saxon and the medieval period noted at St John's Hospital (Vince 1982, 205) has yet to be filled. None of the structures attributed to this period produced contemporary pottery, and there were no residual sherds which could be dated to this period with any certainty. Sherds from glazed, wheel-thrown pitchers occurred in two fabrics (F247, F254) in later contexts, and it seems likely that these vessels belong to the post-Conquest period. There is also as yet no evidence to suggest that the earliest occurring medieval fabrics (F231, F202) were present on the site in the late Anglo-Saxon period.

MEDIEVAL POTTERY

The medieval pottery was unequally distributed through the stratigraphy of the site: the groups used for comparative purposes between periods are derived from assemblages formed artificially from pottery deposited in unconnected features of roughly contemporary date, rather than a number of key groups of similar site and type of deposit (for example, rubbish pits) which were not present here. This method is clearly not a satisfactory way of producing an analysis of the changes in pottery supply over a period of time, and cannot fully take account of the human agency involved in the deposits, but it does enable a certain amount of information to be extracted about the sources of supply, and also to trace change in the uses to which pottery was put over a period of time.

Sources of pottery supply
From the late 11th to the 15th century 'locally' produced wares form the bulk of the pottery assemblages examined. These wares are derived from two sources, one of which supplied predominantly domestic utensils, the other mainly table wares. A coarse limestone-tempered ware (F202), precise source unknown but thought to be local to Cirencester on petrological evidence (Vince 1982) and bearing a marked similarity to wares from the Forest of Wychwood (M. Mellor pers. comm.), first appears on the site in post-Conquest, but pre-abbey contexts in significant quantities. Large 'groups' of vessels in this fabric were present in contexts associated with the construction of the abbey and include some examples of table wares, indicating that finer vessels were attempted. Thereafter a certain proportion of almost every medieval context containing pottery produced some sherds of this ware and it is clearly difficult to know to what extent this material may be residual. Examples of tripod pitchers and a hand-made balluster jug suggest that the pottery was still operating into the 13th century, in which case very little typological change is apparent in the design of simple cooking vessels.

The second source is Minety, in the Forest of Bradon (F200) whose products first appear on the site with the construction of the abbey. This industry is known to have produced a characteristic type of cooking pot in the 12th and 13th centuries, rather more sophisticated in manufacture to those produced by small, local potteries, which it traded over a wide area (Vince 1985) few of which were found here. Similarly the industry produced elaborately decorated tripod pitchers in the 12th and 13th centuries, and in the 13th and 14th centuries, decorated jugs, but most of the sherds from this site suggest plainer wares were supplied to the abbey. However at some point in the 15th century, this industry took account of changing styles in domestic pottery and produced a range of typically 'Tudor' wares - meat dishes, chafing dishes, large conical flanged bowls, pipkins, inkwells and upright cisterns. This 'progressive' urge did not last long because the speckly, pale glazed wares must have looked 'old-fashioned' beside the new fashion for clear glazed red earthenwares which became popular from the early 16th century and there is some typological evidence to suggest that the Minety potters abandoned their traditional area of production around Minety for pastures new at Ashton Keynes some miles away (F201). Examples of these later wares were present in latest abbey and early post-destruction contexts.

In the early medieval period there are few examples of wares reaching the site from further afield. A second type of limestone-tempered ware with added flint (F231) appears only in post-conquest, pre-abbey features, with one or two residual sherds in abbey construction contexts, and representing almost totally sherds from a single beehive base. The source of this fabric is unknown, but it has been noted at Cricklade, Toothill and Swindon (unpublished sites in north Wilts). Five sherds from glazed wheel-thrown pitchers of Stamford type (F247; F254), only one of which was stratified in a post-conquest context, point to more specialised, expensive, table wares being brought in from a considerable distance, suggesting that in the late 11th century no local producer could provide wares of equal quality.

In the 12th century, only one sherd from a type of cooking pot known to have been produced in south Wilts (F240) was noted, with a second from a pit outside the west front of the abbey. This ware is extremely common on sites of the period in Gloucestershire and Wiltshire, and its almost complete absence here is interesting. A similar situation was noted at St John's Hospital, Cirencester, with only single sherds from alternative domestic pottery producers (F203; F205), neither of which occurred at the abbey. Likewise, only two sherds were noted of non-local tripod pitchers, of a type common in Oxford at this period (F221).

By contrast, this pattern begins to alter with the emerging fashion for elaborately decorated and brightly coloured jugs first noticeable in the early 13th century, which local potteries did not seem to provide, although Minety jugs could be highly decorative. The earliest context producing sherds of this type of jug is the courtyard outside the west front, where sherds from bright copper green jugs from Stamford (Lincs) (F268) and highly decorated jugs from Ham Green in Bristol (F206) were recovered, in addition to a further example of a non-local tripod pitcher (F270). By the second half of the 13th century additional, and different, sources of these jugs are represented, and on the limited evidence available from contexts within the abbey, it would appear that the same sources of supply were used in the 14th century also. Minety jugs were more abundant in deposits - but plain. The most common sources of decorated jugs were those potteries at Brill (Bucks) (F207) and Nash Hill (north Wilts) (F219). Evidence for this is augmented by assessing the proportions of sherds in post-destruction pits and rubble layers. Several sources could not be clarified, but are clearly non-local (F223; F233; F234; F235; F269). In addition, sherds of Worcester-type jugs were also present (F239).

There is a transitional period between the late medieval and early post-medieval periods in which wares of medieval appearance and origin clearly linger into the new world of Renaissance refinery with its changing requirements and continental imports. The Minety industry is one of these, although the efforts of the potters to progress into the new age are noticeable. Sherds from 'medieval' style jugs from Bristol potteries (F262) and smaller more fashionable jugs from Malvern Chase, Worcs (F204) occur in latest abbey contexts, which are clearly marked by the almost sudden appearance of new vessel types, potting techniques and styles of wares from a wide range of sources, including the continent. This opening up of trade in pottery marks the end of the traditional potteries which served English markets for many centuries and the adaptation and development of others into the post-medieval world.

Changes in pottery usage in the medieval period
The most noticeable feature of the assemblages of pottery between the late 11th and early 13th centuries is the predominance of the hand-made jar, or cooking pot. These vessels would appear to conform to a demand for specific sizes; although most were similar, some were noticeably larger than others. With few exceptions the vessels were globular with upright or everted rims and sagging bases. Relatively few examples of straight-sided vessels with flanged, or 'club' rims were recovered (c. 1% of the total), and it seems likely that the function of these in the kitchen would have been different. The majority were produced in a coarse limestone-tempered ware (F202), but this pattern is not altered by the appearance of rare cooking pots in other fabrics (F200; F240). Indeed it seems possible that there was no open market in cooking pots at the abbey and that demand was directed to a particular producer. During the 13th century and thereafter until the end of the medieval period, the ceramic cooking vessel is less and less visible in the record. Once F202 ceased production at some point in the 13th century, products from Minety (F200) did not correspondingly rise in subsequent assemblages. Rather the type of vessel changed. Very large

wheel-thrown jars were produced by the Minety potteries during the late 13th and 14th centuries and later. Some of these may have been bung-hole cisterns, or jars for storage. Possibly this decline represents the use of metal cauldrons at this time. However, during the 15th century and into the post-medieval period, small, handled and lidded pipkins, or cooking vessels reappear. These vessels were made by Minety whilst other examples of wheel-thrown cooking wares from other sources are represented by sherds of vessels from Malvern Chase, Worcs (F204).

Domestic utensils apart from jars were very rare until the late medieval period here. In late 11th and 12th-century contexts only a single example of a handle socket for a bowl (fig. 88, 26) and the rim of a shallow bowl or pan was recognised (both in F202). Fourteenth-century contexts in the eastern extension produced a single sherd recognisable from a cistern in F200, although some sherds attributed to large jars may have belonged to cisterns. A small cylindrical cistern on tripod feet was recovered from a late medieval pit outside the west front (F200; fig. 89, 53). It seems likely that some of the large pans or conical bowls produced by the Minety industry in the late medieval period would have been used in dairy production (fig. 90, 60-4).

Until the late medieval period pottery vessels used at table were almost exclusively used to dispense beverages. These vessels were clearly distinguished from domestic pottery by more precise potting and firing; glazes to provide an impervious container, and decorations to delight those who used them. They would have been treasured longer than ordinary earthenwares and were obtained from potteries which specialised in their production, sometimes from far afield. This pattern is visible on the present site together with a greater demand for table wares over a period of time. During the late 11th century such items were rare in the post-conquest contexts. A single sherd from a glazed wheel-thrown, spouted pitcher, possibly from Stamford was noted (F254). Residual sherds produced five examples in total. In abbey construction contexts several examples of unglazed spouted pitchers of a similar form, some with stamped decoration, indicate that small quantities of table wares were produced by the local industry (F202; fig. 88, 22) These vessels were relatively small and open-mouthed, although tall rims may have prevented spillages.

Larger, hand-made tripod pitchers (spouted, although no examples were noted here) with strong handles and constricted necks first appear on the site in contexts associated with the abbey construction. These vessels are glazed partially at the base internally and overall externally and may be elaborately decorated. The majority of examples were produced by the Minety potteries (F200), with one or two 'copies' in the coarser local fabric (F202) and only rare examples from potteries outside the area (F221; F270; ?F232). Where larger fragments of the Minety products were recovered these do not show the elaboration of decoration or of handle construction noted in the 12th century in Gloucester (Vince 1983a, 126) and only pulled spouts were noted here. Tripod pitchers appear to have continued in use well into the 13th century here, with examples occurring in a group of the mid 13th century in the undercroft.

Tripod pitchers are large globular vessels, but at some point in the early 13th century a preference for tall, narrow jugs, with pulled clearly defined spouts came about. Presumably these were lighter and easier to pour, but they could be thrown on a wheel with the emphasis placed upon hand applied decoration. The earliest examples on the present site are sherds from wheel-thrown Stamford jugs in bright copper green (F268) and hand-made vessels with elaborate applied decoration from Ham Green, Bristol (F206). The mid to late 13th-century assemblage in the undercroft and residual material from post-destruction pits in this area indicate that by the second half of the 13th century a few specialist potteries were mass-producing fairly sophisticated products. Examples were reaching the abbey from Brill, Bucks (F207), Nash Hill, Wilts (F219) and the Worcester area (F239), with odd sherds from other jugs from a variety of (unidentified) non-local sources. However, these elaborately decorated pieces would appear to have been a passing fashion, because, amongst the relatively few sherds stratified within the 14th and later century contexts of the abbey, there is a marked preference for plain, dark green glazed jugs, often potted very thinly and precisely on a fast wheel. By the latest contexts in the life of the abbey jug sherds have become a relatively unimportant feature of the assemblages to be replaced by a sudden influx of vessels for the consumption of beverages, in three wide range of forms and from a range of sources including continental Europe. There is insufficient stratigraphic evidence to be able to pin this transition down, or to be able to determine when early types of drinking vessels, such as those produced in 'Tudor Green' (F220) make their first appearance, but sherds of a Cistercian ware cup (F244) were present in silts which had built up behind the choir stalls in which three coins dated to the late 15th century, were deposited. Presumably by the late 15th or early 16th century more sophisticated vessels in other materials were used for the serving of beverages at table in keeping with the general increase in demand for refinements by the wealthy at this time.

Throughout the medieval period miscellaneous vessels were produced in pottery where, presumably, no other material would have been suitable, and which added to the repertoires of the potteries. These miscellaneous products provide an indication of local, specialised, demand and localised 'traditional' products. During the early medieval period, post-conquest contexts produced few such products. A single example of a 'beehive base' or 'West Country Vessel' was noted in F231. This vessel has a shallow form like a truncated cooking pot with a flat base and perforated sides. The function is obscure. Many other, larger, perforated vessels were recovered from contexts between the 12th and late 13th centuries in F200 and F202. These vessels have opposing handles and are oval, rather than circular and have strengthening bands of applied clay around the rim. Some are sooted and burnt internally, and were first recorded as curfews, but they do not have top louvres or a top mounted handle. Others are glazed internally and sooted externally, and have knife-cut sagging bases; perhaps they are pans. The perforations are evenly spaced just below the clay band of the rim. A large group of sherds was stratified in the undercroft and other examples are present in post-destruction contexts in this area. Other examples were found in trenches outside the west front. Similarly, the function remains obscure.

During the late medieval period the number of ceramic oddities increased as though a certain amount of experimentation was taking place. The abbey site provides a glimpse of this with the recovery of an inkwell or condiment set from a Bristol pottery (F262, fig. 91, 73); money boxes, one of which was stratified in the silts below the choir stalls (F250, fig. 93, 114), with other examples in Minety ware (F200) from post-destruction contexts, and a tiny ?chafing dish with a yellow glaze (F200, fig. 89, 56).

TABLE 1: THE CIRENCESTER POST-ROMAN POTTERY TYPE-FABRIC SERIES

For abbreviations used here see page 98. Note that number F246 was not assigned.

TF	NAME & PARALLELS	SOURCE	HARDNESS	COLOUR	INCLUSIONS	VESSEL TYPES	POTTING TECHNIQUE	SURFACE TREATMENT	DECORATION	DATING	REFERENCES
200	Minety wares: 'Selsey common ware' Gloucester TF 44 Bath fabric 'J' Oxford Fabric BB	Minety, NE Wiltshire	Hard	Reduced core, light grey; pinkish buff surfaces (5YR 7/4)	Oolitic limestone, tempering, rare quartz grains	HMTP, HMCP, handled pans or curfews, ridge tiles, dripping pans. Jugs, jars, bowls, pipkins, lids, skillets, cisterns, money boxes, chafing dishes	HM / WT	Lead glaze	Combing, applied strips, slashing	E12-M13 / 13th-E16th	Dunning 1949 Musty 1973 Vince 1979b,29 Vince 1982, 202 Vince 1983a,126,130 Vince 1985
201	Ashton Keynes wares, Gloucester TF 80	Ashton Keynes, NE Wiltshire	Hard	Oxidised Light red (5YR 7/8); can be reduced Dark grey	Sand-tempered with rare chalk, red/black iron ore	Jugs, jars, bowls, pipkins, lids, plates, chafing dishes, tankards, chamber pots, flower pots. Dripping pans, ridge tiles, stove tiles, drains	WT / HM	Lead glaze	Roller stamps	E16-L18	Vince 1983a,132
202	Coarse limestone - tempered ware	?local to Cirencester	Soft to hard	Brownish through to light red (5YR 5/6 - 2YR 5/6) or black & dark grey	Oolitic & other limestone, red iron ore. Quartz grains	HMCP, bowls, lamps, spouted pitchers, tripod pitchers, jugs, handled pans or curfews	HM	Rarely glazed	Stamped	L11-L12? or early 13th	Vince 1982, 203
203	Malvernian cooking pots Gloucester TF 40	Malvern Hills	Hard	Dark brown	Malvernian rock fragments, quartz grains, mica	HMCP	HM			E12	Vince 1977a Vince 1982,203-4 Vince 1983a,126
204	Malvernian glazed wares Gloucester TF 52	Malvern Hills, Herefords & Worcs	Hard	Light red (5YR 7/6) to pinkish (5YR 7/4)	Malvernian rock, quartz grains	Jugs, jars, CP, bowls, pipkins, chafing dishes	WT	Lead glaze with copper green flecks		14-E17th	Vince 1977a Vince 1982,205 Vince 1983a,132
205	East Wilts/Berks, flint-tempered ware: Oxford fabric AQ	?Berkshire	Hard	Dark grey, through buff to pinkish	Quartz sand, grey flint fragments, chalk inclusions	CP	HM			12-13th	Haldon & Mellor 1977,115 Mellor 1980a Vince 1982,204
206	Ham Green ware Gloucester TF 53 Bath Fabric I	Pill, Bristol	Hard	Reduced grey pinkish surfaces where visible	Quartz & limestone sand, clay pellets	Jugs	HM	Lead glaze	combing, incised lines applied pads & strips	E-M13th	Barton 1963 Vince 1979b,29 Vince 1982,204
207	Brill-type wares Oxford fabrics AM & AW	Brill, Bucks & other sources	Hard	Pale creamy buff to pirk (5YR 7/6)	Quartz, rare iron ore	Jugs	WT	Lead glaze with copper	Rouleting stamps, paint, applied strips	M13-14th	Haldon & Mellor 1977 118-119; Mellor 1980b, 177-179; Jope 1954

TF	NAME & PARALLELS	SOURCE	HARDNESS	COLOUR	INCLUSIONS	VESSEL TYPES	POTTING TECHNIQUE	SURFACE TREATMENT	DECORATION	DATING	REFERENCES
208	Cistercian Wares Gloucester TF60?	Unknown	Hard	Dark red/brown (2.5YR 6/6)	Quartz grains, ?sandstone frags, iron ore	Handled cups, goblet?	WT	Iron rich lead glaze	Applied white clay pads	E16-E17	Vince 1983a, 132
209	Tin-glazed wares	London, Bristol & Netherlands	Soft to hard	Off-white to buff & pink	Rare iron ore	'Albarellos', ointment pots, plates, cups, bowls, mugs, chamber pots	WT, moulded	Tin glaze, lead glaze on plate backs	Painted	E16-L18	
210	Verwood ware	Dorset	Hard	Dark pink	Quartz sand	Bowl or jar	WT	Lead glaze		L17th	
211	"Cream wares"	Staffs	Hard	Pale cream		Table services	WT, slip moulded	Glazed		18th	
212	Wheelthrown slip-decorated wares	Staffs	Hard	Pinkish (2.5YR 6/6)	Clay streaks, red iron ore	Plates	WT	Lead glaze	White slip trailing	L17	Celoria & Kelly 1973
213	"Slip-ware"	Staffs	Hard	Pale buff to light brown (10YR 8/4)	Red clay streaks	Circular & oblong plates	Moulded	Lead glaze	Brown & 'red' trailed slip, impressed cockle shells around rims	L17-M18	Kelly & Greaves 1974
214	Transfer printed "China"	Staffs & other sources	V hard	Off white		Table services, chamber pots	Moulded, slip cast	Glaze	Transfers applied	L18-19th	
215	White salt-glazed stonewares	Staffs	V hard	Off white		Table services	WT, turned moulded	salt glaze	Mouldings incised blue filled lines	M-L18th	Kelly & Greaves 1974
216	Frechen stoneware	Rhineland	V hard	Blue-grey		Drinking jugs, bottles	WT	Mottled salt glaze	Applied moulded motifs	M16-M17th	
217	Westerwald	Rhineland	V hard	Blue-grey		Tankards	WT	Blue-grey salt glaze	Incised lines, paint moulded motifs	L17-M18th	
218	Porcelain	China, Japan	V hard	Off-white, translucent		Table services	WT, turned	Clear glaze	Painted	18-19th+	
219	Nash Hill wares	Nash Hill, NW Wilts	Hard	Dark reddish-brown (5YR 7/8)	Quartz sand, sandstone, iron	Jugs, tiles, ridge tile, Louvre	WT, HM	White slip, lead glaze with copper	Paint	L13-14th	McCarthy 1974
220	"Tudor Green"	Surrey/Hants	Hard	Off-white	Quartz sand	Handled cups, jugs, chafing dish?	WT	Copper glaze, lead glaze		15-E16th	Holling 1977
221	Oxford medieval ware?; Newbury fabric S	Unknown	Hard	Grey to brown	Quartz sand			White slip, copper glaze			Vince forthcoming
222	Surrey/Hants border wares	Surrey/Hants	Hard	Off-white to cream	Quartz sand, iron ore & chalk fragments	Tripod pipkins, bowls, chafing dishes, mugs	WT	Lead glaze	Ribbing	E17th	Holling 1971 Haslam 1975

No.	Ware	Source	Hardness	Colour	Inclusions	Forms	WT/HM	Glaze	Decoration	Date	Reference
223		unknown	Hard	Pale grey	Quartz sand, rare black iron	Jug	WT	Lead glaze	Thumbed down base	L13th?	
224	Fine micaceous earthen ware Gloucester TF 54	Gloucs/Herefords border	Soft to hard	Reddish-yellow (5YR 6/6)	Rare iron ore	Copies of Raeren jugs, bowls	WT	Lead glaze	Grilled base	E16-18th	Vince 1977b Vince 1983a,134
225	Raeren stonewares	Rhineland	V hard	Blue-grey		Drinking jugs	WT	Salt glaze	Frilled bases	E-M16th	Hurst 1964
226	Marbled Cistercian ware	Unknown	Hard	Red & cream clays mixed	Quartz grains	Handled cups	WT	Lead glaze		M-L16th?	
227	Merida ware	Iberian peninsular	Hard	Pinkish (5YR 7/6)	Quartz & rock fragments, mica	Costrels, bowls lid	WT turned			15-17th	Hurst 1977
228	Cologne stoneware	Germany	V hard	Brownish grey		Drinking jugs, tankards	WT	Brown salt	Applied moulded motifs	M16th	
229	Martincamp flasks	N France	V hard	Pale grey		Bottles or flasks	WT	Kiln gloss		15-E17th	Hurst 1960-64
230	Early Ashton Keynes	NE Wilts?	Hard	Reduced core, buff to light red surfaces	Quartz & oolitic limestone 'sand'	Pipkins, jugs lids, bowls	WT	Lead glaze	Combing	L15-E16th?	
231		NE Wilts?	Soft	Light brown (5YR 5/3)	Oolitic limestone, flint, shell and quartz	HMCP 'Beehive'	HM			12th or earlier	
232		Unknown	Soft	Pale buff	Quartz sand, rare ?slate, iron ore	Jugs	WT	Lead glaze	Applied strips, finger nail impressions, combing	L13th-?	
233		Unknown	Hard	Pale orange (5YR 7/4) grey core	Quartz sand, (sub-rounded milky & clear grains)	Jugs	WT	Copper glaze	Applied strips	L13th-?	
234		Unknown	Hard	Buff to brown (5YR 6/6) grey core	Quartz sand, rare ?chert & iron ore	Jugs	WT	Lead glaze	Slashing	L13th?	
235		Unknown	V soft	Pale pink (5 YR 8/4)	Fine quartz	Jugs	WT	Copper glaze on interior		L13th-?	
236	Iron-glazed ware	Staffs	V hard	Buff (10YR 8/3)	Clay pellets, iron ore	Tankards, chamber pots	WT	Glaze	Ribbing	L17-M18th	Kelly 1973
237	Miscellaneous, unprovenanced stonewares										

TF	NAME & PARALLELS	SOURCE	HARDNESS	COLOUR	INCLUSIONS	VESSEL TYPES	POTTING TECHNIQUE	SURFACE TREATMENT	DECORATION	DATING	REFERENCES
238	Black-glazed wares	Staffs & Midlands	V hard	Brick red (10YR 6/8)	Quartz grains, sandstone, clay pellets, iron ore	Handled cups, chamber pots	WT	Lead glaze		L17-E18th	
239	Worcester-type jugs	Worcs/Glos?	Hard	Reddish-brown (5YR 7/6)	Quartz sand, rare iron ore and sandstone	Jugs	WT	White slip copper glaze	Rouletting, applied pads & strips	13th	Barton 1967
240	Bath fabric 'A': Gloucester TF 48	W.Wilts	Hard	Dk brown, to black or buff	Polished quartz, flint, mica, chalky limestone in varying amounts						
241	"Slip wares"	Staffs or Bristol	Hard		Clay pellets, rare iron ore	Handled cups, chamber pots	WT	Glazed	Painted slips	L17-18th	Barton 1961 Celoria & Kelly 1973
242	Black-glazed wares	East Anglia	Soft	Brick red (2.5YR 6/6)	Fine quartz	Handled cups	WT	Lead glaze	Ribbing	17th	
243	Miscellaneous, unprovenanced earthenwares										
244	Cistercian ware	?Gloucs	Hard		Rare quartz	Handled cups, goblet? lids	WT	Lead applied white clay pads		L15-16th	
245	'Saintonge' ware	SW France	Soft	Off white	Abundant mica	Jugs, chafing dishes	WT	Lead glaze	Moulded faces, combs stamps	15-16th	Hurst 1974
247		Unknown (similar to Winchester ware?)	Hard	Off-white	Fine quartz-sand, rare black iron ore	Spouted pitcher	WT	Crackled lead glaze		L11th?	Biddle & Barclay 1974
248	French flasks										
249	Nottingham	Notts	V hard		Fine quartz	Tankards	WT turned	Iron wash salt glaze	Rouletting	18th	Hurst 1966
250	Micaceous ware	Unknown ?local	Hard	Light red (2.5YR 6/6)	Oolitic limestone, quartz, iron ore	Jug, money box	WT	Lead glaze	Frilled base	L15-16th	
251	Sandy earthenware	Unknown, possibly Donyatt	Hard	Reddish (2.5YR 6/8)	Quartz sand, iron ore	Jars	WT	Lead glaze		17th?	
252	Miscellaneous flower pots										
253	Siegburg stoneware	Germany	V hard	Cream to grey		Beaker, tankard	WT		Applied moulded friezes	15-16th	Beckmann 1974
254		Unknown (possibly Stamford?)	Hard	Off-white	Fine quartz	Spouted pitcher	WT	Lead glaze		L11th?	

No.	Name	Source	Hardness	Colour	Inclusions	Forms	Manufacture	Glaze/Surface	Decoration	Date	Reference
255	Hand-made early Saxon wares - see p. 103										
256	Black-glazed bowls	Staffs	Hard	Mixed red & cream clays	Quartz grains, iron ore?	Large deep bowls	WT	Red slip		L18th	Celoria & Kelly 1973
257	Brown wares	Staffs	Hard	Chocolate brown		Tea & coffee pots	WT	Glazed	Incised lines	M-L18th	
258	Wedgewood black basalte, jasper ware etc	Staffs	V hard	Charcoal grey, black, blue green		Table services	Slipcast, turned		Moulded	M-L18th onwards	
259	Cream-bodied kitchen wares	Staffs etc	V hard	Buff-cream		Kitchen bowls, plates etc	Moulded	Glazed	Moulded	L18-19th onwards	
260	Sand-free ware	NE Wilts?	V hard	Brick red (10R 6/8)	Rare oolitic limestone, iron ore	Bowls	WT	Glazed		M18th	
261	Early Staffs stoneware	Staffs	V hard	Cream to grey		Drinking cups, tankards	WT turned	Iron & white washes, salt glazed	Ribbing	E-M 18th	Kelly 1973
262	Bristol/Redcliffe ware	Bristol	V hard	Grey core pinkish surfaces (5YR 7/6)	Quartz sand, clay pellets	Jugs, inkwell set	WT, HM	Lead glaze with copper		L13-15th	Dawson, Jackson & Ponsford 1972
263	Fulham stoneware	London	V hard	Pale grey	Black iron specks	Mugs	WT	Salt glaze	Ribbing	L17-E18th	Christophers, Hazelgrove & Pearcey 1974
264	Stoneware	?London	V hard	Cream	Black iron ore	Tankard	WT	White slip, salt glaze		18th	
265	N French Jugs	N France	Hard	Off white	Quartz grains mica	Jug	WT	Lead glaze		13th	
266		?Netherlands	Soft	Off white	V fine quartz	?Albarello	WT	Bright green glaze		16th	
267		Unknown	Soft	Reddish (2.5YR 6/6)	Fine quartz & black iron sand, mica	Ointment pot	WT	White slip		17th?	
268	Developed Stamford	Stamford	Hard	Off-white	Rare iron & ?chalk	Jugs	WT	Copper glaze		L12-E13th	Kilmurry 1977, 1980
269		Unknown, possibly nr Laverstock, S Wilts?	Soft	Buff to cream (7.5YR 7/4)	Quartz sand, rare iron ore	Jugs	WT	Lead glaze	Applied strips, stabbing folded base	L13-14th?	Musty, Algar & Ewence 1969
270		Unknown	Hard	Off-white	Quartz sand, white clay pellets		HM	Lead glaze	Applied pellets, combing	E13th?	

TABLE 2 : INCIDENCE OF FABRICS AND VESSEL TYPES IN POST-CONQUEST CONTEXTS PRIOR TO THE CONSTRUCTION OF THE ABBEY (SHERD COUNTS ONLY)

PHASE 1b VESSEL TYPE	Hand-made CPs			Beehive bases	Glazed pitchers	Intrusions	Total
FABRIC	F255	F202	F231	F231	F254		
ROBBING OF SAXON WALLS	1	47	1		1	F206?	51
'GRAVEYARD' SOILS		17				F269?	18
'NORMAN' STRUCTURE		6		6 ?1Vessel			12
TOTAL	1	70	1	6	1	2	81

TABLE 3: INCIDENCE OF FABRICS AND VESSEL TYPES IN CONTEXTS ASSOCIATED WITH THE CONSTRUCTION OF THE ABBEY (*c.* 1130 to *c.* 1176) (SHERD COUNTS ONLY)

PHASE 2 VESSEL TYPE	Hand-made CPs			Unglazed SP's	Bowl	Lamps	Hand-made TPs			Curfew / Pan	Total
FABRIC	F202	F231	F240	F202	F202	F202	F202	F200	F221	F200	
MAKE-UP LAYERS (TO LEVEL SITE)	106		1	15	1			8	1	1	133
MAKE-UP LAYERS (FOR FLOORING)	286	2		23		2	4	7	1		325
12TH CENT. FLOORS (MORTAR AND CLAY)	3										3
FOUNDATION PACKING OF 12TH CENT. WALLS							?1				1
TOTAL	395	2	1	38	1	2	5	15	2	1	462

TABLE 4 : INCIDENCE OF FABRICS AND VESSEL TYPE DURING THE USE OF THE ABBEY: CONTEXTS OUTSIDE THE WEST FRONT OF THE ABBEY PRODUCING EARLY TO MID 13TH-CENTURY MATERIAL (SHERD COUNTS ONLY)

PHASE 3a VESSEL TYPE / FABRIC	Hand-made CPs				Hand-made TPs			Beehive base	Curfew/ Pan	Spouted pitcher	Jugs						Total
	F255	F202	F240	F200	F202	F200	F270	F202	F202/F200	F202	F200	F206	F268	F265	F233	F243	
PITS/ROBBING EARLIER THAN COURTYARD	1	88	1	2		10			1								103
MAKE UP LAYERS FOR COURTYARD		75				4				1				1			82
COURTYARD SURFACES		50			3	41	1		2		1	9	1				108
POST HOLES/ FEATURES CUT THROUGH COURTYARD				1?		3					3					1	8
MEDIEVAL DITCH CUTTING COURTYARD		2				6		1					1		1		11
PITS LATER THAN COURTYARD		17				2											19
TOTAL	1	232	1	3	3	66	1	1	3	1	4	9	2	2	1	1	331

TABLE 5: INCIDENCE OF FABRICS & VESSEL TYPES DURING THE USE OF THE ABBEY MID 13TH TO 15TH CENTURIES (SHERD COUNT ONLY)

VESSEL TYPE:	HMCP		SP	HMTP		Pan/?Curfew			Jugs								WT Jars	Cistern	Cup	Total
PHASE 3b-d — FABRIC	202	231	202	200	202	202/200	202	200	207	223	219	239	269	233	262	204	200	200	220	Total
REPAIRS TO FLOORING IN UNDERCROFT PRIOR TO ERECTION OF PARTITION — 3b	49	1		36	2	c. 90	1	18	5	6			2							210
ERECTION OF TIMBER PARTITION IN UNDERCROFT — 3b				2					1											3
FLOORING POST-DATING PARTITION — 3c	11			36					6	5	1									59
CONSTRUCTION OF NORTH TRANSEPT APSE EXTENSTION — 3c	7		1									1								9
CONSTRUCTION OF EASTERN EXTENTION; NEW FLOORS; BUTRESSING — 3c				1													1	1		3
INSERTION OF TOMBS IN EASTERN EXTENSION — 3c									1								5			6
TOMB IN SOUTH PRESBYTERY AISLE — 3c	1																1			2
COBBLED AREA OUTSIDE WEST FRONT — 3c									1											1
ALTERATIONS TO CLAUSTRAL RANGE — 3c	6			12							1			10			2			31
PIT OUTSIDE WEST FRONT — 3d																	2	1v		3v
PRE-DESTRUCTION DEPOSITS OUTSIDE WEST FRONT — 3d				1	1				1						3	1			1	8
TOTAL	74	1	1	88	3	c. 90	1	18	15	11	2	1	2	10	3	1	11	2	1	335

TABLE 6: INCIDENCE OF FABRICS & VESSEL TYPES DURING THE LATEST USE OF THE ABBEY (SHERD COUNTS ONLY)

PHASE 3e

VESSEL TYPE	HMCP	HMTP	Jugs			Flask	Cistern	Drinking jugs			WT Jars		Lids	Conical bowl		Money box	Drug jars	Drinking cups			Total
FABRIC	202	200	200	269	201	248	200	225	224	216	200	201	200	200	201	250	209	244	208	220	
RELAID & REPAIRED FLOORING IN USE BEFORE DEMOLITION	3	1			1		1?		1	1	7		1	2	1		1	4	14		38
SOIL BUILT UP ON FLOOR SURFACES			1	1		1	1?			1	1				1				1	4	12
SOIL BUILT UP BEHIND & BELOW CHOIR STALLS																1v		1			2
ALTERATIONS TO THE CHAPTER HOUSE	1		1		1			1		1		1			1			3	8	1	19
TOTAL	4	1	2	1	2	1	2	1	1	3	8	1	1	2	3	1v	1	8	23	5	71

TABLE 7: INCIDENCE OF FABRICS & VESSEL TYPES AT TIME OF ABBEY DEMOLITION AND THROUGHOUT DESTRUCTION PERIOD (SHERD COUNTS ONLY)

PHASE 4a-c VESSEL TYPE	Misc jars					Pipkins			Lids		Chamber pots	Cistern	Jugs			
FABRIC	200	204	201	243	251?	200	230	201	200	201	251	200	200	201	204	230
ROBBING PRE-DATING RUBBLE DEPOSITS 4a			2	1			1v						2	1		
PRIMARY RUBBLE DEPOSITS 4b	5		7		1	1		1	1	1	1?	1	5	11	7	6
ROBBING POST-DATING RUBBLE DEPOSITS 4c	4	1					1						1	8		
TOTAL	9	1	9	1	1	1	2	1	1	1	1	1	8	20	7	6

PHASE 4a-c VESSEL TYPE	Drinking jugs					Flask	Drug jars	Bottle	Cups					Tankards	
FABRIC	224	225	228	216	209	248	209	216	208	220	244	242	238	201	236
Phase 4a				4			2	2	11		1				
Phase 4b	2	7	1	26	1v	1		3	59	5	17	1	1?*	6	
Phase 4c		1	1	9		2			15	1	1		1*	1	1*
TOTAL	2	8	2	39	1	3	2	5	85	6	19	1	2*	7	1*

PHASE 4a-c VESSEL TYPE	Misc bowls							Plates		Chafing dish	Meat dishes		Money boxes		Goblet/ ?figure	Total
FABRIC	200	201	230	251	227	224	222	201	251	201	200	201	200	250	208	
Phase 4a		2	3					2?							1	35
Phase 4b	7	37	1	2		1	1	7	1	2	2	1	1	1		252
Phase 4c		22			1			5								76
TOTAL	7	61	4	2	1	1	1	14	1	2	2	1	1	1	1	363

* = possible intrusions

TABLE 8: INCIDENCE OF FABRICS & VESSEL TYPES IN FEATURES ASSOCIATED WITH GARDENING ACTIVITIES - 17TH TO EARLY 18TH CENTURIES (SHERD COUNTS ONLY)

PHASE 5 VESSEL TYPE	Jars		Lids	Jugs				Drinking jugs					Tankards			
FABRIC	201	204	201	201	220	204	224	225	228	216	217	237	201	253	263	236
FLOWER BEDS & LINEAR FEATURES 5a	1	2		21			1	2	1	21		1	5	1	1	2
GRAVEL PATHS, DRIVES 5a	1			2		1				1	1		2			
CONSTRUCTION OF GARDEN WALLS 5a	1			1						5						
DRAINAGE FEATURES 5a			1	1						9			1			1
REDEPOSITED RUBBLE 5b	7			1		1							2			1
RUBBISH PITS EARLIER THAN c. 1710 5c				2	1	2		3	3	1						
TOTAL	10	2	1	27	1	4	1	5	4	37	1	1	10	1	1	4

PHASE 5 VESSEL TYPE	Cups							Bottles/ Flasks			Chafing dishes		Skillet	Misc bowls			
FABRIC	220	244	208	238	242	241	209	248	216	227	201	245	201	201	222	224	204
FLOWER BEDS & LINEAR FEATURES 5a	3	6	26	2			1	2	11	1	2		1	44	2	2	1
GRAVEL PATHS & DRIVES 5a			3											4			
CONSTRUCTION OF GARDEN WALLS 5a			4											1			
DRAINAGE FEATURES 5a		1	7	2	1						2	1		5			1
REDEPOSITED RUBBLE 5b	3	4	41	3	1	1		1			3			9		1	1
EARLIER THAN c. 1710 5c		2	3	1										6		1	
TOTAL	6	13	84	8	4	1	1	3	12	1	7	1	1	69	2	4	3

PHASE 5 VESSEL TYPE	Plates					Chamber pots		Meat dish	Flower pots	Misc vessels			Total
FABRIC	201	230	209	213	215	209	201	201	252	209	267	266	
FLOWER BEDS & LINEAR FEATURES 5a	16	1	2	1		3		1	3	1	1	1	193
GRAVEL PATHS & DRIVES 5a													15
CONSTRUCTION OF GARDEN WALLS 5a													12
DRAINAGE FEATURES 5a	2		1		2	1							39
REDEPOSITED RUBBLE 5b	3						1						84
RUBBISH PITS EARLIER THAN c. 1710 5c	1								1				27
TOTAL	22	1	3	1	2	4	1	1	4	1	1	1	370

TABLE 9: INCIDENCE OF FABRICS & VESSEL TYPES IN 18TH-CENTURY FEATURES
(SHERD COUNTS ONLY)

PHASE 6 VESSEL TYPE	Kitchen wares						Table wares													
	Jug	Lid	Bowls				Plates						Tankards							
FABRIC	201	201	201	256	259	260	209	213	215	238	214	201	201	241	261	217	236	249	215	238
PIT BP I 4 6a	4		10	1		1	1	2		1			1		2	2	1	1		
STONE STRUCTURE & CULVERT 6b	2	1	2																1	1
LATE RUBBLE SPREADS 6c	2		11						2		1	5		1			1		1	
STONY LAYER 6d	1				1	1														
TOTAL	9	1	23	1	1	1	1	2	2	1	1	5	1	1	2	2	1	1	2	1

PHASE 6 VESSEL TYPE	Tea/Coffee wares				Chafing dish	Drug jars etc	Chamber pots		Flower pots	Drain pipe	Total
FABRIC	215	257	258	218	201	209	209	236	252	201	
PIT BP I 4 6a	6	1				2	2				38
STONE STRUCTURE & CULVERT 6b				1					2		10
LATE RUBBLE SPREADS 6c				1	2					1	28
STONY LAYER 6d			1					1	1		6
TOTAL	6	1	1	2	2	2	3		3	1	82

CATALOGUE OF ILLUSTRATED POTTERY

Fig. 87

1. HMCP/beehive base?, F231, oxidised surfaces, grey core. BH IV 34, pre-abbey 'Norman' structure, phase 1b.
2. HMCP, F202, coarse fabric, fired dark brown. BP VII 10, robbing of Saxon buildings, phase 1b.
3. HMCP, F202, fired black throughout. BP VII 2, robbing of Saxon buildings, phase 1b.
4. HMCP, F202, spalled surfaces, decorated rim top. BT I 17, stony layer pre-dating courtyard, phase 3a.
5. HMCP, F202, join visible where rim moulded to body of vessel. BV II 21, 12th-13th century context, phase 3.
6. HMCP, F202. BV I 6.
7. HMCP, F202, coarse fabric fired grey-brown overall. BV II 19.
8. HMCP, F202. 65 BK V 21/25, make-up layer for abbey construction, phase 2.
9. HMCP, F202, neck slashed at the join of the strip of clay used for the rim and the body of the vessel. 65 BK V 21/25, make-up layer for abbey construction, phase 2.
10. HMCP, F202, the lip of the rim was probably formed by hand rotation. BV III 11, rubble associated with courtyard, phase 3a.
11. HMCP, F202, fired black throughout. BV I 1E.
12. HMCP, F202, wheel-finished rim, reduced grey, burnt? BH V 28, make-up layer for 12th-century flooring, phase 2
13. HMCP, F202, sooting on exterior. BV III 29, pit, phase 3a.
14. HMCP, F202, fired black throughout. BV III 35, robber trench, phase 1b.
15. HMCP, F202, hand-rotated rim with finger tipping. BP I 11, feature associated with a stone drain, phase 6b?
16. HMCP, F202, sooted. BV IV 28, levelling for floor in undercroft, phase 3b.
17. HMCP, F202, blackened overall. BV III 24, trough, possibly robbing trench, phase 3a.
18. HMCP, F202?, blackened overall. BT I 19, stony layer associated with courtyard, phase 3a.
19. HMCP, F202, sooted on exterior. BH IV 28, levelling for floor in undercroft, phase 3b.
20. HMCP, F202, oxidised brown interior, sooted exterior. BH IV 28, levelling for floor in undercroft, phase 3b.
21. HMCP, F202, fired black. BP II 11, robbing feature, phase 1b.

Fig. 88

22. Spouted pitcher, F202, oxidised orangey-brown. BT I 1, U/S.
23. HMCP/pitcher, F202, oxidised surfaces, stamp shown in inset. BG VII 34, make-up layer for 12th-century floor, phase 2.
24. Pitcher, F202, oxidised light brown surfaces, stamp is shown in inset. BT I 1, U/S.
25. Pitcher, F202, oxidised surfaces, interior leached, stamp shown in inset. BH IV 31, make-up level for 12th-century floor, phase 2.

26. Spout from a pitcher or socket handle of a ?bowl, F202, oxidised orange-brown surfaces. BV I 6.
27. Lid or lamp, F202, crudely shaped. BH VII 18, make-up layer for 12th-century floor in chapter house, phase 2.
28. Handle of ?pitcher, F202, oxidised reddish-brown, decorated with rows of stabbing. BJ IX 2, robbing feature, post-abbey destruction, residual, phase 4c.
29. HM bowl, dish or fry pan, F202, sooted exterior. BG III 21, levelling for abbey construction, phase 2.
30. HMTP, F202?, sparse glaze on handle. BG IV 23, pre-dissolution or post-demolition disturbed layer, phase 3e-4.
31. HMTP, F202?, thinly applied glaze to exterior, possibly F200. BV III 11, rubble associated with courtyard, phase 3a.
32. HMTP, F202, pale yellow glaze, comb decoration. BH IX 1, topsoil, U/S.
33. Curfew or pan?, F202, internally sooted and spalled. BH VI 17, levelling in undercroft, phase 3b.
34a. HM jug, F202, patchy spots of glaze, rim wheel-finished, oxidised. BH X 4, rubble deposit, post-dissolution, residual, phase 4b
34b. HM jug, F202, unglazed, oxidised. BH VI 17, levelling in undercroft, phase 3b.
35. Jug or TP, F200, elaborate slashing on handle, applied pellets on rim top, very dark green glaze. BM III 6, rubble deposit, post-dissolution, phase 4b.
36. Globular jar or pitcher, F200, glazed on exterior, leached on interior. BG VII 12, redeposited rubble, post-dissolution, residual, phase 5.
37. HMTP, F200, glazed inside and out. BN IV 10, unphased.
38. HMTP, F200, overall glaze, deep slashes parallel to handle, method of fixing by clay plug visible. BV III 5, courtyard outside west front of abbey, phase 3a.
39. HMTP, F200, handle; deep central slash with side slashing, patchy glaze. BH V 45, make-up layer for 12th-century floor in chapter house, phase 2.

Fig. 89

40. HM jar, F200, reduced, internally glazed, decorated with stabbing and combing. BV III 28, pit, phase 3a.
41. HMCP, F200, ?wheel-finished rim, glazed internally. BV III 28, pit, phase 3a.
42. WTCP/jar, F200, unglazed. BP V 6 Pit, residual, phase 3.
43. WTCP/jar, F200, splash of glaze on rim top. BH X 2, flower bed, residual, phase 5.
44. WTCP/pipkin, with lid-seat, F200, band of glaze on rim top and splashes on exterior. BJ XVII 1, residual, U/S.
45. WTCP/pipkin, with lid-seat, F200, splashes of glaze on rim top and neck. BP I 6, residual, phase 5-6.
46. Pipkin with lid-seating, F200, thin external cover of glaze, sooted. BJ XIV 2, residual, late 18th-century rubble spreads, phase 6c.
47. Lid of pipkin, F200, wheel-thrown and turned, splashes of glaze and considerable sooting on exterior. BL V 14, robbing of crossing area, phase 4a.

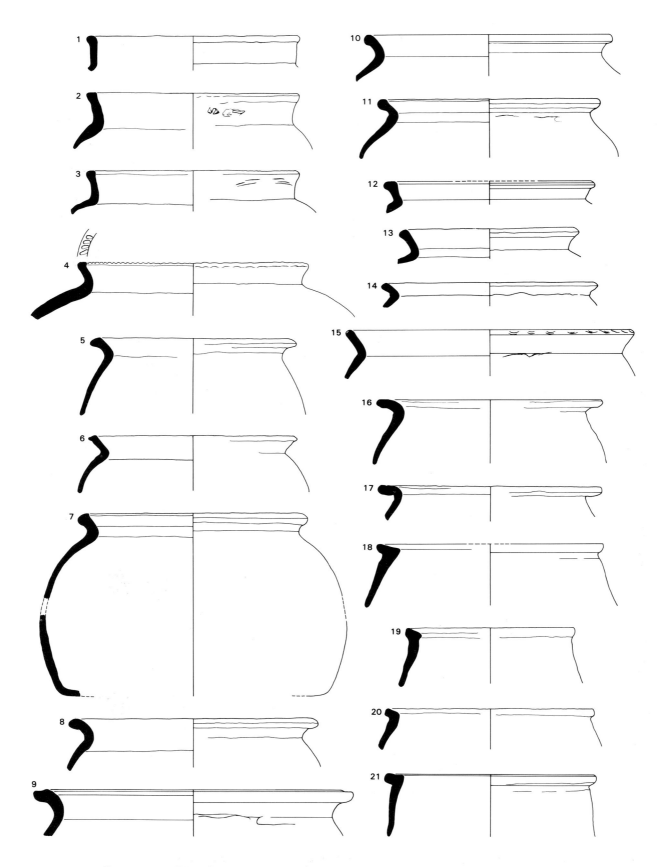

87. Medieval pottery, F202, limestone-tempered ware, 1:4

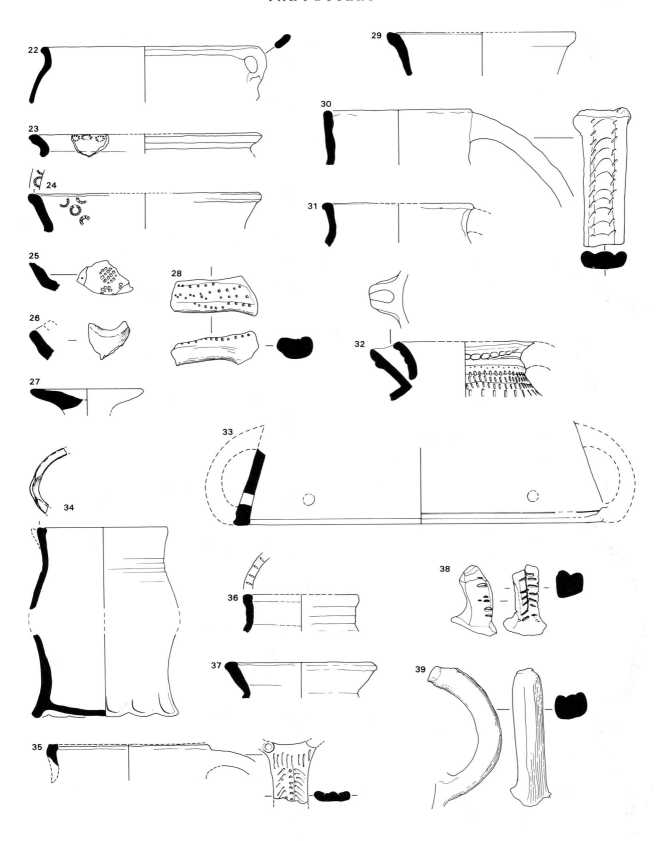

88. Medieval pottery, nos. 22-34, F202, limestone-tempered ware; nos. 35-39, F200, Minety ware, 1:4

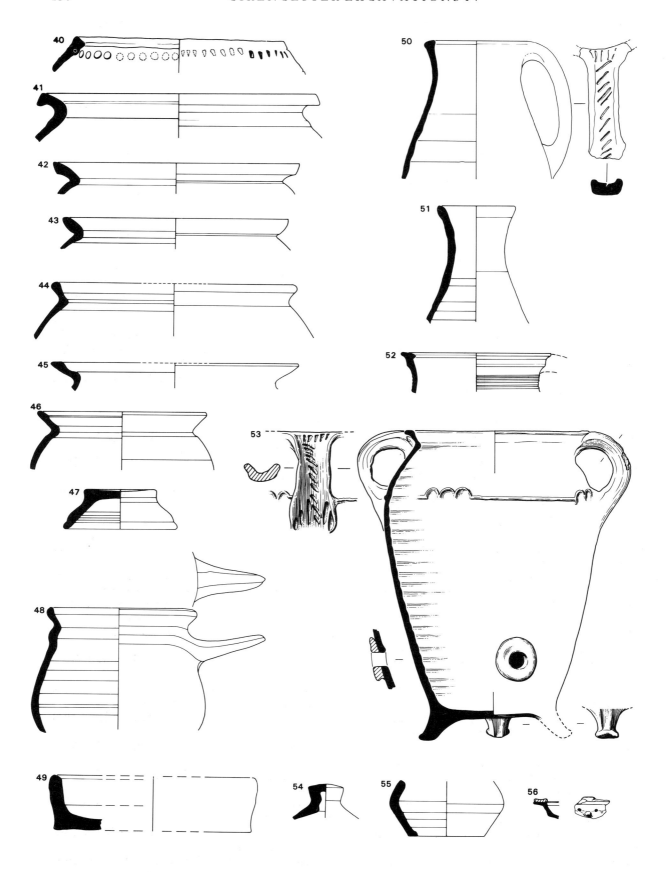

89. Medieval pottery, nos. 40-56, F200, Minety ware, 1:4

48. Pipkin with straight handle, F200, bib of glaze below handle. BJ VIII 7, rubble layer, phase 4b.
49. Dripping pan/meat dish, F200, hand-made, splashes of glaze internally. BH V 8, rubble layer, phase 4b.
50. WT jug, F200, strap handle diagonally slashed, thin, patchy glaze, residual? BG IV 33, pit, phase 4a.
51. WT jug, F200, runnels of glaze in direction of rim mouth. BN I 11, intrusive in mixed layer, phase 2.
52. WT jug, F200, handle scar, oxidised with splashes of glaze. BN IV 8, residual, phase 5-6.
53. Cistern, F200, splashes of glaze on shoulder. BP I 19, 15th-century pit, phase 3d.
54. Top of money box?/lid knob?, F200, thin coating of glaze on the exterior. BP III 4, robber trench, residual.
55. Money box/bottle?, F200, unglazed. BL V 6, rubble deposit, phase 4b.
56. Chafing dish, F200, thick yellow glaze overall. 65 BK I 4, flower bed, phase 5.

Fig. 90
57. Curfew/pan?, F200, internally sooted, splashes of glaze on exterior, hand-made. BH VI 17, levelling in undercroft, phase 3b.
58. Curfew/pan?, F200, internal glazing, horizontal slashes on handle, hand-made. BN I 9, redeposited rubble, residual, phase 5.
59. Curfew/pan?, F200, internally glazed, handle attached to vessel by 'plug', hand-made. BV III 7, pit, phase 3a.
60. Bowl ,WT, F200, unglazed. BP IV 1, residual, U/S.
61. Conical bowl, F200, internally glazed. BJ XIV 2, late 18th-century rubble spreads, residual, phase 6c.
62. Conical bowl, F200, wavey combed decoration, glazed on interior. BM II 1, topsoil , residual.
63. Conical bowl, F200, glazed internally. BJ XIV 2, late 18th-century rubble spreads, residual, phase 6c.
64. Conical bowl, F200, splashes of glaze on interior. BJ XII 2, rubble layer, phase 4b.
65. Conical bowl/platter, F200, combed decoration on flange. BJ XII 2, rubble layer, phase 4b.

Fig. 91
66. HMCP/pitcher, F240, oxidised brown surfaces. BL IX 7, make-up layer for abbey construction, phase 2.
67. HMCP, F240, oxidised brown surfaces. BV III 29, pit, phase 3a.
68. WT jug, F268, patches of copper green glaze on exterior. BT I 21, L-shaped ditch post-dating courtyard, phase 3a.
69a & b. HM jug, F206, external glaze. BV III 6, pit earlier than courtyard, phase 3a.
70a. WT jug, F207, glaze runnels in direction of rim mouth. BG IV 21, rubbish survival?, phase 4a.
70b. WT jug, F207, elaborate decoration: rouletted, applied strips, painted. BG IV 23, 17, disturbed layer, phase 4a.
71. WT jug, F219, white slip under copper green glaze. BG IV 33, pit, phase 4a.
72. WT jug, F262, internal glaze. BP II 8, soil layer, pre-destruction of abbey?, phase 3d.

73. Inkwell set? F262, overall glaze, hand-made. BP II 7, rubble, residual, phase 4b.
74. WT? jug, F269?, stabbed decoration, clear exterior glaze. BP II 11, robbing feature, intrusive, phase lb.
75. WT jug. F269? folded thumbed base, copper speckled glaze. BJ XIV 2, late 18th-century rubble spreads, residual, phase 6c.
76. WT jug, F233, applied strip decoration, copper green glaze. BG V 48, levelling for floor in north end of cloisters, phase 3c.
77. Pipkin, F201/230?, rim glazed on the interior, oxidised surfaces. BL X 4, robbing of rubble, phase 4c.
78. Pipkin/jar, F201, internal glaze on rim, oxidised, residual. BM V 2, redeposited rubble, phase 5.
79. Jar, F201, internal glaze, reduced. BL I 4, redeposited rubble/soils, phase 4b.
80. Jar F201, internal glaze and on exterior shoulder, oxidised. BL XI 3, redeposited rubble, phase 4b.
81. Jar/CP, F201, internal glaze on rim, oxidised. BN III 2, rubble, phase 4b.
82. Jar /CP, F201, internal glaze, stamp on neck of vessel, reduced. BN I 9, redeposited rubble, phase 5.
83. Jar/CP, F201, internal glaze, reduced. BM I 22, gravel path in garden, phase 5.
84. Bowl/jar, F201, internal glaze, oxidised. BN III 2, rubble, phase 4b.

Fig. 92
85. Curving-walled bowl, F201, internal glaze. BJ IX 3, linear feature in garden, phase 5.
86. Curving-walled bowl, F201, internal glaze, oxidised. BG V 8, late pit, phase 6.
87. Curving-walled bowl, F201, internal glaze, reduced. BL IV 5, flower bed, phase 5.
88. Bowl? F201, oxidised. BG V 29, pit in garden, phase 5.
89. Curving-walled bowl/jar, internal glaze, reduced core. BL VI 1, topsoil, residual, U/S.
90. Bowl with moulded rim, F201, internal glaze, reduced core. BM III 1, flower bed, phase 5.
91. Jar, F201, internal glaze, reduced core. BJ XIV 2, late 18th-century rubble spread, phase 6c.
92. Bowl F201, internal glaze, oxidised. 65 BK VII 1, residual, U/S.
93. Bowl, F201, internal glaze, oxidised. BH IV 1, topsoil, residual, U/S.
94. Straight-sided jar, F201, thumbed applied neck strip. 64 BK I 4, flower bed, phase 5.
95. Chafing dish, F201, internal glaze, reduced. BH IX 6, culvert, phase 5.
96. Chafing dish, F201, internal glaze. BN IV 7, 18th-century layer, phase 5.
97. Chafing dish, F201, unglazed, reduced. BM V 2, redeposited rubble, phase 5.
98. Shallow bowl, F201, internal glaze, oxidised. BH V 5, linear feature, phase 5.
99. Bowl/cup? F201, internal glaze, reduced core. BH V 12, rubble deposit, phase 4b.
100. Jug, F201, overall dark green glaze, oxidised fabric. BM II 6, garden soil, phase 5.
101. Jug/tankard, F201,overall glaze, oxidised fabric. BM III 2, flower bed, phase 5.

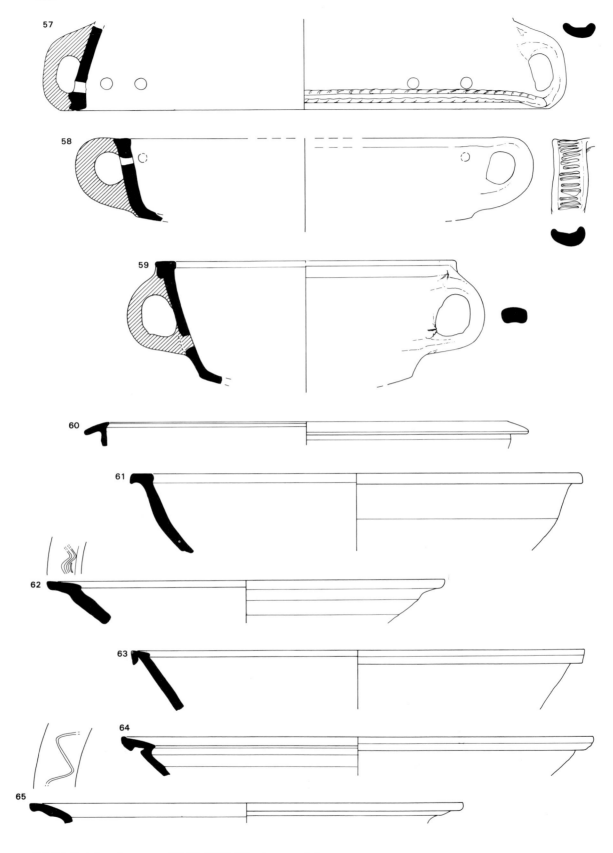

90. Medieval pottery, nos. 57-65, F200, Minety ware, 1:4

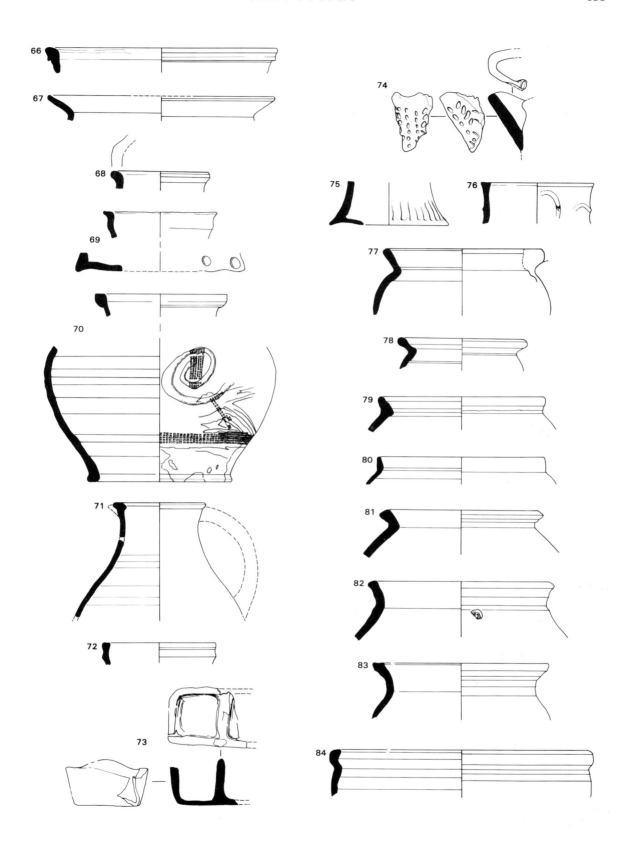

91. Medieval pottery, nos. 66-67, F240, Bath fabric 'A'; nos. 68-76, various fabrics; nos. 77-84, F201, Ashton Keynes ware, 1:4

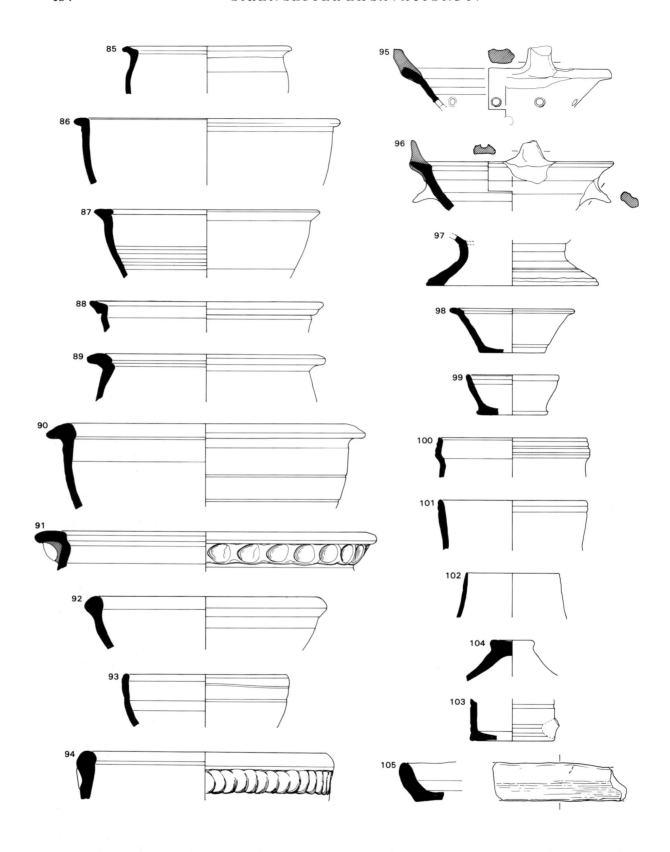

92. Medieval pottery, nos. 85-105, F201, Ashton Keynes ware, 1:4

102. Tankard, F201, imitation of stoneware form? overall clear glaze, oxidised. BJ II 2, topsoil.
103. Tankard, F201, overall glaze, reduced. BJ XIII 1, topsoil.
104. Lid, F201, splashes of glaze on top only, oxidised. 65 BX IX 2, rubble deposit, phase 4b.
105. Dripping pan/meat dish, F201, internal glaze, reduced core. BJ XIV 3, rubble deposit, phase 4b.

Fig. 93
106. Conical bowl, F201, internal glaze, burnt exterior, reduced. BM II 6, garden soil, phase 5.
107. Conical bowl/dish, F201, internal glaze, reduced. BM I 2, garden soil, phase 5.
108. Conical bowl, F201, internal glaze. BJ XIV 2, late 18th-century rubble spreads, phase 6c.
109. Conical bowl/plate, F201, glaze splashed onto interior, reduced. 65 BK II 7, robbing post-dating primary destruction rubble, phase 4c.
110. Conical bowl/pancheon, F201, internal glaze, reduced core. BM V 2, redeposited rubble, phase 5.
111. Plate, F201, decorated with chevron stamping, internal glaze, reduced. BL XI 3, redeposited rubble, phase 4b.
112. Plate/bowl, F201, decorated with chevron stamps, glazed interior, reduced. BM III 1, flower bed, phase 5.
113. Conical bowl, F230, combed decoration, internal glaze. BJ XIV 2, late 18th-century rubble spreads, phase 6c.
114. Money box, F250, overfired with black core and brown surfaces, glaze on exterior top. BL V 7, 6; silts below choir stalls, phase 3e.
115. WTCP, F204, unglazed, oxidised, light brown. 64 BK I 4, flower bed, phase 5.
116. Chafing dish, F204, internal clear glaze, oxidised light brown. BH XI 2, culvert, phase 5.
117. Bowl, F204, internal glaze, oxidised. BM IV 7, redeposited rubble, phase 5.
118. Cooking pot/jar, F204, internal glaze, oxidised. BM I 37, late abbey or post-destruction context, phase 3e/4.
119. Jar, F204, internal glaze, external sooting, oxidised. BJ II/III 1, topsoil, U/S.
120. Jar, F204, internal glaze, oxidised. BM II 6, garden soil, phase 5.
121. Jar, F204, internal glaze, oxidised. BM II 7, soil, phase 5.
122. Pipkin? F204, dark brown internal glaze, stacking mark on handle. BP I 6, soil, phase 5-6.

Fig. 94
123. Lobed cup, F220, overall bright green glaze. BN V 1, residual, U/S.
124. Lid of posset pot, F244, external glaze, light brown fabric, traces of applied white clay decoration. BG I 16.
125. Posset pot, F244, dark brown fabric and glaze. BJ IV 3, rubble deposit, phase 4b.
126. Three-handled cup, F214, light brown fabric, overall glaze. BL V 6, rubble deposit, phase 4b.
127. ?Posset pot lid, F244, dark blackish glaze on exterior only, applied white clay decoration; knob is bare of glaze and cut into a point. BH IX 1, topsoil.

128. Goblet/salt cup? F244, external clear glaze, light brown fabric. 65 BK IV 4, flower bed, phase 5.
129. Two-handled cup, F244, dark and overfired fabric, traces of applied white clay pads on girth of vessel. BG VII 15, rubble deposit, phase 4b.
130. Figurine? F208, vertical ribbed conical 'vessel', black glaze. BL IV 6, robbing of abbey stones, phase 4a.
131. Handled cup, F208, black firing. BN III 2, rubble, phase 4b.
132. Corrugated cup, F208, overfired, 'metallic'. BM V 2, redeposited rubble, phase 5.
133. Posset pot, F208, 'metallic' glaze. BM I 1, topsoil.
134. Corrugated cup, F226, dark brown glaze. BG V 6, rubble deposit, phase 4b.
135. Jug, F224, glazed on neck. BL IV 5, flower bed, phase 5.
136. Drinking jug, F224, thick external glaze and inside base, traces of incised decoration. BP I 16, sandy soil, phase 5?
137. Bowl, F224, internal glaze, oxidised. BJ XIII 1, topsoil.
138. Two-handled cup, F242, dimples below handle bases, black glaze, oxidised fabric. BM I 28, rubble deposit, phase 4b.
139. Ointment pot, F267, oxidised earthenware, covered by a cream slip, glazed overall. BH II 2, garden context, phase 5.
140. Tripod pipkin, F222, pale green internal glaze, sooted on exterior. 64 BK II 1/2, topsoil.
141. Beaded rim bowl, F222, horizontal handle, internal glaze. BP II 7, rubble, phase 4b.
142. Flange rim bowl, F222, finely potted, yellow internal glaze. BN I 2, stony layer, phase 5?
143a. Barrel mug, F222, brown mottled glaze. BN I 1, garden context, phase 5.
143b. Barrel mug, F222, dark brown glaze. BN I 1, garden context, phase 5.
144. Barrel mug, F209, mauve tinged tin glaze, kicked-up base. BG V 8, late pit, phase 6.
145. Drug jar, F209, blue, purple and yellow painted decoration. BH XI 1, U/S
146. Tea cup? F209, blue painted decoration, glaze 'bubbled' in places. BP I 8, late pit, phase 6.
147. Chamber pot, F209, blue-tinged glaze, ?Bristol. 64 BK II 1, topsoil.
148. Tankard, F263, brown iron wash, salt-glazed. BH IV 1, topsoil.
149. Tankard, F263, brown iron wash, salt-glazed. BH IX 4, garden context, phase 5.
150. Tankard, F236, dark brown glaze. BP I 1, U/S.
151. Tankard, F236, ribbing up entire vessel. BN VII 3.
152. Tankard, F261, brown wash, salt glaze. BN V 1 U/S.
153. Tankard, F261, white slipped, brown paint on rim, salt-glazed. BP II 4, garden context, phase 5.
154. Bowl/cup, F261, very finely thrown and turned, brown wash and salt glaze. 64 BK II 1, topsoil.
155. Handled cup, F238, thick black glaze. BJ IX 3, linear feature in garden, phase 5.
156. Handled cup, F238, thick black glaze. BH II 2, garden context, phase 5.

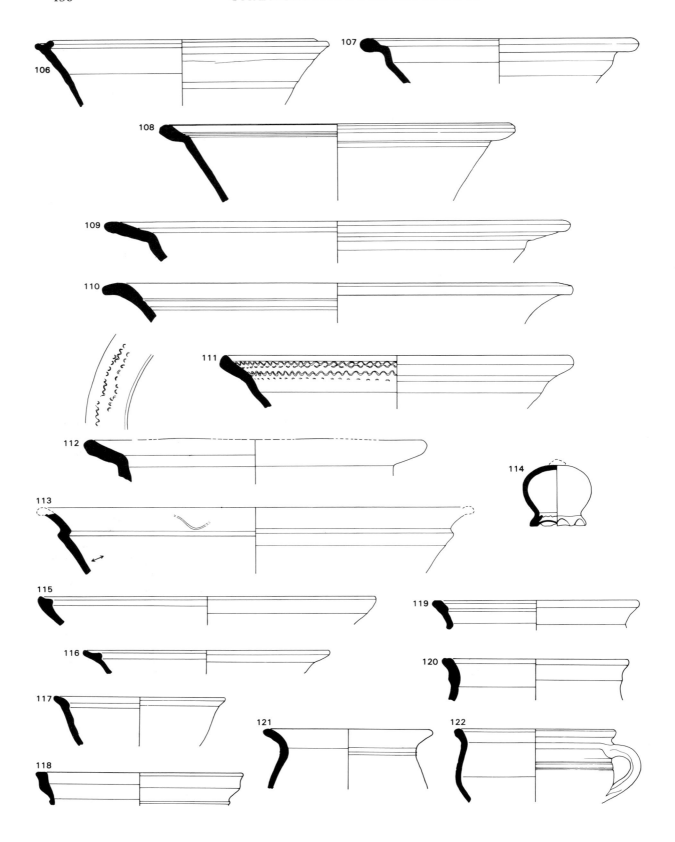

93. Medieval pottery, nos. 106-112, F201, Ashton Keynes ware; no. 113, F230, early Ashton Keynes ware; no. 114, F250; nos. 115-122, F204, Malvernian Glazed ware, 1:4

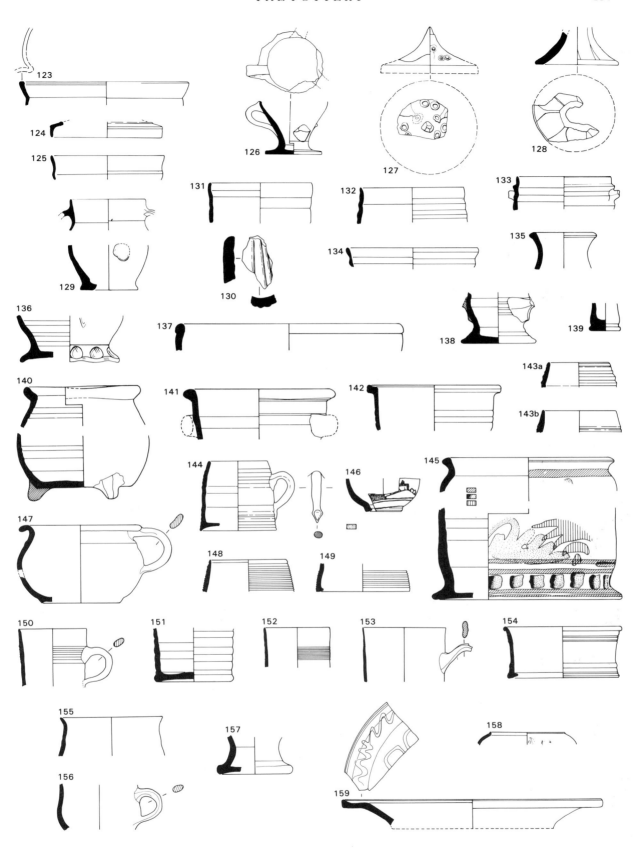

94. Late medieval pottery, 1:4

157. Tyg, F238, black glaze. BN II 2, robbing, phase 4c.

158. Globular cup or mug, F241, brown combed slip decoration. 65 BK III 3, rubble, phase 4b.

159. Wheel-thrown plate, F212, white trailed slip decoration. BG VII 3, later rubble, phase 6.

Fig. 95

160. Chafing dish, F245, comb-stamped decoration, splash of glaze on rim. BH XI 2, culvert, phase 5.

161. Globular jug, F225, ribbed vessel, patchy iron wash. BJ VII 4, rubble layer, phase 4b.

162. Globular jug, F225, ribbed vessel, patchy iron wash. BJ VII 4, rubble, phase 4b.

163. Globular jug, ?F216, brown salt glaze. BH XI 2, culvert, phase 5.

164. Globular jug, F225, ribbed vessel, wire cut and cracked base. BH IV 2, garden context, redeposited rubble, phase 5b.

165. Globular jug, F228, applied decoration of four-petalled roses and twisting stems. BN III 2/II 3, rubble, phase 4b.

166. Globular jug, F228, matt grey finish, applied oak sprigs and leaves. BL I 3, robbing, phase 4c.

167. Tankard, F228, brown salt-glazed stoneware, moulded figure of Eve. BM III 1, flower bed, phase 5.

168. Ovoid jug, F216, applied raised spiral bosses surrounded by petals. BL III 3, U/S.

169. Globular jug, F216. BM V 15, robbing, phase 4a.

170. Globular jug, F216, 'tiger skin' salt glaze. BG V 10.

171. Bottle ?/flask, F216, 'tiger skin' salt glaze. BM I 20, garden context, phase 5.

172. Bottle/flask, F216, fine ribbing up to rim. BM I 26, garden context, phase 5.

173. Bottle/flask, F216, applied small bearded faces below collar. BH III 4, U/S.

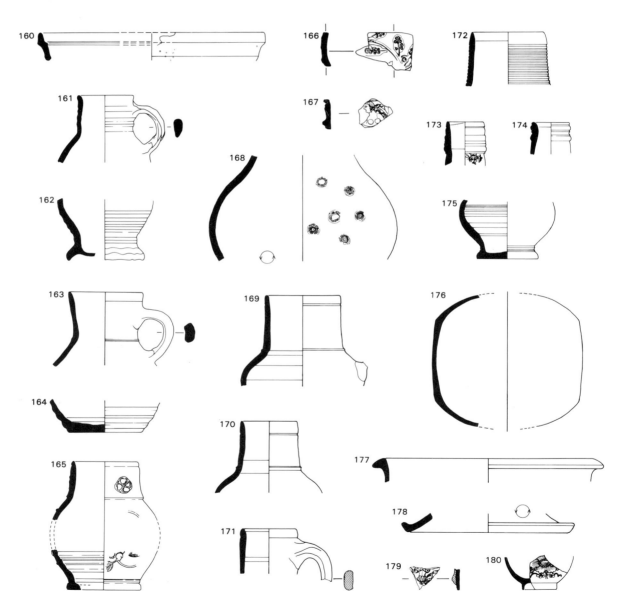

95. Post-medieval pottery, 1:4

174. Bottle/flask, F216, brown speckled salt glaze. BG V 8, late pit, phase 6.
175. Jug base, F216, wire-cut footring base. BJ I 4, late pit, phase 6.
176. Costrel, F227, heavily knife-trimmed sides, unglazed. BH X 2, flower bed, phase 5.
177. Bowl, F227, unglazed. BN I 6, late pit, phase 6.
178. ?Lid/bowl, F227, unglazed. BG V 8, late pit, phase 6.
179. Tankard, F253, white unglazed stoneware, applied decoration - an urn with foliage? BL V 3, garden context, phase 5.
180. Tea cup, F218, blue-painted decoration of a flower. 64 BK II 1, topsoil.

Fig. 96
181. Wide bowl with flanged rim, F201, internal glaze, oxidised. BP I 4, mid 18th-century pit, phase 6.
182. Conical bowl, F201, internal glaze, oxidised. BP I 4, mid 18th-century pit, phase 6.
183. Bowl, F201, thumbed rim, internal glaze. BP I 4, mid 18th-century pit, phase 6.
184. Bowl base, F201, internal glaze, oxidised. BP I 4, mid 18th-century pit, phase 6.
185. Straight-sided bowl, F201, grooved lines on exterior, internal glaze. BP I 4, mid 18th-century pit, phase 6.
186. Jug, F201, internal glaze, oxidised. BP I 4, mid 18th-century pit, phase 6.
187. Shallow dish/bowl, F260, reduced, internal glaze. BP I 4, mid 18th-century pit, phase 6.

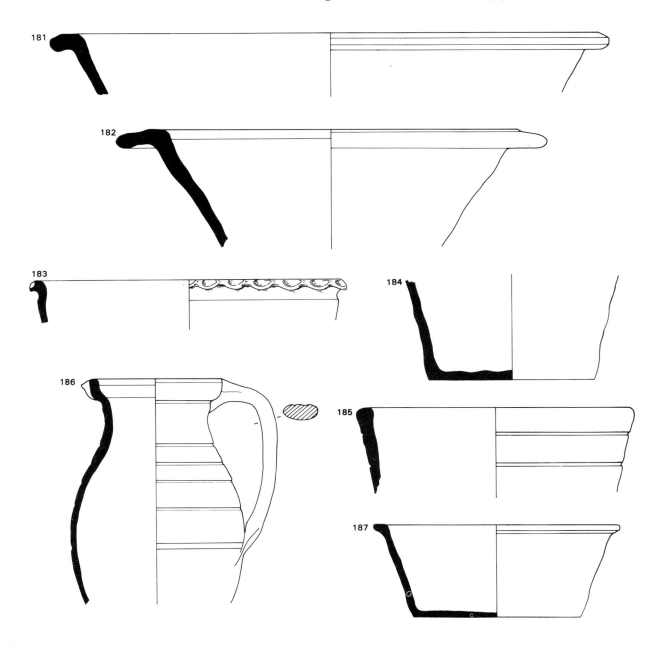

96. 18th-century pottery, 1:4

Fig. 97

188. Tea pot, F257, chocolate brown fabric with overall clear glaze. BP I 4, mid 18th-century pit, phase 6.

189. Tea pot/coffee pot lid, F215, knob missing, crudely finished steam hole. BP I 4, mid 18th-century pit, phase 6.

190. Chamber pot, F209, blue-tinged tin glaze. BP I 4, mid 18th-century pit, phase 6.

191. Drug jar, F209, pale blue-painted decoration. BP I 4, mid 18th-century pit, phase 6.

192. Ointment pot, F209, white tin glaze. BP I 4, mid 18th-century pit, phase 6.

193. Tankard, F217, incised lines painted with blue chequered design. BP I 4, mid 18th-century pit, phase 6.

194. Bowl, F215, pulled out spout. BP I 4, mid 18th-century pit, phase 6.

195. Bowl, F215, angled spout. BP I 4, mid 18th-century pit, phase 6.

196. Chamber pot, F236, scoured interior. BP I 4, mid 18th-century pit, phase 6.

197. ?Bowl/jar, F215, scratched blue-filled decoration. BP I 4, mid 18th-century pit, phase 6.

198. Bowl, F249, brown iron wash. BP I 4, mid 18th-century pit, phase 6.

199. Tankard, F215, turned base. BP I 4, mid 18th-century pit, phase 6.

200. Tankard, F201, stacking mark on base, overall dark glaze. BP I 4, mid 18th-century pit, phase 6.

201. Plate, F209, blue-painted decoration. BP I 4, mid 18th-century pit, phase 6.

202. Plate, F213, marbled slip decoration. BP I 4, mid 18th-century pit, phase 6.

203. Oblong plate, F213, combed slip decoration. BP I 4, mid 18th-century pit, phase 6.

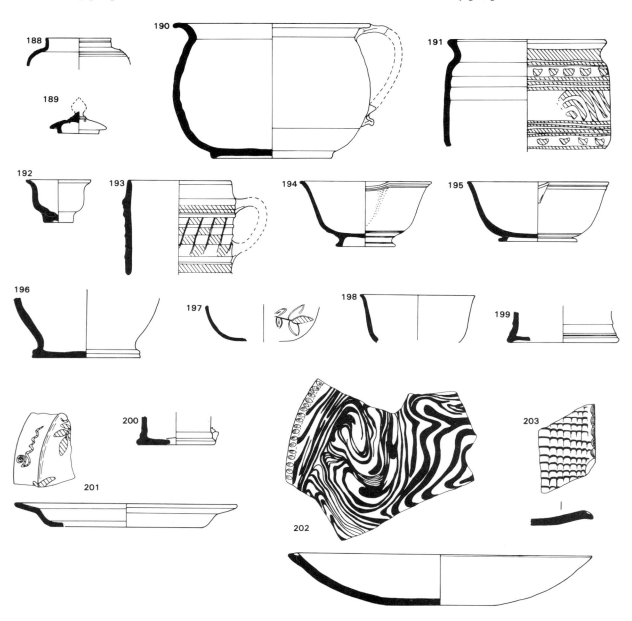

A SAMPLE OF THE ROOF TILES

The illustrated examples (fig. 98) consist of fragments of four crested ridge-tiles with traces of glaze. The crests are knife-cut, and two of the fragments (fig. 98, nos. 1 and 2) also show thumb-impressions. Jope suggested (Jope 1951, 86) that knife-cutting, at least in Oxfordshire, started to appear in the late 13th century. Nos. 1 and 4 preserve the end-crests of the tiles, and no. 1 has, in addition, a deliberately cut circular aperture, approximately 22 mm. in diameter, separated from the end of the tile by one straight-topped crest. This is likely to be the setting for a ceramic finial, the lower part of which would be shaped to fit the aperture. Such finials were studied by Dunning (1971).

An elaborately decorated ridge-tile found at the Laverstock pottery has a larger aperture with cut marks around the edges (Musty, Algar and Ewence 1969, 140). No. 1 has a single incised line across the surface but it is uncertain if this is decoration.

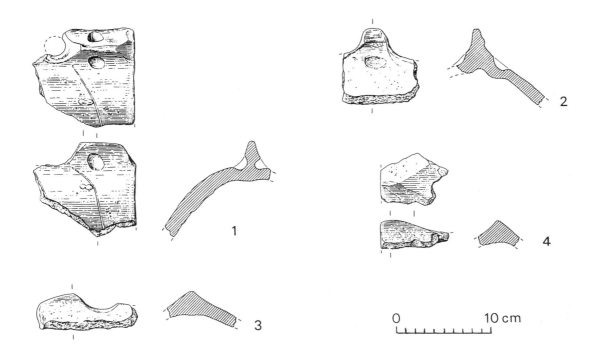

98. Roof furniture

THE MEDIEVAL FLOOR TILES

A. G. Vince

INTRODUCTION

A large number of fragments of medieval floor tile were recovered from the 1964-66 excavations representing at least 651 separate tiles. They were divided into design groups by David Wilkinson and the dimensions, thickness range, average degree of bevel, number of keying scoops and minimum number of tiles in each group were recorded (Wilkinson 1983b). A sample of each design group, amounting to the total number present for all but the largest groups, was examined by the author and assigned to fabric groups. In no case did tiles with the same design occur in more than one fabric and it is therefore probable that the unexamined tiles can also be assigned to a fabric group on the basis of design.

The tiles range in date from the mid 13th century or later through to the later 15th or early 16th century but do not appear to represent a continuous use of decorated tiles during this period. Rather, it seems that the tiles may represent as few as four or five consignments of tiles. The groups are described below in apparent chronological order, followed by a discussion of the supply of tiles and a comparison with tile use on other west country monastic sites.

The designs are assigned numbers prefixed CTD (Cirencester Tile Design); figs. 102-110.

Floor tiles *in situ*

Three main tile floors survived *in situ*, with the tiles embedded in mortar:

1. In the 14th century extensions to the presbytery north aisle: two tile areas and several patches (figs. 47, 99)

2. In the north transept (fig. 100; Wacher 1965, Plate XXXIVa)

3. In a room on the north side of the north claustral range (figs. 64, 101)

Floor 1 was of Nash Hill tiles, and was in several parts. One fragment of it (Floor 1a) lay over the original 12th-century east wall, W407, and so post-dates the presbytery eastern extension. The original floor was composed of CTD 38, although later some of the border tiles were replaced with other designs. Another area, 6ft x 4ft 6ins (1.8 x 1.4m) (Floor 1b), contained a large number of re-used tiles, suggested by the high number of designs used (CTD 3, 6, 9, 13-14, 22-4, 37-8, 44-5, 47, 52, 92, 94).

Floor 2 of Nash Hill tiles was in the north transept. Most of the floor was composed of CTD 19. A border was formed of plain tiles bounding a row of CTD 11

99. Medieval floor tiles: floor 1, in east extension to abbey church

and CTD 18; both these were originally designed to be used in four-tile layouts and were here either used singly or halved. This border was parallel to the step in the north transept, west of the transept chapel.

Floor 3, in a room in the north claustral range was entirely composed of re-used tiles including CTD 1, 3-7, and plain tiles. It measured 3ft x 4 ft (0.9m x 1.2m).

Southern Wiltshire

Tiles from a southern Wiltshire source were recognisable through their light colour and the presence of abundant fragments of reddish clay/iron ore and cream clay pellets, both often several mm across. The light-coloured clay was in some cases laminated and is probably relict clay from the original clay source rather than fragments of the white clay used as inlay. Large red/brown and black rounded flint fragments in the order of 10 to 20mm across were present. These indicate that cleaning of the clay was not very effective. The tiles contained abundant quartz sand, not present in the relict clay and therefore probably deliberately added to the tile fabric.

The tiles usually had four scooped keys on the base which in comparison to those found on Nash Hill tiles were deep and regular. The base of the tiles had originally been sanded (as a result of the tiles being laid on a sanded surface to dry) but this sand was usually trimmed off. Seven designs were present in the southern Wiltshire fabric group, all used on tiles of similar size, *c.* 145mm square. They all belong to the 'Wessex School' and are paralleled at a number of southern Wiltshire sites, including the kiln site at

Clarendon Palace, where tile-making is documented in 1250-52. Undecorated border tiles, scored and snapped into small triangles, were also present in this fabric as were plain green-glazed tiles of the standard size.

The tile designs can be divided into two groups: those intended to be used in groups of four and those intended to be used singly. The fact that the four-tile designs (CTDs 6 and 7) are both approximately four times as common as the remaining tiles does suggest that they were used in such groups. Most of these tiles were found relaid in a room on the north side of the north claustral range (floor 3). Two of the designs used at Cirencester could be matched precisely with those found on sites in south Wiltshire. These were CTD 6, found at Clarendon in the Queen's chamber pavement dated 1250-52 and at Ivychurch Priory (Eames 1991, Design No. 107) and CTD 7, found at Amesbury (Eames 1991, Design No. 147). None of the designs are known from either of the known Clarendon kilns but a south Wiltshire origin seems assured. Furthermore, in Eames' discussion of these Wessex School tiles a date in the 1250s-1260s is postulated. This group of tiles is therefore certain to have been the first to have been used at Cirencester.

Nash Hill

Amongst the most distinctive features of tiles from the Nash Hill tilery, situated near Lacock in west Wiltshire, are large angular red sandstone fragments up to 6mm across. Rounded red clay pellets up to 3mm across, turning dark purple when over-fired,

100. Medieval tile floor, floor 2, in north transept

are also found together with an abundant rounded quartz sand. The quantity of sand varies somewhat from tile to tile and in extreme cases the tiles are quite friable as a result. Many of the Nash Hill tiles were over-fired and of a very dark colour but they could be fired to an even red colour, providing a strong contrast with the white slip. A distinct variant on this fabric contains moderate fragments of bivalve shell, up to 3mm long, in addition to the red sandstone and clay pellets noted above.

The tiles almost all had some sort of knife-cut keying scooped into their bases, varying from two perfunctory scoops on some of the rectangular border tiles to the standard four scoops found on the majority of tiles. CTD 34 was the only square design to have three scoops rather than four and these were present on at least two separate tiles, indicating that these two tiles were made as part of a single batch where the tiler had decided to veer from standard practice. In comparison with the southern Wiltshire tiles, the scoops on the Nash Hill tiles were irregular and shallow.

Large heraldic tiles on quarries between 204mm and 213mm square form the most distinct members of the Nash Hill group. The Cirencester examples include not only the arms of England (CTD 8) and an unidentified coat of arms bearing three lions rampant (CTD 10) but also examples of both designs in reverse (CTD 9 and 11 respectively). Interestingly, the incorrect versions are more common than the correct ones at Cirencester. The other two large heraldic tiles vary somewhat in their design. CTD 12 appears to have been used with others of the same type in a carpet pattern whereas CTD 13 has its shield set upright on the tile. One indistinct example of a four-tile quatrefoil design was found on a similar size tile (CTD 14). Three border tiles made for use with this large quarry size were found. Two were produced by scoring and snapping a large square tile into two equal-sized rectangles (CTD 15 and 16) whilst the third (CTD 17) may have been produced by scoring and snapping a large tile into three, to judge by more complete examples from Huish Church (Thompson 1967, 60-1). All the tiles with the shelly variant of the Nash Hill fabric were of a similar large quarry size, although on average up to 20mm narrower. The designs are a mixture of single or repeating carpet patterns (CTD 18, 19 and 20) and four-tile quatrefoils (CTD 21 and 22). Two of these designs occur together at Huish Church and all are likely to have been produced using a batch of clay and therefore were in contemporary use.

The remaining Nash Hill tiles are mainly of a smaller square quarry size, c. 140mm (i.e. just slightly narrower than the southern Wiltshire tiles). The wide range of single and repeating designs include free-standing mythical beasts (CTD 24), castles (CTD 25 and 26) and other designs (CTD 27-31),

101. Medieval tile floor, floor 3, in north-east range of cloister

but the most common designs are variations on the theme of a circle with trefoils at the four corners. These include a foliated cross (CTD 32), three dies of the same design of two birds and a tree (CTD 5, 33, 34), three griffins (CTD 35-37), three lions (CTD 38-40) and what has been interpreted as a letter I (CTD 41; McCarthy 1974, 141, Fig. 28, no 38). Four-tile designs consist of five variations on the theme of a quatrefoil within a pelleted circle (CTD 42-46), a pelleted circle containing sixfoils and a trefoil (CTD 47), two birds and a tree (CTD 48-9), floriated crosses (CTD 50-52), a pelleted quatrefoil containing fleurs de lys (CTD 53), and an unidentified four-tile pattern (CTD 54).

Border tiles of four different types were found. First were square tiles bearing four similar elements suitable for scoring and snapping into four small squares or eight small triangles but also capable of being used whole (CTD 55, 56, 57 and 58). CTD 58 is probably a Lombardic letter. The second type consists of designs which could be subdivided into two rectangular tiles. Examples include normal and reverse frets (CTD 59 and 60) and a row of circles between parallel lines (CTD 61). The third border type consists of square or rectangular tiles decorated with foliage scrolls usually between plain or pelleted lines (CTD 62-67). The latter has a rebated back indicating its use as the riser of a set of steps. The fourth border type consists of running animals, probably dogs, in a foliage background. These were probably produced as part of a hunting scene (CTD 68-9). A large number of unidentifiable fragments were also present, some of which have been illustrated (CTD 70-81).

Two fragments of what may be original Nash Hill tile pavement were found. The first, in the presbytery north aisle of the east end extension (floor 1) consisted of the smaller tiles, of designs CTD 38, 42, 44 and 47 and was laid diagonally to the walls. The second patch (floor 2) was in the north transept and consisted of the larger tiles, including both shelly and standard fabrics. It appeared to have been relaid. CTD 11, 18 and 19 were present but not used in the originally intended manner.

The origin of these tiles is not in serious doubt since many of the Cirencester examples can be matched in both fabric and die to material from the kiln site (McCarthy 1974; Griffiths and Robinson 1991). The shelly variant of the fabric has not been noted elsewhere and clearly links together all the tiles made from it. This is confirmed by the fact that two of the designs found on the shelly variant tiles occur together at Huish, and in Floor 2 at Cirencester. The group is represented as Nash Hill only by a fragment of one four-tile pattern (Griffiths and Robinson 1991, Fig 4 no 87). It may or may not be significant that the remaining large tiles do not contain the shelly version of the Nash Hill fabric. One of the border tiles from this group was found associated with two of the dies used on the shelly tiles at Huish and both shelly and standard fabrics were present in the Cirencester floor 2. In either case, the dating of the tiles to the later part of the 13th century or early in the following century

seems likely. Just how far into the 14th century the Nash Hill tilery was operating is unknown. The presence of two versions of two of the heraldic tiles is a possible indication that the dies were recut after the originals had worn out, although the contemporary use of multiple dies for common designs is also suspected. Cirencester includes several examples of such multiple dies but provides no evidence for whether they were used sequentially or side by side.

Droitwich/South Worcestershire

The production of tiles in Worcester is known from documentary sources and from the discovery of a kiln for the production of flat roof tiles at Sidbury, to the south of the city. Decorated medieval floor tiles, however, are not documented as the products of this industry nor is there any positive archaeological evidence from Worcester, such as wasters. At St Mary Witton, Droitwich, however, a tile kiln was discovered in the mid 19th century and some of the tiles from this kiln exist in the British Museum collection. The fabric of these tiles has been used to define a 'Droitwich type' tile industry which certainly included the products of the Droitwich kiln but probably also included tiles from other kiln sites in the Droitwich/Worcester area. The petrological characteristics of these tiles are not easy to see with the naked eye, since rounded quartz sand is practically the only inclusion type visible. However, thin-section analysis has shown that a significant proportion of the quartz grains in this sand had a metamorphic origin and include impurities in the form of minute (c. 0.05mm long) greenish or reddish flakes of ?chlorite. Rare, large rounded quartz/quartzite pebbles up to 10mm across are sometimes present. The Droitwich-type floor tiles were laid to dry on a surface coated with this quartz sand and can vary in both texture and firing. The Cirencester examples have a relatively low frequency of quartz sand and had firing temperatures towards the middle of the range. They were also all verging towards the thicker end of the thickness range for tiles from this industry. These traits suggest that the tiles formed a single consignment, a suggestion given further weight by the similarity in date of the decorated examples.

The Cirencester examples are all of similar size, c. 120mm square. Designs include two heraldic shields set upright on the tile: the arms of de Clare (CTD 82) and the crossed keys and sword used as the arms of St Peter and St Paul (CTD 83). Three designs from sixteen-tile patterns include one with the arms of Beauchamp (CTD 84, 85, 86). Square tiles designed to be usable as small square border tiles also occurred, although none had actually been scored or cut (CTD 87, 88 and 89). Droitwich-type tiles apparently had a long period of production, from some time in the early to mid 14th century through to the second half of the 15th century. The Cirencester assemblage can be placed towards the end of this period but not at the end itself, since there are tiles which are typologically later from sites such as Keynsham Abbey, Somerset (Lowe 1979).

Malvern Chase

The production of floor tiles alongside pottery in the Hanley Castle potteries of south Worcestershire is proven both by a comparison of pottery and tile fabrics and by the discovery by P. Ewence and others of fragments of floor tile and pottery in the same waste heaps at Hanley. A study of the fabrics found amongst the Gloucester Blackfriars Malvern Chase tiles shows that there are three distinct variants: a sandy version found exclusively on early to mid 14th-century tiles; a less sandy variant found predominantly on 14th-century tiles and a fine version found predominantly on later 15th and 16th-century tiles. The Cirencester examples belong mainly to this third sub-group. They contain angular fragments of acid igneous rock, often over 10mm across, but these are sparse to moderate in frequency. Rounded quartz sand is present in all the tiles but is very particularly noticeable in the Cirencester tiles. A large number of designs are represented at Cirencester, often by a single incomplete fragment. Single patterns include two birds and a tree (CTD 90) and a fish in a vesica (CTD 91). Four-tile patterns include one pelleted circle with quatrefoil (CTD 92) and three others (CTD 93-5). CTD 95 is similar in style to the Great Malvern school and includes an unidentified coat of arms. Two tiles from a four-tile pattern comprising the arms of England and France quartered were found (CTD 96 and 97). A large number of designs from sixteen-tile patterns were found (CTD 98-9, 101-110).

Tiles decorated with dies originally used at the Great Malvern tilery or its offshoots at Monmouth or Lenton Priory, form a distinct sub-group although there is no evidence that they were distinguished in quarry size or method of manufacture and they may well have been brought to Cirencester alongside the remaining designs. These Great Malvern derived designs include CTD 111, the crowned IHS monogram between segments of quatrefoils, a crowned M (CTD 112), a crowned IHC monogram (CTD 113), the Stafford knot (CTD 114), a fleur-de-lys in a diagonally-set square (CTD 115) and a floral pattern (CTD 116). Four-tile patterns include a black-letter inscription, DOMINE JHU MISERERE (CTD 117) (known from Gloucester Cathedral Lady Chapel), and the arms of Beauchamp (CTD 118). Fragments of sixteen-tile patterns with a band of black-letter inscription were too fragmentary for reconstruction (CTD 119-125) whilst two tiles from the centre of a sixteen-tile pattern in which four tiles made up the arms of Beauchamp were found (CTD 126 and 127). Fragments of similar style to the Great Malvern tiles were also found (CTD 128-9, no. 129 known from Gloucester Cathedral Lady Chapel) together with a large number of unidentifiable fragments (CTD 110, 130-140).

None of these Malvern Chase tiles was found *in situ* at Cirencester except where clearly used to patch earlier Nash Hill pavements. The fact that there were so many designs in use and never more than five examples of a design raises the possibility that the tiles were never laid in the intended groups, but merely used as fillers. Alternatively, the surviving collection may be a very small sample of the original consignments. The Cirencester collection of Malvern Chase tiles forms a useful assemblage for studying the development of the history of tile production at Hanley. The similarity in quarry size and appearance suggests that all the Cirencester tiles came to the site as a single consignment and yet they include examples with designs that would stylistically be dated to a much wider date-range, for example the pelleted circle is typical of 13th-14th century Wessex school pavements whereas some of the four-tile patterns are similar to, if not from the same dies as, later 15th-century Droitwich type tiles in addition to the Great Malvern derived dies. The latter can definitely be dated to the closing years of the 15th century at the earliest since they must have had a long life following their initial use for Abbot Sebroke's pavement at Gloucester. It is likely that the entire collection can be dated to the very late 15th or early 16th century. Large tiles with designs influenced strongly by the Great Malvern tiles were being made at Hanley Castle in the 1530s but are absent at Cirencester. This may simply be a matter of preference but may indicate that this final production phase began after the Cirencester consignment had been completed.

Source

All the tiles from Cirencester can be attributed with some degree of certainty to a known tile industry. The abbey was therefore supplied with its floor tiles entirely from within the established market. There are tile designs found at Cirencester that have not been recorded elsewhere but this is probably due to the relatively limited knowledge of medieval floor tiles, and not a result of tiles being commissioned especially for the abbey. Certainly, to the best of our knowledge, the heraldic tiles found are either already known as part of the stock in trade of the tilery where they were made, or are unlikely to have had any especial connection with the abbey (for example the reversed shields found on the large Nash Hill tiles). There is an apparent pattern in the change of supply, in that in the 13th and 14th centuries the tiles were obtained from southern sources, close to the centres of innovation in Winchester and Clarendon, whereas by the 15th century, supply was from tileries in southern Worcestershire. These were able to utilise the river Severn to establish an extensive market for their products, reaching as far west as Pembrokeshire. Cirencester is, however, the only known site to the east of the Cotswold scarp to have produced these particular Severn Valley products in any quantity (a few may have found their way into central Wiltshire via Bristol). Products of later medieval north Wiltshire (an unknown source supplying Malmesbury Abbey), Berkshire (i.e. Newbury) or south Buckinghamshire (i.e. Penn) tileries were conspicuously absent from the excavated assemblage.

Date

The broad date range of the Cirencester tiles can be summarised in the table below. Before the middle of the 13th century floor tiles were so scarce that their absence is of no surprise. In the later 14th century, however, other local religious houses were receiving floor tiles and their absence from Cirencester must indicate a low level of building or repairs. Similarly, floor tiles were used extensively in the west country in the early 16th century and their absence from Cirencester must also be significant, especially considering that some west country houses were investing heavily in floor tiles at this time (for example Hailes Abbey and Llanthony Priory, Gloucester).

Quality

It is impossible to tell precisely what the relative value of different types of floor tile might have been. An idea of the value placed upon particular types of tile might be gained by examining the distance over which they were transported, especially if there were other potential sources which might have been tapped. For the mid 13th century there were few other sources of floor tiles in the west country and the presence of floor tiles of this date at Cirencester suggests that it was at the forefront of fashion at this time. By the later 13th and early 14th centuries there were other possible sources, including the 'stabbed Wessex' tiles found at sites to the north of Cirencester and the Chertsey-Halesowen tiles found locally at Hailes Abbey, Evesham Abbey and Kenilworth Priory. To the modern eye these tiles appear to be of extremely high quality and therefore presumably desirable. Their distribution does suggest that people were prepared to order their transportation over considerable distances (although the number of sources in addition to Halesowen and Chertsey is

unknown). Cirencester Abbey may therefore already have lost its innovative position in the use of floor tiles, or it may be that by the time the Halesowen-Chertsey tiles were being made, at the turn of the 14th century, the abbey was already fully paved. Similar alternative possibilities exist at the end of the 15th century. From the 1450s until the 1480s it would have been possible to obtain Great Malvern floor tiles, or tiles produced in the Malvern School at one of its daughter tileries. However, it may be that the Malvern Chase tiles from Cirencester are just slightly later than the final end of the Great Malvern school (which, with a duration of c. 30 years, could easily have been under the control of a single master tiler). Conventional dating of the Canynges pavement would suggest that these would have been available at the same time as the Malvern Chase tiles, and both the distribution of these tiles (as far as Heytesbury in Wiltshire and to St David's in Pembrokeshire) and their technical quality, suggest that they should have been preferred if available. By the late 15th century, it seems, Cirencester was obtaining second rate floor tiles. However, since the original location of the areas paved with these tiles is not known it is difficult to take this conclusion any further. It may well be that a small number of tiles was obtained for an unimportant location whereas the Canynges-type tiles were clearly being produced for church and cathedral floors and that we are not here comparing like with like. Nevertheless, the increasing volume of data on the source and distribution of medieval floor tiles in the west country, when used in conjunction with evidence from the study of decorated window glass and architectural mouldings, is opening up the possibility of studying changing patterns of wealth and patronage in religious houses.

TABLE: DATE RANGE OF THE CIRENCESTER TILES

Date	Tile group	Minimum number	Percentage	Comments
Mid 13th century, c. 1250s to 1260s	Southern Wiltshire	141	21.4	Probably from a single consignment
Later 13th or early 14th century; post 1271	Nash Hill	426	65.4	Probably from a single consignment. Certainly all the large tiles made and in use at the same time.
Later 14th century	None	0	0	
15th century	Droitwich	9	1.3	Probably from a single consignment
Late 15th century	Malvern Chase	76	11.6	Low ratio of fragments to designs
Early 16th century	None	0	0	

102. Medieval floor tiles, CTD 1-7, Nash Hill 'light'; CTD 8-10, Nash Hill, 1:4

103. Medieval floor tiles, CTD 11-18, Nash Hill; CTD 18, 'shelly', 1:4

104. Medieval floor tiles, CTD 19-32, Nash Hill; CTD 19-23 'shelly', 1:4

33

34

35

36

37

38

39

40

41

42

43

44

45

46

47

105. Medieval floor tiles, CTD 33-47, Nash Hill, 1:4

106. Medieval floor tiles, CTD 48-67, Nash Hill, 1:4

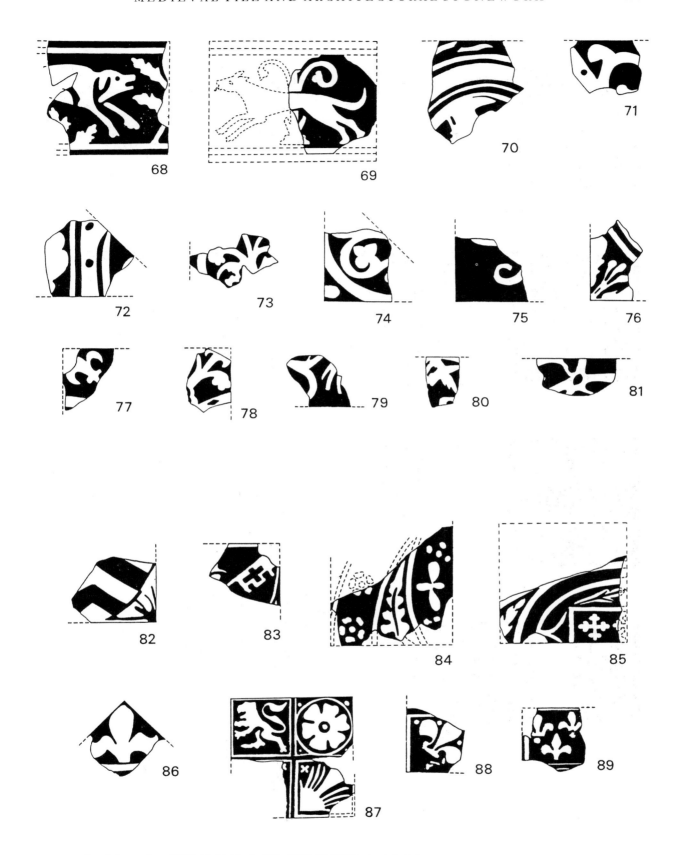

107. Medieval floor tiles, CTD 68-81 Nash Hill; CTD 82-89 Droitwich, 1:4

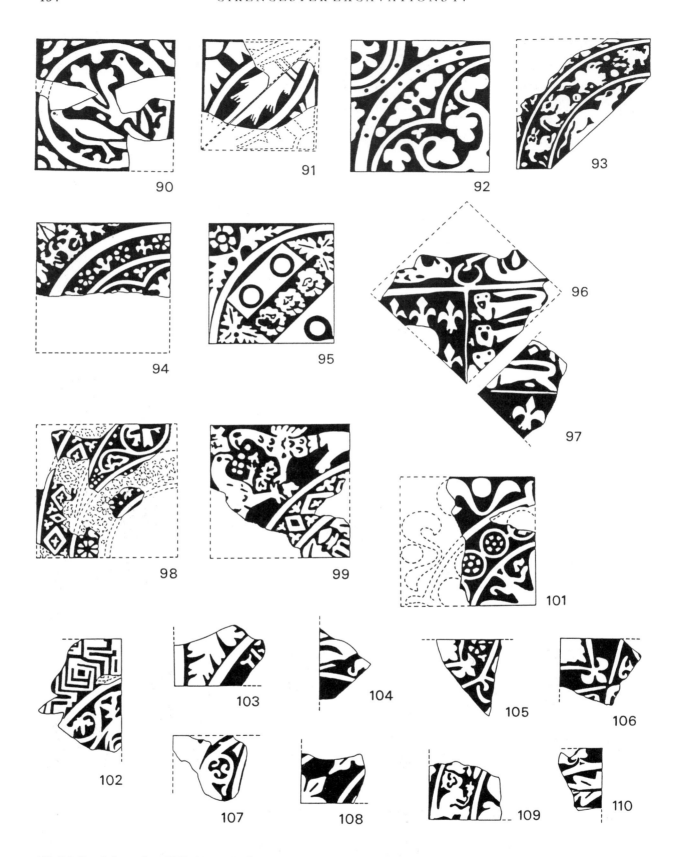

108. Medieval floor tiles, CTD 90-110 Malvern (CTD 100 not illustrated), 1:4

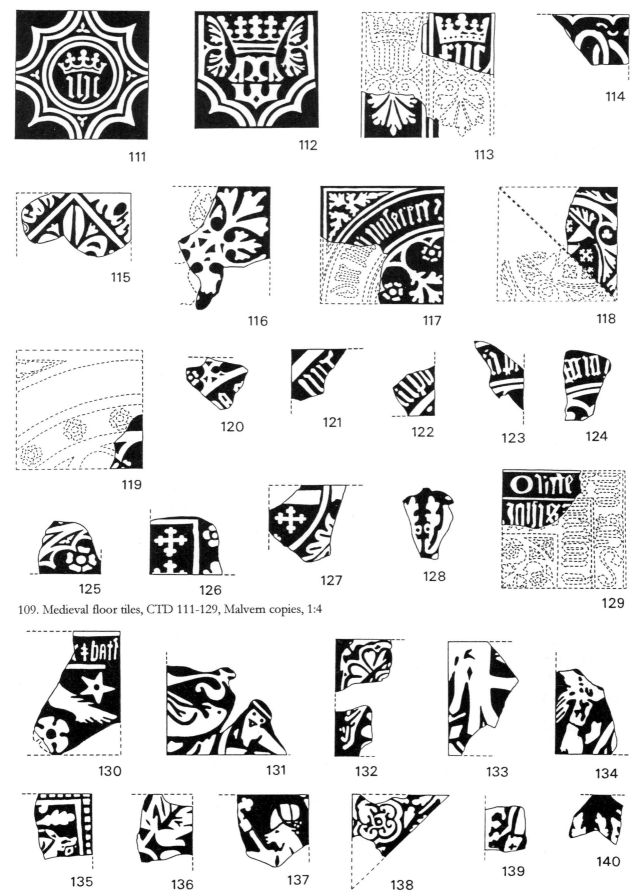

109. Medieval floor tiles, CTD 111-129, Malvern copies, 1:4

110. Medieval floor tiles, CTD 130-140, miscellaneous fabrics, 1:4

ARCHITECTURAL STONEWORK: AN ASSESSMENT

D. J. Wilkinson

A large proportion of the stonework which was excavated between 1964 and 1966 was reburied at the end of the excavation because of the lack of storage space; the remainder is at the Corinium Museum. The total number of fragments is probably in excess of 1000. Only a small proportion of the stonework had a recorded context; most of it seems to have come from the post-1539 destruction deposit.

Architectural stonework from the abbey has been found over the years in the gardens of Abbey House; many of these found their way to either the Bathurst or Cripps collections, both of which were brought together when the Corinium Museum was resited in 1938 in Park Street, Cirencester. None of these pieces is discussed here.

In 1975 and 1976 fragments of stonework from the excavations were studied as part of an undergraduate thesis at University College, Cardiff (Wilkinson 1977); that paper forms the basis of the following report. It should be emphasised that this report is the result of examining less than 10% of all the architectural fragments in store; there is thus considerable potential for future study.

Most of the stone is Jurassic limestone of the oolitic series. Some is good quality white limestone of Bathonian type containing little fossiliferous shell, whilst some contains not only much fossiliferous shell but is also iron-stained, probably by limonite. There are a few fragments of polished grey limestone known as 'Purbeck Marble'. A few pieces of stonework are sculptural rather than architectural.

In the following discussion the numbers used in Wilkinson 1977 are retained, preceded by the letters AF (Architectural Fragment). The stylistic terms are as follows:-

Romanesque/Early English	1189-1307
Geometrical: decorated	1280-1360
Geometrical: Curvilinear	1320-1400
Perpendicular	1377-1485
Late Perpendicular	1485-1550

The Romanesque or Norman pieces are generally easy to identify. AF 20, 86 and 87 are all voussoirs with chevron or zigzag decoration. AF 20 comes from the soffit of a small window or doorway. AF 87 is from an arch with a span of c. 18ft (5.4m). AF 5 is an engaged shaft or bowtell perhaps part of a doorway using orders. AF 32 appears to be a simple billet mould. AF 92 is part of a scallop-shell capital.

Early English style is not so conspicuous. AF 16 is a classic keel moulding. AF 13 appears to be typically Early English and is composed of three round mouldings, the centre one of which is a circular engaged shaft. AF 57 is a rib or arch moulding composed of undercut rounds and fillet and is probably Early English. AF 67 is a vault rib moulding with a radius of 2.8m. It is chamfered and the soffit is

a two-thirds round. Similar ribs have been found in Norman work, but this example is most probably Early English or early Decorated.

AF 3 and 7 display examples of the wave moulding which was commonly employed in late Curvilinear and early Perpendicular arches. Both look like ribs, but they are not noticeably curved. AF 68, 70 and 71 make use of the sunk chamfer and are probably 14th century.

Fragments displaying typical elements of the Perpendicular style, particularly the ogee and the broad fillet, are numerous. AF 60 is an unusual piece in that it uses old-fashioned elements such as rounds and hollows as well as typically Perpendicular features including the bracket moulding and casement.

There are several Perpendicular window mullions with tracery, for example AF 73. AF 53 is a fragment of panel tracery displaying a less popular but diagnostic Perpendicular moulding. AF 39, 47 and 51 are all pieces from the same fan vault. AF 29 is panel tracery, possibly from the central panel of a fan vault. AF 9 clearly comes from a different fan vault. AF 8, 58, 82, 83, 84 and 85 all come from the same late Perpendicular screen.

Excavation of the abbey foundations suggested that apart from the extension of the chancel to the east there were few major alterations, but the architectural fragments show that there was considerable improvement above foundation level, and that successive abbots introduced a variety of new styles. The Perpendicular style is well represented. It seems probable that Perpendicular styles such as panel tracery and fan vaults were imposed on a Norman structure. Some removal of Norman stonework would have been necessary to install large glazed Perpendicular windows. In this sense Cirencester may have been copying Gloucester, although at Gloucester there was more money available to transform the Norman choir and presbytery into the Perpendicular masterpiece and later to pay for the Lady Chapel as well (Verey and Welander 1979, 21-9).

Alterations may have taken place on the tower to let in more light, a necessity as the increasing number of chapels reduced the amount of light in the choir and crossing. The twelfth-century nave may have had a clerestory, but this would not have provided much light. The improved techniques of building of the fifteenth century may have prompted the monks to embark upon improving the upper stages of the nave.

It is clear from the variety of panel tracery alone that the austerity exhibited in the plain moulding of the 12th-century abbey precinct north gateway was not maintained in the abbey of the 15th century. The Perpendicular styles exhibited seem to be most closely paralleled in St Mary's, Oxford, and the parish church of St John the Baptist, Cirencester. It is interesting that Bridlington Priory, which shows styles very similar to those of Cirencester, was also of the Augustinian Order. Gloucester too must surely have been a major source of inspiration.

CATALOGUE

AF 20   Fig. 111. Unprovenanced. Voussoir from Norman arch. Badly damaged. The piece is the common chevron form of decoration which occurs in so many doorways. This piece, however, comes from the soffit plane, so that the decoration would only be appreciated by a person standing in the doorway. The use of chevron decoration in two planes is not unattested, for example it occurs in the chancel arch at Elkstone, c. 1160-70 (Verey 1970, pl. 15). It is used in door and window arches, for example Iffley church (Oxon) c. 1160. The radius of the arch, although difficult to measure, was 390mm. Since Norman arches were invariably semi-circular, this means the distance spanned was 780mm. The narrowest jamb may have been smaller still, this appears to have come from a window or very small doorway. Only twelve such pieces would have been required to form the arch. Width in arch 107mm. Depth 164mm.
Date: 1120-1200.

AF 86   Not illustrated. U/S, east end of church. Voussoir from Norman arch, badly damaged. The piece displays chevron decoration, but unlike AF 20 and 87 it is in the more usual plane. It is from a small arch, radius 370mm, very similar in size to AF 20. Twelve pieces would have been required to form the semi-circular arch. Very pale pink paint.
Date: 1120-1200.

AF 87   Not illustrated. South side of chapter house. Voussoir from Norman arch, very badly damaged. The piece displays chevron decoration like pieces AF 20 and 86, and it occurs in the soffit plan as on AF 20. However, the arch in this case is very much larger. The radius is approximately 2.70m, and the span would have been 5.4m if the arch was perfectly semi-circular. Approximately thirty-six voussoirs would have been required to form the arch.
Date: 1120-1200.

AF 5   Fig. 111. BH XI 8, north side of chapter house apse. Mainly small grains, but shelly. Engaged shaft, slightly damaged, slightly 'pitted'. An engaged circular shaft occurs at the corner of what is otherwise a plain ashlar block. If the block is part of a pier, the shaft is decorative rather than structural, since a plain ashlar would do. The shaft is worked on the recessed plane, indicating the use of orders; the shaft is also poorly undercut. Distance between bedding plane 136mm. Length 280mm. Width at least 155mm. Red paint.
Date: 1115-1160, probably c. 1125.

AF 32   Not illustrated. Unprovenanced. Hollow mould with billet, fairly damaged. The billet is a fairly early form of Norman ornament and, when used in a single row, is merely an intermittent round moulding, as at Malmesbury Abbey (Wilts), c. 1130 (Parker

1891, 77). Often it was used in combination with other forms of decoration such as at Walmer (Kent), c. 1120.
Date: 1115-1150, probably c.1125.

AF 92   Fig. 111. Unprovenanced. Piece of Norman capital, very badly damaged. Slightly pitted. The capital has scallop-shell decoration. This is a common form of decoration and occurs on both large square and round piers in late Norman work. Examples occur at St John's Hospital, Cirencester (McWhirr 1973, 215). The scallop-shell decoration is found on flat capitals at Kirkstall Abbey (Yorks), c. 1152-1160 (Parker 1891, 69) and in the arcading of the porch at the west end of Fountains Abbey church (Cook 1961, pl. xxxvii). The workmanship is of low quality.
Date: 1120-1200.

AF 16   Fig. 111. Unprovenanced. Piece with keel moulding. Badly damaged and heavily weathered. The piece may be part of a pier or arch moulding. Keel or pear mouldings seem to be a characteristic of Early English style. It was used in a suite of mouldings at Haseley (Oxon) c. 1220 (Parker 1891, 114). It also occurs in the door and window jambs of West Walton (Fletcher 1960, 507). Minimum height 230mm.
Date: 1200-1280.

AF 13   Fig. 111. Unprovenanced. Fragment of composite pillar moulding, very damaged. The moulding is composed of three circular shafts, the central being larger than the other two, which are of equal size. The shafts are close, but divided by hollows. There are two additional half-round hollows. The layout is based on the equilateral triangle. Piers with engaged columns are a feature of Early English Gothic. Examples occur at the Temple Church, London, in the choir c. 1240 and at Netley Abbey c. 1250. The type also occurs at Pershore c.1230. Overall surviving dimensions 331 x 216 x 150mm. Whitewash.
Date: 1190-1300, probably c. 1240.

AF 57   Fig. 111. Unprovenanced. Voussoir of archivolt of arch or rib. Complete. Rib or arch moulding composed of undercut rounds and fillet. The hollows may have been carried into neighbouring blocks. Radius of intrados 2.1m. Similar examples occur at Bordesley (Rahtz and Hirst 1976, 144, stone no 13) and in the choir of Whitby Abbey (Bond 1906, 675). The piece seems to exhibit Early English moulding types. Whitewash.
Date: 1220-1370.

AF 67   Fig. 111. Unprovenanced. Section of rib from vault. Slight surface damage. While chamfered ribs with rounds are known to have occurred in late Norman work, for example at Kirkstall Abbey (Yorks) (Bond 1906, 673); the rounds in such vaults were large, c. 125mm radius. Round mouldings were used in Early English and early Decorated work and these tended to be of a more similar size to this piece (radius 39mm). The chamfers too tended to be more generous. Central setting-out line on bedding plane. Radius of intrados 2.8m. Whitewash and white paint.
Date: 1210-1320.

AF 3   Not illustrated. Possibly from nave or south side of chapter house. Arch or rib mould, slightly damaged. This is a very unusual moulding for a pier or rib. The wave moulding is common in late curvilinear and early Perpendicular arches. It occurs at Leadenham and Beverley St Mary chancel. Here it is set deeply into the chamfer plane, which suggests that this might be an early form. This leaves a very curious end moulding. The piece has all the appearance of being a rib, except that it is not noticeably curved. Dimensions 515 x 271 x 168mm. White paint.
Date: 1300-1400.

AF 7   Not illustrated. BJ V 2. South side of chapter house. Arch or rib mould. Almost complete. The piece is essentially the same as AF 3. For some reason it has been chamfered off obliquely. The piece also exhibits slight variations in detail, but this may be due to poor workmanship. Central. Setting-out line on bedding plane. Length 515mm. Other surviving dimensions 225 x 165mm. Whitewash and white paint.
Date: 1300-1400.

AF 68   Not illustrated. Unprovenanced. Wall rib of vault. Slightly damaged. Overall this piece is not dissimilar to AF 67. However, it has a narrow fillet on the round and a sunk chamfer. Broad fillets on rounds occur on AF 1, AF 29 and AF 81. AF 57 has the same round and fillet, while AF 71 has a similar sunk chamfer. AF 70 and 90 come from the same scheme, as may AF 57. A good parallel for this is a window mullion from Maidstone All Saints (Kent), c. 1390. This piece is shorter than the main rib AF 70. Radius approximately 4m. Whitewash and white paint.
Date: 1300-1400

AF 70   Fig. 111 Unprovenanced. Rib of vault. Slightly damaged. See AF 68 for discussion. This piece is slightly chamfered off obliquely, where it abutted up to another piece of stonework, possibly another rib or roof boss. Radius approximately 3m. Whitewash and white paint.
Date: 1300-1400.

AF 71   Not Illustrated. Unprovenanced. Rib and tracery, badly damaged. This piece seems more similar to AF 70 than to AF 67. It seems to fulfil the purpose of either arch or jamb as well as that of being a piece of panel tracery. The bedding plane is the springing line for a curved rib to depart from the vertical rib. Also a subsidiary rib springs at the same level from the recessed fillet, presumably as a piece of tracery. Perhaps the piece was situated somewhere in the triforium or clerestory stages. Central setting-out line with another at right angles on bedding plan. See AF 68. Radius of main rib 630mm. Radius of subsidiary rib 255mm. White paint.
Date: 1280-1400.

AF 60   Not illustrated. Unprovenanced. Moulding of large composite pier. Fairly damaged. The moulding is composed of three rounds divided by two small circular hollows and flanked by two larger circular hollows. The bracket moulding is flanked by two broad straight fillets. Another ogee curve is undercut by a recessed fillet which is in turn cut into by a casement.

At least one other piece is likely to have been required to complete the pier. The pieces are very large, however, and this is a feature of the Perpendicular style of construction. Neither the recessed order nor the chamfer plane appears to have been the basis for cutting the mouldings. This may indicate both early preconception and confidence in design. The moulding system seems to lack symmetry.

The three rounds and intermediate hollows are reminiscent of the Early English style, and in particular of the western school of using engaged columns in triplets, for example in the choir of Lichfield Cathedral c. 1195 and in the choir of Pershore Abbey 1223-1229. However, other features indicate a later date. The bracket (or double ogee) moulding is essentially a characteristic of the Perpendicular style. The single ogee mould parallels half of the bracket mould. The use of a round with a thin straight fillet was introduced in Early English style, but this mould is characterised by the two convex rounds having separate centres and the fillet being broad. This allows for a reverse curve to link the convex round with the fillet. This is a Perpendicular feature, as is also the use of recessed fillet to undercut and therefore emphasise the ogee mould, as at Chelmsford (1489), although here the centres of the convex rounds are further apart still. There are several elements, therefore, which suggest that the piece is only likely to have been constructed after 1400. The group of three rounds and intermediate hollows must therefore be regarded as a residual feature incorporated in a new design. Possibly it was incorporated to echo the use of the same type of moulding element elsewhere in the church (see AF 13). The retention of a close group of three engaged columns occurs also at St George's Chapel, Windsor (1473-1516), which also exhibits the ogee, the bracket and the casement. Central setting-out line. Whitewash. Best parallels in Cirencester parish church, west window, c. 1420, and St Mary, Oxford, chancel 1462.
Date: 1420-1500. Probably c. 1450.

AF 73   Fig. 111. Unprovenanced. Mullion of window with tracery. Slightly damaged. The piece is a long bar of window mullion. Two circular tracery elements spring from the mullion to form partially circular elements. The higher springs at the same level at which the lower circle finally departs from the vertical mullion. Although both arches are of a similar size (radius 498mm) the lower seems to be much wider. Both circles probably enclose cinquefoils. Neither arch has bars the same depth as the main mullion (255mm as opposed to 356mm). The piece is probably Perpendicular in style, since the shaft continues vertically even though it is amongst other tracery forms. The mullion is deep in comparison with its width; it displays the ogee and fillet mould. Two bonding marks. Length between bedding planes 615mm. Depth 356mm. Width 166mm.
Date: 1370-1520.

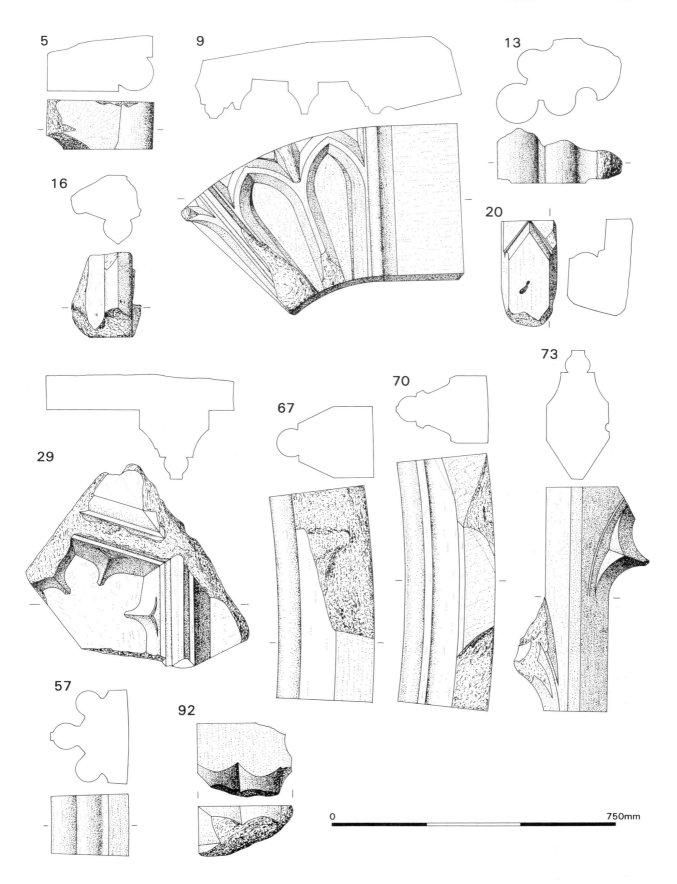

111. Architectural stonework

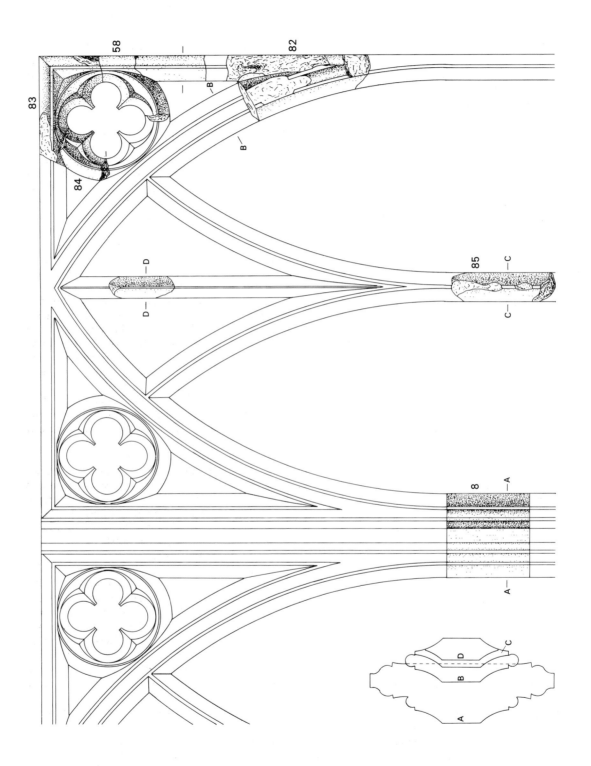

112. Suggested reconstruction of tracery screen, possibly from the north transept

AF 53 Not illustrated. Unprovenanced. Rib of panel tracery. Fairly damaged. The moulding type is similar to that of AF 39 and 51. It is used in the windows of the George Inn at Glastonbury. The mullion is probably straight and almost certainly forms Perpendicular style panels, which occur frequently on towers. Central setting-out line of bedding plane and along centre of rib.
Date: 1380-1520.

AF 39 Not illustrated. Possibly apse of south transept (see AF 51). A piece of fan vaulting. Very badly damaged. See AF 51 for description. Overall surviving dimensions 225 x 230 x 185mm. Same scheme as AF 47 and 51.
Date: 1360-1500. Probably c. 1440.

AF 47 Not illustrated. Unprovenanced. Central panel between fans of a fan-vault. Very damaged. The panel exhibits the secondary rib form of the scheme, but fits behind (i.e. above) the main rib which overlaps (see AF 51). In this too the ogee tracery form is dominant. The cusps seem to terminate in simple knobs rather than raised flower designs. Roughly scored cross. Setting-out lines along centres of ribs and on the side bedding plane. Same scheme as AF 39 and AF 51.
Date: 1360-1500, probably c. 1440.

AF 51 Not illustrated. BL XI 2, from apse of south transept. A piece of fan vaulting. Not complete, much surface damage. Slightly pitted. The key elements in the tracery design are the ogee form and the rectilinear struts. The ogee is used in fan vaulting commonly, but is usually subdued and occurs only in inner circles. This is true even of the Gloucester cloister, which is 14th century. The dominance of the ogee curve, being used on the periphery of the fan, seems to be a hangover from curvilinear window tracery design. Moreover, the use of crossing straight ribs is a distinctly rectilinear feature, common in the second half of the 15th century. The best parallel available for dating purposes is not a vault, but a pair of windows. When the north porch and Trinity Chapel were built at Cirencester parish church c. 1430, new windows were placed in the clerestory of the aisle as well as in the Trinity Chapel. The Trinity Chapel windows are not strictly speaking Perpendicular in style, since no single mullion runs straight from top to bottom. However, while the windows make good use of the 'dagger' and the 'ogee' they also make use of the rectilinear strut. Another clue to dating lies in the moulding form of the clerestory windows built at the same time. The moulding on the exterior of the main mullion exactly parallels that of the main circular rib from AF 51. The moulding is a rare type. The masons involved in the construction of both the abbey vault and the parish church windows were borrowing elements of style without comprehending the spirit of the styles they were using. The workmanship is poor. The use of flower decoration is unusual in a vault although it occurs at Gloucester. The radius of the fan is 1.80m. The span will therefore have been 3.60m. Setting-out line along centre of central rib. Distance between bedding planes 440mm. Other surviving dimensions 505 x 210mm. Same scheme as AF 39 and 47.
Date: 1360-1500, probably c. 1440.

AF 29 Fig. 111. Unprovenanced. Piece of panelled tracery, fairly damaged. The main rib form is the same as on AF 1 and 81. The hollow on piece AF 1 is of a very similar size. The rib form is similar to that on pieces AF 73 and 77, but on this piece it is perfectly round, with a fillet, whereas on pieces AF 73 and 77 the ogee curve is used.

The tracery pattern is formed of straight main ribs which cross, in between which there is a cinquefoil of pointed foils. The tracery is on a flat panel, but could still have occurred in the central infill of a fan or ribbed vault, as at St George's chapel, Windsor (Bond 1906, 332). Possibly part of the same vault as AF 1. The same rib moulding occurs at Vale Royal (Thompson 1962). The bedding planes form a wedge shape. Depth of piece at least 285mm.
Date: 1400-1520.

AF 8 Fig. 112. Possibly from the north transept area. The main mullion in a stone screen. Complete. This piece is a course in the main mullion of either a rood or chapel screen. The piece again makes use of the broad fillet and ogee forms. The use of bead is commonly found in wooden screens of the 15th century. The beads also define the depth of the secondary mullion (see AF 58, 82 and 83). The third mullion type (AF 85) uses the element between the beads. It seems likely, therefore, that the main mullions formed a rectangular tracery form 552mm wide, or a multiple thereof, with the secondary mullion dividing it into equal sized tracery designs defined by transoms. It is not clear how the third mullion type (AF 85) relates to the other two. The mullion is characterised by its large size and complexity of form. The screen would have been 362mm deep, and was probably an impressive structure of the Perpendicular style. Central setting-out line. Distance between bedding planes 166mm. Depth 362mm. Width 178mm. Whitewash. Same scheme as AF 58, 82, 83, 84 and 85.
Date: 1430-1530, probably c. 1500.

AF 9 Fig 111. Unprovenanced. Piece of fan vaulting. In three pieces, but nearly complete. This piece of vault seems to have been bedded into the wall. It is also quite close to the springing line. However, the vault must have been quite flat since the curve is very gentle in section. While the piece takes up a quarter of the fan, it does not curve 45 degrees. The fan may have been based on a four-centred arch, so that the inner sections were more sharply curved.

There is a lip for the piece to overlap the inner sections. The outer panels were probably divided into two. The outer radius is 798mm, but the distance between the outer and inner is only 420mm. The circles therefore have different centres (30mm apart). The vault is of a late Perpendicular refined type. The piece is closely paralleled by the vault in St Catherine's chapel in Cirencester parish church. Length 740mm. Depth 200mm.
Date: 1420-1500.

AF 58   Fig. 112. ?BL II 17. North side of nave, possibly in area of north transept. Piece of mullion and tracery of screen. Badly damaged. The piece is formed of a straight secondary mullion (see AF 8) and part of a quatrefoiled circle. The circle has a narrow fillet and is the fourth mullion element in terms of depth (140mm) and moulding form. The circle is linked to the secondary mullion on at least one side, but was not substantially linked on all four sides to a secondary mullion. It may have touched another quatrefoiled circle. The foils are circular and although not filleted, provide a fifth separate mullion depth (118mm). The radius of the circle was 104mm.

Quatrefoiled circles were a common tracery form in perpendicular stone screens and examples can be seen at the Audley chantry chapel at Salisbury Cathedral, *c.* 1515 and at Bath Abbey *c.* 1515. Same scheme as AF 8, 83, 82, 84 and 85. Chantry chapel of William Birde, Bath Abbey *c.* 1515 (Wright 1973, 15). Date: 1430-1530. Probably *c.* 1500.

AF 82   Fig. 112. Possibly from the north transept area. Piece of mullion and tracery from screen. Badly damaged. This is a piece of secondary mullion (see AF 8) with a tracery mullion branching off in the form of a curve (radius 867mm). This could form a large reverse curve or an equilateral pointed arch form. It could form a pointed arch over a door. In theory it could form a round arch and this would allow for the possibility that the straight mullion is in fact a transom. The mullion appears to have backed into another piece, which suggests that it might occur at the end of the screen. Depth 222mm. Whitewash. Same scheme as AF 8, 58, 83, 84 and 85. Date: 1430-1530, probably *c.* 1500

AF 83   Fig. 112. Possibly from the north transept area. Piece of mullion and tracery from a screen. Badly damaged. This piece is formed of two straight secondary mullions at right angles to each other, with a quatrefoiled circle set into the corner (see AF 8 and 58). One of the secondary mullions is therefore a transom. The true mullion is not freestanding, since it is cut off at the back, like AF 82, and the piece may have been a 'respond' at the end of the screen. The quatrefoiled circle may not have joined the same secondary mullion element on the other two respective sides. It may have been linked to another quatrefoil circle or to another tracery element. Originally 223mm deep. Same scheme as AF 8, 58, 82, 84 and 85.
Date: 1430-1530. Probably *c.*1500.

AF 84   Fig. 112. Possibly from the north transept area. Piece of tracery from a screen. Very badly damaged. This piece is part of a quatrefoiled circle. See AF 58 for discussion. Depth 133mm. Same scheme as AF 8, 58, 82, 83 and 85.
Date: 1430-1530, probably *c.* 1500.

AF 85   Fig. 112. Possibly from the north transept area. Piece of mullion from a screen. Badly damaged. The piece is part of a bar from the mullion of a screen. From the size of the hollow (radius 88mm) and the depth of the mullion it can be directly related to AF 8. The mullion is the minor one of three. Depth 178mm. Width 66mm. Same scheme as AF 8, 58, 82, 83 and 84.
Date: 1430-1530, probably *c.* 1500.

THE BURIALS

C. M. Heighway, M. Harman, L. Viner, and D. J. Wilkinson

INTRODUCTION

This report is compiled from an archive report by Linda Viner, which in turn derived from the stratigraphic analyses of David Wilkinson, and a report on the human skeletal material by Mary Harman (Harman 1966).

The original excavation had not anticipated the excavation of large numbers of burials. Not all burials were recorded or lifted, and those in special graves such as stone cists were more often recorded than plain earth burials. After excavation, human bone was assigned H numbers. These total 157, of which many were disarticulated fragments. For the purposes of the present study, unlocated burials and those consisting only of bone fragments have been disregarded; the total burials considered in this report therefore represents a minimum of 60 individuals.

The burials were originally designated by their somewhat cumbersome context numbers; for this report the H numbers, which were strictly speaking assigned to bones only, have been used to apply also to the grave in which the skeleton was found. In cases where no bones were recovered, it has been necessary to assign new H numbers which run from H200 onwards. Where the grave had more than one occupant, the H number of the most complete skeleton has been used, on the assumption that the most complete remains represent the primary occupant. Where this assumption cannot be made, a new H number has been assigned.

The report on the human skeletal material (Harman 1966) divided the articulated skeletons into Saxon (21), medieval (32) and post-medieval groups (9) and analysed the various characteristics including height, age, sex and dental health. However, subsequent work has shown that the distinction between 'Saxon' and medieval graves is uncertain (see below); some 'Saxon' burials are now thought to be 13th century, while some 'post-medieval' burials may be medieval. It has, therefore, been decided not to publish the skeletal report in full, although much information from it has been incorporated in what follows.

Types of coffins

There were various types of coffins and other containers:
1. Grave lined with stones, oval or rectangular in shape
2. Grave lined with stones, tapered in shape
3. Solid stone coffin
4. Wooden coffin
5. Earth grave.

Both types 1 and 2 occasionally had a rectangular recess created for the head.

Type 1 may be late Saxon onwards. Type 2, tapered graves are thought to apply to high-status graves of the late medieval period (Litten 1991, 89); the usual medieval coffin shape was rectangular. However, stone-lined tapered graves were found at St Andrew, Fishergate where they are dated 12th-16th century (Stroud and Kemp 1993, 153). Plain stone-lined graves at Fishergate numbered only two which contained children; their date range was also 12th-16th century. A rectangular mortared stone-lined grave with head recess at St Oswald's Priory, Gloucester was of late 11th to 12th-century date (Heighway and Bryant forthcoming).

The distribution of the different types of coffin through time is expressed in the following table. Much of the dating is uncertain, so this is only a general indication of periods of use.

What is noticeable is the lack of wooden coffins in the earlier periods (although they were perhaps unexcavated), and the increase in variety of container in the late medieval period. The increase of earth graves in the late medieval period is distorted by the large number in the burial pit: there must have been many more earth burials in all periods which have not been excavated.

At Cirencester there is a notable absence of burials with 'earmuffs' - stones propping the head, usually a 10th to 11th-century rite - and of charcoal burials (usually a high-status 10th to 12th-century rite). If Cirencester was indeed an Anglo-Saxon minster church, some such burials would be expected, as at the late-Saxon minster of St Oswald's Priory,

TABLE TO SHOW DIFFERENT TYPES OF BURIAL CONTAINER THROUGH TIME

Type	Date			
	11th century	11th-12th century	13th-16th century	Total
Stone-lined grave	4	12	4	20
Rectangular or oval stone-lined grave with head recess		3		3
Tapered stone-lined grave with head recess		1		1
Wooden coffin			5	5
Wooden coffin in stone-lined grave with head recess			1	1
Wooden coffin in stone-lined grave without head recess			3	3
Solid stone coffin			1	1
Earth grave	6	5	15	26
Totals	10	21	29	60

Gloucester. Stone-lined graves at Gloucester only occur in the late 11th century, and then rarely. Cirencester clearly had plenty of these; perhaps earlier burials with different rites do exist at Cirencester, but have not been excavated.

Burial rites and attributes
Since there was insufficient record made of body positions, no study of this has been possible.

'Saxon' burials (late Anglo-Saxon to c. 1130)
In his report, David Brown (1976, 41-2) described stone-lined graves which he thought were associated with the intermediate church, or possibly with the phase 1a Anglo-Saxon church. He pointed out that some stone-lined graves appeared to define the east end of the Anglo-Saxon church (ibid, p. 42). The graves west of the Anglo-Saxon church were set in a dark burial soil (fig. 19, context BP VII 1) which in turn was sealed by the courtyard surface outside the west end of the 12th-century abbey nave (Brown 1976, 41). Brown acknowledged that the stone cist H139 was inserted when the Saxon church had already been robbed, and assigned H139 to the phase 1b church. However, the courtyard surface sealing the burials (BP IV 10, fig. 19) appears from the associated pottery to carry a *t.p.q.* of the 13th century, so the latest of the graves at the west end of the abbey could be of 12th to 13th-century date. A group of graves in trench BP II and BP I (not planned in Brown 1976, Fig 3.8, or Brown and McWhirr 1966, Fig 3) were originally designated 'Saxon' presumably because they were set in the dark burial soil . However, pottery analysis ascribes these burials (H148, 147, 94, 104, 107, 108) to the 13th century. It must be borne in mind that the pottery evidence is of uncertain reliability in the case of graveyards, since there is a high likelihood of unseen grave cuts and consequent introduction of intrusive material. Nevertheless, some of the burials in this dark burial soil (e.g. H147, H144, fig. 29) were stone cists with recessed heads which might be expected to be 12th century or later (above p.163). It seems likely that the 'dark burial soil' (or as much as was excavated) spans a period from the Anglo-Saxon through to the 12th or perhaps 13th century.

There were, however, certainly burials on the site before the 12th-century abbey was begun. Some at least of these burials were in stone cists. At least seven burials (H200, 203, 205, 206, 207, 208, and 210) were cut by abbey walls of *c.* 1130. H200 and H203 were stone cists (fig. 40); H205 (Wacher 1965, plate xliii) was in a stone-lined grave and clearly earlier than the 1130 church. H210 was a stone-lined grave covered with a slab. These pre-abbey burials suggest that an unknown number of the burials west of the 12th-century west end were also pre-1130 in date.

It should also be noticed that a number of burials within the area of the 12th-century nave were on curious alignments, which do not relate to the 12th-century nave as one would expect were they buried inside the church. Some of these oddly aligned burials are among the six mentioned above which are certainly pre-1130. Burials with this alignment have therefore been assumed to be 11th century.

There are no burials which could certainly be said to be contemporary with the phase 1a church: however, it should be noticed that few of the trenches were taken to natural. Section 120 (fig. 19) shows the bottom of the 'Saxon graveyard' labelled 'unexcavated' at about 6ft (2m) depth, and in trench BP I where there was dense medieval burial, there was 'no natural at 11ft 6 ins (3.5m)'. It is to be noted that this considerable depth of burial is in the area *outside* the phase 1a church. No doubt early burials exist which would take the history of the site back to the foundation of the first church.

Medieval burials (*c.* 1130-*c.*1530)
The most significant grave excavated was H118 at the centre of the nave (fig. 33) (Brown and McWhirr 1966, plate xliiic). The tomb was built of large slabs set on edge with smaller stones filling the gaps. The stones were mortared together and the inside of the tomb was coated with white plaster. The tomb contained the remains of at least three individuals, a male aged 35-40, a male aged 30-35, and a male adult.

It was noted (Brown and McWhirr 1966, 248, note 2) that the position of this tomb corresponded with the position of the burial of Regenbald as described by Leland (Leland, *Itin.* **1**, 129). Regenbald was a priest high in royal administrative service in the reigns of Edward Confessor and William I who is thought to have left handsome endowments to Cirencester church (Evans 1989, 116) but he must have been dead for a generation when the new abbey of *c.* 1130 (? or 1117, see Evans 1991, 99) was built. He might have been buried in the old church, and his bones moved (Evans 1991, 101). However, it is more likely, as David Brown asserts, that the association with Regenbald was simply incorrect, and that Leland was reporting a tradition current in his time, that whatever body this tomb contained was moved from the previous church (Brown 1976, 42). It is, of course, totally unknown who the founders and benefactors of the old Saxon church might have been, but if the body of one of them had been revered in the crypt, it could well have been moved

113. Early 13th-century grave cover of burial H160

to the new church in the 12th century, and to a new location little removed from its position in the crypt of the old church.

West of the west end of the 1130 church was a group of burials in the 'dark earth' mentioned above. H148 was a stone-lined cist, H147 a cist with recessed head (fig. 29). The two cist burials (of adults, one male) appear to have been under or earlier than the other skeletons, which were earth burials. Most of the earth burials were of children (H94, H95, H104, H107, H108). If the pottery evidence can be depended on, then these burials belong to the 13th century, or perhaps later. The presence of children of course suggests a lay population. It should be noticed that this group is very close to the abbey south boundary: it is possible that these were parish burials; the boundary between abbey and parish may not always have been definitively marked.

Some burials in the 12th-century nave, which are aligned on it, could be 12th century or later. There was in the north transept a burial in a wooden coffin, H61, containing a male aged more than 30.

Two graves were excavated well to the south-east of the abbey church (fig. 33). Both had stone grave-covers. H160 had a decorated grave slab (fig. 113), incomplete, covering a solid stone coffin base. Inside was the skeleton of an adult male, and the skull fragment of another individual. The slab was said to be early 13th century (Brown and McWhirr 1966, 253). H101 was a monolithic rectangular coffin, with drain holes in the base and a recess for the head. Inside the coffin was the skeleton of a complete male adult, and odd bones from at least three other individuals.

The cover was inscribed +HIC IACET WALTERUS: DE : CHELT[E(N)]HAM : QUONDAM : CLERICUS : NOSTER :[CUIU]S : ANIME PROPICIETUR[R : D]E [S (Here lies Walter of Cheltenham formerly our clerk to whose soul may God be merciful).

Walter of Cheltenham was a member of the Abbot's Council in 1285. In 1298 he was securing for the abbey the restoration of the church of Ampney St Mary, of which he was rector. In 1302 he procured a licence to alienate in mortmain to the abbey a house and carucate of land in Sapperton. By 1269 he held the churches of Ampney St Mary and Withington. In 1291 he obtained the church of Coates, and in 1298 that of Sapperton. He was already dead in 1306. Walter only received orders as a subdeacon in 1284 and priest in 1300. He was clearly not a canon but a secular priest. His property may have been given to help build the abbey choir (Radford 1966; *CC* **3**, 1977, no 195; Evans 1993, 126-7).

It was the view of the excavators (Brown and McWhirr 1966, 253) that the tombs were not in their original positions. These were evidently high-status tombs, and it was thought unlikely that they would originally have been positioned in this corner of the cemetery. It is not clear why or when they were moved.

In the north presbytery aisle there were three recorded burials. H106 (fig. 47) cut the sleeper wall on the threshold of the new eastern chapels: a tiled floor of the early 14th century, thought to be original, covered the tomb, which thus should be of late 13th-century date. Inside the stone-edged tomb was a wooden nailed coffin and part of a rectangular copper alloy plate (not illustrated). The skeleton was male, aged 25 or over. H202 cut the same wall and is perhaps of similar date. H201 (fig. 47) could have belonged to the central aisle of the 12th-century presbytery and so is of 12th-16th century date: it is stone-lined with a recessed head (fig. 34) and is a parallel for stone-lined burials outside the west end.

There were a number of burials in the area of the claustral buildings. In the chapter house a burial, H49, preceded the 14th-century construction of the vestibule walls. The burial (fig. 57) was of a male, aged 35-40, in an oak coffin, with the remains of a pewter chalice on the knees and a penannular iron buckle above the pelvis (finds not illustrated). This burial is thought to be 13th century. Burial H219, in the cloister walk, was in a stone coffin, and presumably dates to between the 12th and the 15th centuries.

Set in the south wall of the south presbytery aisle was a tomb H59 (fig. 115) which was entered down steps (Wacher 1965, plate xxxviiib). The provision of steps suggests access to the tomb, which is presumably why the excavators described this as a 'chantry tomb'. The backfill of the tomb contained floor tiles of the early 14th century. The tomb contained a male, aged 25-30, laid in a wooden coffin in a stone-lined cist. With the burial were a copper alloy fastening (fig. 69, no. 24), and a 14th-century pewter chalice (fig. 83, no. 141). The chantry chapel also seems to have contained 14th to 15th-century architectural fragments, which are published in Wacher (1965, plate xl) but are not otherwise commented on.

114. Grave cover of Walter of Cheltenham, burial H101

115. Burial H59, with chalice, in 'chantry' chapel built into wall 302, the south wall of the south presbytery aisle

Late medieval or early post-medieval burials

In the south-west corner of the site, there was a large pit, BP I 24 (fig. 8), which contained a collection of burials (H113-115, H124, H137-8). Though all in one pit, the burials were individually disposed, one even being in a coffin. There was one adult, the rest of the six skeletons were juveniles. This group is very reminiscent of 'plague pits' recently excavated of late medieval date in Hereford (Stone and Appleton-Fox 1996, 24-5). The pit was only partly excavated, and no doubt more burials remain south of the limit of excavation. The pit contained 13th-century pottery (Minety ware) and could have been dug in the 13th-14th century. The situation of this pit is south-west of the abbey church, and south of the borough boundary. This tract of land may have been part of the medieval parish cemetery.

In trench BP I, post-dating the burial pit just mentioned, there were several burials. Earth grave H97 contained the remains of a male and two juveniles. H79, an adult male, was also in an earth grave and was curiously oriented north-south. H222, positioned over the 'plague pit', was the platform for a tapered stone-lined burial. This group of burials was sealed by the floor of a 17th-century building.

116. Burial H144 in cist: 11th-12th century

This group of burials may be 15th-16th century and belong, like the burial-pit, to the parish churchyard.

Age and sex of burials

All but two of the adult burials were male. The two females, H139 and H149, were in stone-lined graves. H139 is on section (fig. 19); the grave is stone-lined with a head-recess and overlies the Saxon church robbing. H149 is also stone-lined, and could predate the 12th-century abbey. These two are the only evidence that there was any lay burial connected with the abbey. Both could be 11th century, and belong to the period when this was the graveyard of the minster church, which would have buried lay persons from the minster parish as well as canons. Of the two groups of children, one was 13th century, described above, and possibly part of the parish cemetery, the other was in the burial pit and late medieval, also possibly part of the parish cemetery. Apart from these, all the burials within church and claustral buildings were adult and male, as is to be expected of a community of Augustinian canons, since by the middle ages most lay burial was presumably carried out in the parish churchyard. However, lay persons who had been conspicuous benefactors of the abbey, and their families, as well as the families of secular clerks such as Walter of Cheltenham, would occasionally have been buried in the abbey or its churchyard. Leland asserted that the heart of Sanchia of Provence, wife of Henry III's brother Richard of Cornwall, was buried in Cirencester abbey church (Evans 1993, 127).

The skeletal material by Mary Harman

The height of adult skeletons was calculated from the total length of the long bones, using the formulae of Trotter and Gleser (1958, 79-123). The average height of 26 Saxon/medieval skeletons (all male) was 5ft 5½in (171.45cm).

Most persons over 30 years had some slight evidence of osteo-arthritis. Two, H118a and H143, had most of the vertebral column fused by osteophytic growth, with the rest of the vertebrae less seriously affected. Some persons over 30 years (H91, H147, H121) were not noticeably affected. There was little other evidence for disease affecting the bones; H140 had a lesion on the right lower leg, H74 (a child) suffered from a localised infection of the humeri, H101 may have had rheumatoid arthritis or possibly gout, as well as osteo-arthritis, while H50 probably had congenital dysplasia of the left hip. No fractures were noted.

Post-medieval skeletons?

About 24 skeletons were excavated in trench 64 BK II, thought to be about 60ft west of 64 BK I/IV, but otherwise unlocated. The skeletons were densely packed, and included only one grave with a stone lining. The grave density seems to indicate that this was part of the parish graveyard; the finds suggest that the burials were post-medieval.

ABBREVIATIONS

Antiq Journ	Antiquaries Journal
Arch J	Archaeological Journal
Archaeol	Archaeological
BAR	British Archaeological Reports
BGAS	Bristol and Gloucestershire Archaeological Society
BMC	British Museum Catalogue
CAT	Cotswold Archaeological Trust
CBA Res Rep	Council for British Archaeology Research Report
CRAAGS	Committee for Rescue Archaeology in Avon, Gloucestershire and Somerset
Eng Hist Rev	English Historical Review
GRO	Gloucestershire Record Office
JBAA	Journal of the British Archaeological Association
JRS	Journal of Roman Studies
Med Arch	Medieval Archaeology
Proc Prehist Soc	Proceedings of the Prehistoric Society
Publ Thoresby Soc	Publications of the Thoresby Society
Record Bucks	Records of Buckinghamshire
TBGAS	Transactions of the Bristol and Gloucestershire Archaeological Society
TWAS	Transactions of the Worcestershire Archaeological Society
VCH	Victoria County History
WAM	Transactions of the Wiltshire Archaeological and Natural History Magazine
Worcs Hist Soc	Worcestershire Historical Society

BIBLIOGRAPHY AND REFERENCES

Anon 1795 Plan of the Borough Town of Cirencester shewing the Property of T. B. Howell Esq (1795). GRO D2525

ASC The Anglo-Saxon Chronicle, in C. Plummer (ed), *Two of the Saxon Chronicles Parallel*, 2 vols (Oxford 1892, 1899, reprinted 1952). English translations by D. Whitelock (London 1961), M. J. Swanton (London 1996)

Atkyns, R. 1712 *The Ancient and Present State of Gloucestershire* (reprinted Wakefield 1974)

Atkinson, D. R. 1965 'Clay Tobacco Pipes and Pipemakers of Marlborough', *WAM* **60**, 85-95

Atkinson, D. R. 1980 'More Wiltshire Clay Tobacco Pipe Varieties', *Archaeology of the Clay Tobacco Pipe iii*, BAR **78**, 293-304 (Oxford)

Barnard, F. P. 1917 *The casting counter and the counting board* (Oxford)

Barton, K. J. 1961 'Some evidence for two types of pottery manufactured in Bristol in the early 18th century', *TBGAS* **80**, 160-168

Barton, K. J. 1963 'A medieval pottery kiln at Ham Green, Bristol', *TBGAS* **82**, 95-127

Barton, K. J. 1967 'The medieval pottery of the City of Worcester', *TWAS* 3rd Series **1** (1965-7), 29-44

Beckmann, B. 1974 'The main types of the last four production periods of Siegburg pottery', in Evison, Hodges and Hurst 1974, 183-220

Beecham, K. J. 1887 *History of Cirencester and the Roman City of Corinium* (reprinted Gloucester 1978)

Berry, G. 1974 *Medieval English Jetons* (London)

Biddle, M. and Barclay, K. 1974 'Winchester Ware', in Evison, Hodges and Hurst 1974, 137-66

Biek, L. and Gillies, X. n.d. 'Sherds from Pit BG IV 33 [at Cirencester Abbey]' (Ancient Monuments Laboratory Report no AM777732)

Bigland, R. 1791 *Historical, monumental, and genealogical collections relative to the county of Gloucester*, 2 vols (London, 1791-2), re-issued by BGAS, 4 vols (1989-95)

Birch, W. de Gray 1900 *Catalogue of Seals in the Department of Manuscripts in the British Museum* **VI** (London)

Blockley, K. *et al* 1997 *Canterbury Cathedral: Archaeology, History and Architecture* (Archaeology of Canterbury, New Series, **1**)

Bond, F. 1906 *Gothic Architecture in England* (London)

Brears, P. C. D. 1971 *The English Country Pottery: its History and Techniques* (Newton Abbot)

Brown, P. D. C. 1976 'Archaeological evidence for the Anglo-Saxon period', in McWhirr (ed) 1976, 19-45

Brown, P. D. C. and McWhirr, A. D. 1966 'Cirencester 1965', *Antiq Journ* **46**, 240-254

Brown, P. D. C. and McWhirr, A. D. 1967 'Cirencester 1966', *Antiq Journ* **47**, 185-7

Caley, J. 1821 'Copy of a Survey of the Priory of Bridlington in Yorkshire, taken about the 32nd year of Henry VIII', *Archaeologia* **19**, 270-5

Cal. Pap. Lett. 1342-62 Calendar of entries in the Papal Registers relating to Great Britain and Ireland: Papal Letters **3**, ed W. H. Bliss and C. Johnson (HMSO, 1897)

Cal. Pat. Calendar of the Patent Rolls preserved in the Public Record Office, 1232-1509, 52 vols (1891-1916); *1547-1582,* 19 vols (1924-86) (HMSO)

Camden, W. 1586 *Britannia* (London)

CC The Cartulary of Cirencester Abbey, **1** and **2** ed C. D. Ross (1964), **3** ed M. Devine (1977, Oxford). References are to document numbers unless otherwise stated.

Celoria, F. S. C. and Kelly, J. H. 1973 *A Post-Medieval Pottery Site with a Kiln Base found off Albion Square, Hanley, Stoke-on-Trent, Staffordshire* (City of Stoke-on-Trent Museum Archaeol Soc Rep **4**)

Cheney, C. R. 1973 *Medieval Texts and Studies* (Oxford)

Christophers, V., Hazelgrove, C. and Pearcey, O. 1977 *The Fulham Pottery, a preliminary account* (Fulham and Hammersmith Historical Soc Archaeol section, revised and amended 1977)

Cirencester Cartulary, Reg. A. MS deposited by Lord Vestey, Bodleian Library, Oxford, Dep C 392

Clay, P. 1981 'The small finds', in J. E. Mellor and T. Pearce (eds) *The Austin Friars, Leicester* (CBA Res Rep **35**, London)

Clifton-Taylor, A. 1984 *Another Six English Towns* (London)

Collinson, J. 1791. *The History and Antiquities of the County of Somerset,* 3 vols (Bath)

Cook, G. H. 1961 *English Monasteries in the Middle Ages*

CS Cartularium Saxonicum, ed W. de Gray Birch, 3 vols (1885-93, reprinted 1963)

Darvill, T. and Gerrard C. 1994 *Cirencester: Town and Landscape* (Cirencester)

Dawson D. P., Jackson, R. G. and Ponsford, M. W. 1972 'Medieval Kiln Wasters from St Peter's Church, Bristol', *TBGAS* **91**, 159-67

DB Domesday Book, 4 vols (Record Commission, 1783-1816). English translation for individual counties in *VCH,* and in Domesday Book series published by Phillimore (Chichester, 1975 et seqq.)

Dep. Keeper's Rep. 1846 *Seventh Report of the Deputy Keeper of the Public Records* (HMSO)

Dunning, G. C. 1949 'Medieval pottery from Selsey Common, near Stroud', *TBGAS* **68**, 30-44

Dunning, G. C. 1971 'A ridge-tile crest from Lyveden, with notes on ridge tiles with knife-cut crests in England and Wales', in J. M. Steane and G. F. Bryant 'Excavations at the deserted medieval settlement at Lyvedon', *Journal Northampton Museum* **12**, 97-105

Eames, E. 1991 'Medieval tiles', in P. and E. Saunders (eds) *Salisbury and South Wiltshire Museum Medieval Catalogue: Part 1* (Salisbury)

Egan, G. 1994 *Lead Cloth Seals and Related Items in the British Museum (*British Museum Occasional Paper **93**)

Egan, G. 1995 'England's Post-Medieval Cloth Trade: A Survey of the Evidence from Cloth Seals', in D. R. Hook and D. R. M. Gaimster (eds) *Trade and Discovery: The Scientific Study of Artefacts from Post-Medieval Europe and Beyond* (British Museum Occasional Paper **109**), 315-26

Egan, G. forthcoming 'Report on Lead Seals found at Kingsholm, Gloucester'

Egan, G. and Pritchard, F. 1991 *Dress Accessories c. 1150-c. 1450: Medieval Finds from Excavations in London* **3** (London)

Endrei, W. and Egan, G. 1982 'The Sealing of Cloth in Europe, with Special Reference to the English Evidence', *Textile History* **13**(1), 47-75

Evans, A. K. B. 1989 'Cirencester's Early Church', *TBGAS* **107**, 107-122

Evans, A. K. B. 1991 'Cirencester Abbey: the first hundred years', *TBGAS* **109**, 99-116

Evans, A. K. B. 1993 'Cirencester Abbey: From Heyday to Dissolution', *TBGAS* **111**, 115-142

Evison, V. I., Hodges, H. and Hurst, J. G. (eds) 1974 *Medieval pottery from excavations: studies presented to G C Dunning*

Finberg, H. P. R. 1957 *Gloucestershire Studies* (Leicester; 2nd edn)

Finberg, H. P. R. 1961 *The Early Charters of the West Midlands* (Leicester, 2nd edn 1972)

Fletcher, B. 1960 *A History of Architecture on the Comparative Method*

Florence of Worcester Florentii Wigorniensis Monachi Chronicon ex Chronicis, ed B. Thorpe, 2 vols (English Historical Society 1848-9)

Fowler, E. 1964 'Celtic metalwork of the 5th and 6th centuries', *Archaeol Journ* **120**, 98-160

Fuller, E. A. 1885 'Cirencester - The Manor and Town', *TBGAS* **9**, 298-344

Fuller, E. A. 1893a 'Cirencester Abbey Church', *TBGAS* **17**, 45-52

Fuller, E. A. 1893b 'The Parish Church of St John the Baptist, Cirencester', *TBGAS* **17**, 34-44

Fuller, E. A. 1893c 'Cirencester Hospitals', *TBGAS* **17**, 34-44

Fuller, E. A. 1894 'Cirencester Guild Merchant', *TBGAS* **18**, 32-74

Gem, R. D. H. 1993 'Architecture of the Anglo-Saxon Church 735 to 870 from Archibishop Ecgherht to Archbishop Ceolnoth', *JBAA* **146**, 29-66

Gesta Henrici II   Gesta regis Henrici secundi Benedicti abbatis. The chronicle of the reigns of Henry II and Richard I, A.D. 1169-92, known commonly under the name of Benedict of Peterborough, ed W. Stubbs, 2 vols (Rolls Series, 1867)

Gesta Stephani Ed and trans K. R. Potter, with a new introduction and notes by R. H. C. Davis (Oxford Medieval Texts, 1976)

Gibbs, M. 1939 (ed) *Early Charters of the Cathedral Church of St Paul, London* (Royal Historical Soc Camden 3rd Series **58**)

Goring, J. J. 1971 'The General Proscription of 1522', *Eng Hist Rev* **86**, 681-705

Green, R. 1977 *Bottle Collecting: Comprehensive Price Guide* (Old Bottles and Treasure Hunting Publications)

Griffiths N. and Robinson P. 1991 'A Re-examination of the Tile Designs from the Medieval Kiln at Nash Hill, Lacock', *WAM* **84**, 61-70

Haldon, R. and Mellor, M. 1977 'Late Saxon and Medieval Pottery', in B. Durham, 'Archaeological Investigations in St. Aldates, Oxford', *Oxoniensia* **42**, 83-203

Harman, M. 1966 [Report on burials from Cirencester Abbey: Corinium Museum archive]

Harvey, J. H. 1969 (ed) *William Worcestre Itineraries* (Oxford)

Haslam, J. 1975 'The Excavation of a 17th-century pottery site at Cove, East Hampshire', *Post-Medieval Archaeology* **9**, 164-187

Hassall, M. 1973 'Inscriptions 1969-1973', in McWhirr 1973, 211-14

Heighway, C. M. and Bryant, R. forthcoming *The Anglo-Saxon minster and medieval priory of St Oswald at Gloucester* (CBA, York)

Holbrook, N. and Wilkinson, K. forthcoming   'The topography and hydrology of the Cirencester area', in Holbrook (ed) forthcoming

Holbrook, N. and Salvatore, J. P. forthcoming 'The Street Grid', in Holbrook (ed) forthcoming

Holbrook, N. forthcoming (ed) *Cirencester: The Roman Town Defences, Public Buildings, and Shops* (Cirencester Excavations **V**)

Holling, F. W. 1971 'A preliminary note on the pottery industry of the Hampshire-Surrey borders', *Surrey Archaeol Collections* **68**, 57-88

Holling, F. W. 1977 'Reflections on Tudor Green', *Post-Medieval Archaeology* **11**, 61-7

Howden   Chronica Rogeri de Houedene, ed W. Stubbs, 4 vols (Rolls Series, 1868-71)

Hurst, J. G. 1964 'Medieval Pottery', in B. Cunliffe (ed), *Winchester Excavations 1949-1960*, **1**, 123-44

Hurst, J. G. 1966 'Imported flasks', in C. V. Bellamy, 'Kirkstall Abbey Excavations 1960-64', *Publ Thoresby Soc* **51**, no 112, 54-9

Hurst, J. G. 1974 'Sixteenth and seventeenth-century imported pottery from the Saintonge', in Evison, Hodges and Hurst 1974, 221-56

Hurst, J. G. 1977 'Spanish pottery imported into medieval Britain', *Med Arch* **21**, 68-105

Ireland, C. 1984 'Roman and medieval pottery', in A. P. Garrod and C. M. Heighway, *Garrod's Gloucester* (Bristol), 73-84

John of Worcester The Chronicle of John of Worcester, 1118-1140, ed J. R. H. Weaver (Oxford, 1908)

Jones, F.E. 1966 'A rare penny of William I from Cirencester', *Spink and Son's Numismatic Circular* **74**, 92

Jope, E. M. 1951 'The development of pottery ridge tiles in the Oxford region', *Oxoniensia* **16**, 86-88

Jope, E. M. 1954 'Medieval pottery kilns at Brill, Bucks: Preliminary report on Excavations in 1953', *Record Bucks* **16** (1953-4), 39-42

Keely, J. 1986 'The Pottery', in McWhirr (ed) 1986, 153-189

Kelly, J. H. and Greaves, S. J. 1974   *The Excavations of a Kiln Base in Old Hall Street, Hanley, Stoke-on-Trent, Staffordshire* (City of Stoke-on-Trent Museum Archaeol Soc Rep **6**)

Kelly, J. H. 1973 *A Rescue Excavation on the Site of the Swan Bank Methodist Church Burslem, Stoke-on-Trent, Staffordshire* (City of Stoke-on-Trent Museum Archaeol Soc Rep **5**)

Keynes, S. 1988 'Regenbald the Chancellor (sic)', *Anglo-Norman Studies* **10**, 185-222

Keynes, S. and Lapidge, M. 1983 *Alfred the Great* (Penguin Classics, Harmondsworth)

Kilmurry, K. 1977 'An approach to pottery study: Stamford ware', *Medieval Ceramics* **1**, 51-62

Kilmurry, K. 1980 *The Pottery Industry of Stamford, Lincs c. AD 850-1250*, BAR **84** (Oxford)

Leland, *Itin. The Itinerary of John Leland in or about the years 1535-43*, ed L. Toulmin-Smith, 5 vols (1907-10, reissued 1964)

Lindley, E. S. 1957 'A Short Study in *Valor Ecclesiasticus*', *TBGAS* **76**, 98-117

Litten, J. W. S. 1991 *The English Way of Death: the common funeral since 1450* (London)

Lowe, B. 1979 *Medieval Floor Tiles of Keynsham Abbey* (privately published)

LP Calendar of Letters and Papers Foreign and Domestic of the reign of Henry VIII, ed J. S. Brewer, J. Gairdner, and R. H. Brodie, 23 vols (HMSO 1862-1932; Kraus reprint 1965)

McCarthy, M. R. 1974 'The medieval kilns on Nash Hill, Lacock, Wiltshire', *WAM* **69**, 97-45

McLees, D. 1988 'Cirencester: Church of St John the Baptist', in N. H. Cooper (ed), *The Cirencester Area* (Royal Archaeological Institute, supplement to **145**)

McWhirr, A. D. (ed) 1976 *Archaeology and History of Cirencester*, BAR **30** (Oxford)

McWhirr, A. D. (ed) 1986 *Houses in Roman Cirencester* (Cirencester Excavations **III**)

McWhirr, A. D. 1973 'Cirencester 1969-72: Ninth Interim Report', *Antiq Journ* **53**, 191-218

Mellor, M. 1980a 'Late Saxon pottery from Oxfordshire: evidence and speculation', *Medieval Ceramics* **4**, 17-28

Mellor, M. 1980b 'Pottery', in N. J. Palmer, 'A Beaker burial and medieval tenements in The Hamel, Oxford', *Oxoniensia* **45**, 160-82

Mellor, M. and Oakley, G. 1984 'A summary of the key assemblages', in T. G. Hassall, C. E. Halpin and M. Mellor, 'Excavations in St. Ebbe's Oxford 1967-1976: pt II : Post-medieval domestic tenements and the post-dissolution site of the Greyfriars', *Oxoniensia* **49**, 181-219

Mon. Angl. W. Dugdale, *Monasticon Anglicanum*, ed J. Caley, H. Ellis and B. Bandinel (6 vols in 8, 1817-30. Reprinted, 6 vols 1846)

Moorhouse, S. 1970 'Finds from Basing House, Hants, Pt 1', *Post-Medieval Archaeology* **4**, 31-91

Moorhouse S. 1971 'Two late and post-medieval pottery groups from Farnham Castle, Surrey', *Surrey Archaeological Collections* **68**, 39-56

Musty, J. W. 1973 'A preliminary account of a medieval pottery industry at Minety, North Wilts', *WAM* **68**, 79-88

Musty, J. W. G., Algar, D. J. and Ewence P. F. 1969 'The medieval pottery kilns at Laverstock, near Salisbury, Wiltshire', *Archaeologia* **102**, 83-150

North, J. J. 1960 *English Hammered Coinage* (London)

Obedientiaries' Accounts. Cirencester Abbey Obedientiaries' Accounts. MS in Staffordshire Record Office, D (W) 1788. 54. 8.

OS 1875 Ordnance Survey 1st edition map of Cirencester 1875

Oswald, A. 1975 *Clay Tobacco Pipes for the Archaeologist*, BAR **14** (Oxford)

Parker, J. 1891 *An Introduction to the Study of Gothic Architecture*

Peacey, A. 1979 *Clay Tobacco Pipes in Gloucestershire* (Bristol)

PR 31 Henry I Magnum Rotulum Scaccarii vel rotulum pipae anno tricesimo-primo regni Henrici primi, ed J. Hunter (Record Commission 1833. Reissued with corrections by C. Johnson, HMSO 1929)

PR 33 Henry II; PR 16 John Pipe Roll for the 33rd year of King Henry II; Pipe Roll for the 16th year of King John, Pipe Roll Society, **37** (1915) and **73** (1962)

Pretty, K. 1975 *The Welsh border and the Severn and Avon Valleys in the Fifth and Sixth Centuries AD: An Archaeological Survey* (unpublished PhD Thesis, University of Cambridge, January 1975)

P.R.O. E 315 Public Record Office, Augmentation Office, Miscellaneous Books

P.R.O. E 321 Public Record Office, Proceedings of the Court of Augmentations

Radford, R. C. A. 1966 'Appendix: the tomb cover of Walter of Cheltenham', in Brown and McWhirr 1966, 253-4

Rahtz, P. and Hirst, S. 1976 *Bordesley Abbey*, BAR **23** (Oxford)

Reece, R. 1962 'The Abbey of St Mary, Cirencester', *TBGAS* **81**, 198-202

Reece, R. and Catling, C. 1975 *Cirencester: Development and Buildings*, BAR **12** (Oxford)

Reg. Arundel The Register of Thomas Arundel, Archbishop of Canterbury, 1396-7, 1399-1414, Lambeth Palace Library MS, 2 vols

Reg. Bransford A Calendar of the Register of Wolstan de Bransford, Bishop of Worcester, 1339-49, ed R. M. Haines (Worcs Hist Soc New Series **4** , 1966)

Reg. Morton The Register of John Morton, Archbishop of Canterbury 1486-1500, Lambeth Palace Library MS. 2 vols. A *Calendar* of this Register, in 3 vols, ed C. Harper-Bill, is in process of publication (Canterbury and York Soc **75** (1987), **78** (1991)

Reg. Reynolds The Register of Walter Reynolds, Bishop of Worcester, 1308-13, ed R. A. Wilson (Worcs Hist Soc **39**, 1927)

Reg. Wakefield A Calendar of the Register of Henry Wakefield, Bishop of Worcester, 1375-95, ed W. P. Marett (Worcs Hist Soc New Series **7**, 1972)

Rot. Claus. Rotuli litterarum clausarum in turri Londinensi asservati, 1204-27, ed T. D. Hardy, 2 vols (Record Commission, 1833-4)

Slater, T. 1976 'The town and its regions in the Anglo-Saxon and medieval periods', in McWhirr (ed) 1976, 81-108

Stone, R. and Appleton-Fox, N. 1996 *A View From Hereford's Past: A report on the archaeological excavation in Hereford Cathedral Close in 1993* (Woonton Almeley)

Stroud, G. and Kemp, R. 1993 *Cemeteries of St Andrew Fishergate* (Archaeology of York, Fascicule **12/2**, York)

Thompson, F. H. 1962 'Excavations at the Cistercian Abbey of Vale Royal, Cheshire', *Antiq Journ* **42**, 183-207

Thompson, F. H. 1967 'Huish church: excavation of the original foundations and an early chapel', *WAM* **62**, 51-66

Trotter, M. and Gleser, G. C. 1958 'A re-evaluation of estimation of stature based on measurement of stature taken during life and long bones after death', *American Journal of Physical Anthropology* **16**, 79-123

VCH Gloucs 2 Victoria County History: A History of the County of Gloucester **2** (1907)

VCH Staffs 3 Victoria County History: A History of the County of Stafford **3** (1970)

Verey, D. 1970 *The Buildings of England: Gloucestershire: The Cotswolds* (Harmondsworth)

Verey, D. and Welander D. 1979   *Gloucester Cathedral* (Gloucester)

Vince, A. G. 1977a 'The Medieval and Post-Medieval Pottery Industry of the Malvern Region', in D. P. S. Peacock (ed), *Pottery and Early Commerce* (London)

Vince, A. G. 1977b *Newent Glasshouse* (Bristol, CRAAGS Occasional Papers **1**)

Vince , A. G. 1979a 'The Pottery', in C. M. Heighway, P. Garrod and A. G. Vince, 'Excavations at 1 Westgate Street, Gloucester 1975', *Medieval Archaeology* **23**, 170-181

Vince, A. G. 1979b 'The Medieval Pottery', in B. Cunliffe (ed), *Excavations in Bath 1950-1975* (Bristol), 27-51

Vince, A. G. 1982   'Post-Roman pottery', in R. H. Leech and A. D. McWhirr, 'Excavations at St John's Hospital, Cirencester', *TBGAS* **100**, 202-7

Vince, A. G. 1983a 'The medieval pottery'; 'The post-medieval pottery', in C. M. Heighway (ed), *The North and East Gates of Gloucester* (Bristol), 125-140

Vince, A. G. 1983b   *The medieval pottery industries of the Severn Valley: 10th to early 17th centuries* (unpublished PhD thesis, University of Southampton)

Vince, A. G. 1985   'The ceramic finds', in R. Shoesmith, *Hereford City Excavations: 3: The Finds* (CBA Res Rep **56**), 34-82

Vince, A. G. forthcoming 'Excavation at Bartholomew Street 1979', in A. G. Vince, S. J. Lobb, J. C. Richards and L. Mepham, *Excavations in Newbury 1979-1990* (Wessex Archaeology)

Wacher, J. S. 1965 'Excavations at Cirencester, 1964', *Antiq Journ* **45**, 97-110

Wacher, J. S. 1976 'Late Roman Developments', in McWhirr (ed) 1976, 15-18

Wadley, T. P. 1886. *The Great Orphan Book, Bristol* (Bristol)

Werner, O. 1977 'Analysen mittelalterlicher Bronzen und Messinge', *Archaologie und Naturwissenschaften* **1**, 144

Wilkinson, D. J. 1977 *The History and Architecture of Cirencester Abbey* (unpublished BA Thesis, University of Cardiff)

Wilkinson, D. J. 1983a [draft report on Cirencester abbey excavations: 12th century and later phases: in Corinium Museum archive]

Wilkinson, D. J. 1983b [report on medieval floor tiles: in Corinium Museum archive]

Willis, Browne 1718 *An History of the Mitred Parliamentary Abbies and Conventual Cathedral Churches*

William Worcestre *Itineraries*, ed J. H. Harvey (Oxford 1969)

Wood, J. 1835 John Wood, Surveyor: Plan of Cirencester 1835. GRO D 6746/P48

Worc. Reg. s.v. Worcester Register sede vacante 1301-1435, ed J. W. Willis-Bund (Worcs Hist Soc **8**, 1897)

Wright, W. M. R. 1973   *Bath Abbey*

Youings, J. 1971 *The Dissolution of the Monasteries* (London)

Zeepvat, R. J. 1979 'Observations in Dyer Street and Market Place, Cirencester, in 1849, 1878, and 1974-5', *TBGAS* **97**, 65-73

INDEX